AF352637

MORE THAN AN ATHLETE

MORE THAN AN ATHLETE

Jim Brown, Black Capitalism, and the Black Economic Union

Robert A. Bennett III

UNIVERSITY PRESS OF KENTUCKY

A note to the reader: This volume contains references to racially motivated violence and oppression. Some of the quotations and passages include outdated terminology, racial slurs, and other insensitive language. The original terms are retained here for historical context. Discretion is advised.

Copyright © 2026 by The University Press of Kentucky

Scholarly publisher for the Commonwealth,
serving Bellarmine University, Berea College, Centre College of Kentucky,
Eastern Kentucky University, The Filson Historical Society, Georgetown College,
Kentucky Historical Society, Kentucky State University, Morehead State University,
Murray State University, Northern Kentucky University, Simmons College,
Spalding University, Transylvania University, University of Kentucky,
University of Louisville, University of Pikeville, and Western Kentucky University.
All rights reserved.

Frontispiece: The Negro Industrial and Economic Union "Ali Draft Summit" meeting on June 4, 1967, in Cleveland, Ohio. Front row (*left to right*): Bill Russell, Muhammad Ali, Jim Brown, and Lew Alcindor (Kareem Abdul-Jabbar). Back row (*left to right*): Carl Stokes, Walter Beach, Bobby Mitchell, Lorenzo Ashley, Sidney Williams, Curtis McClinton Jr., Willie Davis, Jim Shorter, and John Wooten. (Robert Abbott Sengstacke/Getty Images)

Unless otherwise noted, photographs are from the Cleveland Press Collections, courtesy of the Michael Schwartz Library Special Collections, Cleveland State University.

Editorial and Sales Offices: The University Press of Kentucky
663 South Limestone, Lexington, Kentucky 40508-4008
www.kentuckypress.com

Cataloging-in-Publication data is available from the Library of Congress.

ISBN 978-1-9859-0374-6 (hardcover)
ISBN 978-1-9859-0375-3 (paperback)
ISBN 978-1-9859-0378-4 (epub)
ISBN 978-1-9859-0377-7 (pdf)

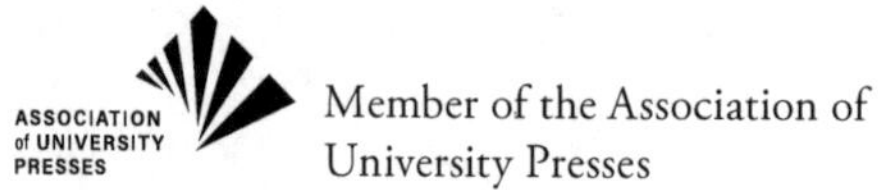

Member of the Association of
University Presses

Contents

Illustrations follow page 92

Introduction

On a sunny afternoon on Sunday, June 4, 1967, a group of prominent Black athletes met in Cleveland, Ohio, at the headquarters of the Negro Industrial and Economic Union (NIEU) located at East 105th Street and Euclid Avenue. This meeting was not a gathering to discuss their leisure activities in the city but rather a critical moment for the role of Black athletes in the struggle for justice, freedom, and equality. Photographs of the meeting show thirteen men gathered around a table, reminiscent of the Last Supper. There is Bill Russell, player and head coach of the Boston Celtics, seated next to Muhammad Ali, the heavyweight boxing champion. Adjacent to Ali is Jim Brown, founder of the NIEU and former Cleveland Brown running back, and Brown is sitting next to college basketball star Lew Alcindor (later Kareem Abdul-Jabbar) from the University of California, Los Angeles. Before these four men are microphones and recorders, and behind them are eight other athletes: Curtis McClinton, a running back with the Kansas City Chiefs; Willie Davis, a defensive lineman with the Green Bay Packers (formerly with the Browns); Walter Beach III, who was out of the National Football League (NFL); Jim Shorter and Bobby Mitchell of the Washington Redskins; Sidney Williams and John Wooten, who were members with of the Cleveland Browns; and Lorenzo Ashley, a former member of the Browns. Carl Stokes, a legal adviser for the NIEU and Ohio state representative during his mayoral campaign, was also present at the press conference. He would eventually become the city's first Black mayor and the first of a major city in the United States five months later.

Many scholars and popular media labeled the meeting the Ali Draft Summit.[1] NIEU executive vice president John Wooten convened everyone at the urging of Jim Brown. The goal was to discuss heavyweight boxing champion Muhammad Ali's refusal on religious grounds to enlist in the US Army during the Vietnam War. Facing jail time, Ali, a devout member of the Nation of Islam and financial supporter of the NIEU, had reached a crossroads. The boxer's actions were a federal offense. He risked losing his heavyweight title and his career after boxing commissions across the United States refused to grant him the necessary boxing licenses. Many opposing voices questioned his loyalty, and national news outlets ran stories with such headlines as "Athletes Fail to Sway Clay," "Negro Stars Fail to Talk Ali into Joining the Army," and "Jim Brown to Urge Clay to Enter Army." Locally, the *Cleveland Press* reported a "group of top-flight Negro athletes" was set to meet at the NIEU office to "persuade the deposed heavyweight boxing champion to accept induction into the Army." The biggest hype came from an NIEU spokesperson who guaranteed a "revealing announcement" after the meeting egregiously alluding to Ali changing his position. Yet, after several hours, Brown, Russell, and the other attendees were convinced that Ali was convicted in his stance and agreed to support him publicly, thereby putting them and the NIEU at the center of a media firestorm.[2]

This moment in the NIEU's history has received considerable attention, while the group's broader efforts have been overlooked, specifically its activism in Black communities and the development of Black businesses. As the demand for Black Power grew strong during the 1960s, there was also a call for "green power." This ideology was promoted under the guise of "Black capitalism," a strategy of President Richard Nixon's administration to support Black business development as a solution to racial inequality across America.[3] Jim Brown and members of the NIEU believed they could use their cache as professional athletes to promote a philosophy of economic self-sufficiency as a strategy for racial advancement. Strategists within the civil rights movement used nonviolent tactics like marches, sit-ins, picketing, and boycotts. While appreciating the utility of these actions, many NIEU members were not comfortable embracing the philosophy of turning the other cheek. They were under the belief that Black capitalism and the promotion of economic opportunities were more effective.

At its core, the NIEU had three objectives:

1.   Use the finances of African Americans collectively for the benefit of all.
2.   Assemble loans with particular attention to favorable interest rates for Black entrepreneurs in business and industry.
3.   Create clinics and workshops to provide African American youth guidance and education on job opportunities and entrepreneurship.

Although economic empowerment did not threaten the order of White racial dominance in the same spirit as armed self-defense or Black Nationalism, the NIEU became involved in the Black freedom struggle at a critical time. Its members established a broad support base, using their fame and notoriety as professional athletes to call attention to social issues, connecting with other professional athletes, politicians, community organizers, and businesspeople nationwide. They launched job programs for Black youth, business development programs, and a national campaign, Food First, to combat poverty. The NIEU also promoted the need for Black people to do more business with each other. However, the goal of economically self-sufficient Black communities proved to be elusive.

Many scholars and journalists have paid considerable attention to the subject of Black athlete activism. Much of the work prior to this time has focused on the 1968 Summer Olympic protests spearheaded by the Olympic Project for Human Rights, while other studies have examined athlete activism at different times. The former topic is covered in such works as Harry Edwards's *The Revolt of the Black Athlete* (1969); Amy Bass's *Not the Triumph but the Struggle: The 1968 Olympics and the Making of the Black Athlete* (2002); Douglass Hartmann's *Race, Culture, and the Revolt of the Black Athlete: The 1968 Olympics and Their Aftermath* (2003); Tommie Smith and David Steele's collaborative *Silent Gesture: The Autobiography of Tommie Smith*; and John Carlos's memoir with Dave Zirin, *The John Carlos Story: The Sports Moment That Changed the World* (2011). These texts and many other books and articles illustrate why the 1968 Games are paramount to understanding the journey of the Black athlete. Regarding athlete activism, there are several works that students of sports history can explore. For example, Damion Thomas's *Globetrotting: African American Athletes and Cold War Politics* (2012); Louis Moore's *We*

Will Win the Day: The Civil Rights Movement, the Black Athlete, and the Quest for Equality (2017); Howard Bryant's *The Heritage: Black Athletes, a Divided America, and the Politics of Patriotism* (2018); and Gregory Kaliss's *Beyond the Black Power Salute: Athlete Activism in an Era of Change* (2023) provide fascinating accounts of how the civil rights and Black Power era has shaped much of the social and political consciousness of African American athletes in the twentieth and twenty-first centuries.[4]

More Than an Athlete examines the intersection of politics, economics, and sports, particularly through the lives of NIEU members. Specifically, I focus on how they leveraged their platforms as professional athletes during the civil rights and Black Power movements of the 1960s and 1970s to improve the conditions of African Americans on and off the field. Their efforts were grounded in a tradition of racial uplift that sought individual and collective success. Over the twentieth century, Black athletes joined organizations and created myriad spaces to address social and bureaucratic issues at local and national levels. This book chronicles the NIEU's formation from 1967 to the mid-1970s, details NIEU members' lived experiences as professional athletes, and outlines their work with the NIEU, examining the various programs and business ventures they created throughout the United States. I argue that the NIEU served as an impetus for the activism of Black athletes in their careers and their communities. The book also explores the successes and failures of the NIEU. Sports leagues and the media responded in different ways to Black athletes' involvement in the civil rights and Black Power movements. Some were receptive, while others feared Black athletes' engagement in the Black freedom struggle.

Chapter 1, "Standing on Their Image," introduces the formation of the NIEU around two events in 1966: Jim Brown's retirement from professional football and the civil unrest from the Hough riots. The civil rights and Black Power movements became part of the national conversation in the 1960s as African Americans began concerted efforts to oppose White discrimination. This chapter examines the role Brown, John Wooten, and Walter Beach, members of the Cleveland Browns during the 1950s and 1960s, played in the fight for economic empowerment and equality for African Americans in Cleveland, Ohio, through the NIEU. Their involvement was not spontaneous but connected to the larger Black freedom struggle. Although Jim Brown closed a figurative door on his athletic exploits when he retired, he set in motion a new career: working for the NIEU. The Hough riots, a period of distress in one of Cleveland's poorest Black communities, were used by the organization to combat the economic inequities in the city.

Chapter 2, "The Ali Draft Summit," chronicles the relationship between Muhammad Ali and Brown and details how their friendship intersected in business terms through Main Bout, a management group they initiated with the support of other NIEU members. The chapter follows the events that led to the NIEU private meeting with Ali, where they discussed his stance on the military and whether to support his right to not enlist, and the results of their decision. This chapter explores the intersection of race, religion, and sports in the case of one of the union's most prominent financial supporters.

In 1968, the NIEU changed its name to the Black Economic Union (BEU), representing the shift in identity from "Negro" to "Black." The group heightened its capitalist efforts in Black communities and professional sports. Chapter 3, "Challenging the National Football League," examines how members of the BEU contested the NFL's status quo approach to player compensation. Black athletes were often paid less than their White teammates and were usually the first to be cut from squads. Their movement and ability to profit from their labor were limited in the first half of the twentieth century and through much of the 1960s. Yet with the rise of professional football's popularity, profits increased as well. Black and White players knew these realities and confronted NFL ownership over their compensation and lack of retirement benefits. As a result, they formed the National Football League Players Association. Two BEU members, John Mackey and Brig Owens, played an integral part in developing the players' union. Their involvement illustrates how the labor fight in the 1970s changed the financial realities of professional athletes in one of the country's most lucrative sports.

Outside the sporting realm, the BEU expanded its operations nationally, opening offices in several cities with high Black populations: Washington, DC, Kansas City, Oakland, and New York. Chapter 4, "In the Community," explores two foci: First, the BEU developed community engagement programs that addressed poverty and created job opportunities for Black youth. These efforts are exemplified through Project Job Interest and Motivation (JIM) and

Food First, which garnered national attention for the BEU and its community activism. Second, the group helped numerous Black people by providing technical aid and financial support. The BEU had significant successes with companies like Magnificent Natural, Namax Builders, and Brady Keys' All-Pro Chicken. There were also some failures. This chapter demonstrates Black athletes' struggle to implement strategies for business development in the communities where they lived.

While much of the book focuses on the foundational efforts in Cleveland and the group's transition to Los Angeles, chapter 5, "Two Different Worlds: Kansas City and the BEU," examines the efforts of Curtis McClinton, who led the Kansas City chapter of the organization, which was arguably its most successful. The segregated culture of Kansas City and the growing influence of professional football (through the Kansas City Chiefs) influenced the work and capabilities of the group. This chapter centers on McClinton to illustrate the relationship Black athletes had with the economic development of the Black community. It also explores the trials and triumphs of his experiences, which were influenced by external and internal forces.

The book concludes with an epilogue, "More Than an Athlete," which assesses the work many of the key players in the organization, such as John Wooten, Walter Beach, and Jim Brown, have done since they left the BEU. It also considers the ties between Black athlete activism in the 1960s and 1970s with the Black Lives Matter movement and Colin Kaepernick's 2016 protest as well as how Jim Brown contributed significantly during this historic moment, beginning a new conversation about Black athlete activism and Brown's legacy during Donald Trump's first presidency.

My influence for this topic came from two moments as a graduate student: reading Jim Brown's 1989 autobiography with Steve Delsohn, *Out of Bounds*, and watching Spike Lee's film *Jim Brown: All-American*. Both explore the NFL Hall of Famer's life and give considerable attention to his activism. There was also mention of his role in the formation of the BEU. There are numerous autobiographies and biographies that focus on his exploits on the football field and his acting career. While they discuss his activism and work with the union, none of them explore the day-to-day work of the organization or its members. I recognize the complexity of the private and public lives of Jim Brown and other BEU members. Some of these aspects are explored in depth in this book, while other matters remain unaddressed. Given the focus of this work, I have intentionally avoided exploring personal or legal matters. This position allows the book to remain centered on its primary scope and purpose.

More Than an Athlete explores how the BEU constructed its efforts to contribute to a movement that challenged US institutions to uphold the nation's mandate of freedom and equality for all. Moreover, its central focus is on how Black athletes assessed their positions as citizens and athletes within the Black freedom struggle during the 1960s and 1970s. Throughout the twentieth century, Black male athletes have used sports as a tool for racial equality. Their lives, whether on the playing field or in their communities, have served as the foundation of activism for future generations of Black athletes. While the experiences of athletes during the civil rights and Black Power era are different from athletes' in the twenty-first century, athletes today face many of the same dilemmas (e.g., racial wealth disparities, denial of voting rights, lack of educational opportunities and funding).

This book's goal is to provide a historical arc for the place of Black athletes in the social, political, and economic landscape of the United States: What is the role of the Black athlete? Should they be confined to what they exhibit through their sport, or are they more than an athlete? This book explores the heavily articulated debate about the social responsibility and relationship of Black athletes to the various Black communities they represent. This book argues that as Black athletes became well-paid celebrities after World War II, some maintained social relevance in African American communities through nonprofit advocacy, entrepreneurship, and philanthropy. This work illustrates the twenty-first-century arc of modern-day Black athlete social involvement, as demonstrated by Colin Kaepernick, Maya Moore, Eric Reid, Malcolm Jenkins, Venus and Serena Williams, Jaylen Brown, Steph Curry, Kyrie Irving, and LeBron James, among others.

1

Standing on Their Image

On the night of Monday, July 18, 1966, in the Hough area, located on the east side of Cleveland, Dave Feigenbaum asked a Black female prostitute to leave his and his brother's bar, the Seventy-Niners Café. The woman allegedly had entered to request donations to support the children of another prostitute who had recently died. The two engaged in a heated verbal exchange, in which Feigenbaum "muttered something about serving Negroes" to one of his workers, and some of the Black patrons of Seventy-Niners overheard his conversation. Later that night, an African American man visited the establishment, bought a pint of wine, and asked for a pitcher of water with a glass. Feigenbaum denied his request since the customer had a takeout order and then informed his workers not to serve "no niggers no water." The man who bought the wine, angered by the comments, made a sign out of a brown paper bag reading "No water for Niggers" and posted it on the bar's front door.[1]

Several Black residents who walked past Seventy-Niners Café noticed the sign and began to point it out to other onlookers. Destruction ensued. Responding angrily, some of the Hough residents defaced and broke windows of the Feigenbaum establishment, and the police were called to calm

8

the crowd. By the time local forces arrived, they were greeted with fire. The café and other adjacent businesses had been vandalized and set ablaze. Police used their guns to quell the unrest in the community. One person the police targeted was a Black woman who was the mother of three children. She was killed in the cross fire between the police and armed residents. Eyewitnesses reported she had no part in the disturbance. The mayor of Cleveland, Ralph Locher, hesitated to call on the Ohio National Guard. He hoped the city's law enforcement could subdue the conflict. However, the racial imbalance in the police department was a significant barrier.[2]

The following day, Tuesday, July 19, Ohio governor James Rhodes sent the Ohio National Guard to the Hough area to relieve the tensions and prevent further damage to businesses. They were not successful. Rioting continued for several more days, ending on Monday, July 25. At the end of nearly a week of rebellion, four Black people had been killed, hundreds injured, and numerous arrested. The financial impact was nearly $2 million in damages. While many White businesses were targeted, community institutions also bore the brunt of the rage. A vocational planning center that provided Hough residents employment training was firebombed. Thus, original animosities centered on the Seventy-Niners Café spread to places promoting the Hough community's greater good, like schools and churches.[3]

After the disturbances subsided, numerous investigations sought to find the source of the violence. A Black Nationalist organization, Afro Set, was a target. This group embraced a position of armed struggle and rejected the call for nonviolence that had been promoted by groups like the local chapter of the National Association for the Advancement of Colored People (NAACP) and the Southern Christian Leadership Conference (SCLC), the national organization led by Martin Luther King Jr. Harllel Jones, also a member of Afro Set and the supervisor of the Jomo Freedom Kenyatta Youth Center (JFKYC), was summoned and testified before a grand jury about his role during the rebellion. After the hearing, Jones was met by reporters as he left the courtroom. To their surprise, he told them the violence would continue. He told them, "There will be riots here next week, next month, next year. . . . Conditions which caused the riots haven't been eliminated." As a result of the grand jury investigation, Cleveland law enforcement closed the JFKYC. Authorities feared Black residents were using the location to make firebombs. When questioned about that claim, Jones stated, "I have a gun. I don't trust any white man. Police shot all the people who were shot in the Hough riots. Check the bullets."[4]

City officials placed the blame for the upheaval in Hough at the feet of the Black Nationalists. Yet many African Americans throughout Cleveland contended that the failure of legislators to address the numerous concerns of their communities, particularly of racial discrimination and its intersection with policing, was the problem. The Hough area was considered a "northern cesspool of misery." It was an economically poor community saturated with White business owners who charged high prices in grocery stores and high rent for tenements infested with roaches and rats. There was also a high rate of crime and juvenile delinquency, as a substantial number of youths had given up on school and dropped out by the eighth grade. While Cleveland was considered "the Best Location in the Nation" as an urban center, it ranked last in "education, housing, employment, health, welfare, law enforcement, and municipal services." In 1966, a study by the Cleveland Subcommittee of the Ohio State Advisory Committee to the US Commission on Civil Rights highlighted this point. The Hough riots brought these issues to the forefront and quickly got the attention of city officials. In the wake of the violence, they could no longer dismiss their constituents' frustrations. Before a Senate subcommittee, Locher argued federal stipulations on city spending were to blame. He stressed that the "red tape" associated with federal aid needed to be eliminated. This allowed city officials the authority to do with the money as they chose. The mayor placed the blame on the lack of federal aid, not on the climate of racial inequities that crossed social, economic, and political lines, demonstrating his administration's inability to recognize the realities and concerns of Black folks in the city.[5]

The fallout from the Hough riots brought members of the Cleveland Browns and their newly found NIEU to the conversation about finding solutions for the social ills in Black urban communities. A week after the Hough riots, Hal Lebovitz, a writer for the *Plain Dealer*, interviewed Walter Beach, John Brown, and John Wooten. The three members of the Cleveland Browns voiced their concerns. They concluded the following:

1. If the amount of money local officials spent to stop the riots had been used to alleviate the conditions that caused them, the violence that ensued would not have happened.

2.   Housing and jobs, or the lack thereof, were a significant reason for the violence.
3.   While they were against the rioting and lawbreaking that ensued, they understood the "discontent" of the people.
4.   Walter Beach identified that the weakness of Black communities was the lack of "any grassroots leader."

The aftermath of Hough could have negatively impacted the efforts of the NIEU's Cleveland office. Instead, they used the incident to position themselves to be part of improving the political and economic inequalities in Black neighborhoods. They used their clout as professional athletes to call on city politicians and businessmen to begin solving the problems from which the earlier violence stemmed. As African Americans fought for social, political, and economic equality through various local and national movements, Black professional athletes through the NIEU found ways to insert themselves in these spaces as well. Formed in 1966 by Jim Brown, the organization was created with the goal of finding solutions to the financial problems that had plagued Black communities since the end of the Civil War in 1865.[6]

For more than half a century, athletic competitions, especially professional sports, served as entertainment, bringing significant profits for White businessmen. The NIEU was founded during a time of intense political agitation that reflected the profound social conflict and transformation during the modern civil rights era. During the first half of the 1960s, the struggle for Black freedom, justice, and equality centered on the desegregation of public facilities and accommodations. The goal was to address the morally corrupt practice of segregation through nonviolent direct action. There was also a focus on promoting equal access to jobs and economic justice across the country. Not swayed to uphold the movement's call for "turning the other cheek," Black men like Jim Brown, John Wooten, and Walter Beach used their platforms, financial assets, and professional connections to address poverty in Black communities across the United States. This chapter explores their lives in Cleveland as members of the Cleveland Browns as they served critical roles with the formation and expansion of the NIEU. Examining their early lives and undertakings with respect to race, gender, and sport is essential to help us understand how Black professional athletes placed themselves in the Black freedom struggle.[7]

Being Black in Cleveland

Cleveland, Ohio, was one of several major northern cities that was a new home for African Americans leaving the South after World War II during the Great Migration. By 1940, Cleveland had a population of 878,336 people. African Americans made up nearly 10 percent of the citizenry. As the *Chicago Defender* influenced many Black folks from the South to move north to cities like Cleveland, another Chicago-based publication, *Jet*, solidified the Ohio industrial town. The featured story for November 25, 1954, was entitled "Cleveland: The Friendly City to Negroes." The editor opined that Cleveland was "not on par" with Los Angeles, Chicago, or Detroit but that "money doesn't talk as loudly in Cleveland's Negro society as it does in other cities. . . . Society here is based more on what you are." The heart of the Glenville community was deemed "the Mecca for Negroes" as one could capture there and throughout the city "the sweat of honest hard work and pride in a town that is not too big to be friendly, old enough to be matured, good enough to live in forever." One of the other promising points of the city was that it boasted the NAACP chapter with the largest number of lifetime members.[8]

The sports scene presented the city as a beacon of racial progress. Jesse Owens, a native of the city (by way of Alabama), won four gold medals at the 1936 Summer Olympics in Nazi Germany. The Cleveland Buckeyes were a fixture with the Negro American League and won the Negro World Series in 1945, defeating the six-time champion Homestead Grays led by Josh Gibson and losing two other trips in 1944 and 1947. Football was also a draw in the city, as Black communities across the United States had an allegiance to the Cleveland Browns. The Browns were the first team to integrate professional football. In 1946, they signed Bill Willis and Marion Motley. Both played critical roles on a Browns team that won five straight championships (four in the All-American Football Conference and one with the NFL). They were indeed Black America's team. A year later, Jackie Robinson made his Major League Baseball debut on April 15, 1947. Nearly three months later, on July 5, 1947, Larry Doby played for the Cleveland Indians, the first American League team to integrate. On the surface, these sporting realities made Cleveland look like a great place for African Americans.[9]

Despite their relative successes, African Americans in Cleveland experienced limitations. By 1960, the Black population had increased to more than

30 percent. The industrial pull of the city had changed its racial makeup as White residents fled to the suburbs. Voting was not an issue in Cleveland as it was in Lowndes County, Alabama, nor was access to accommodations like buses, hotels, and recreational venues. In principle, public schools were integrated, but because of de facto segregated housing, the schools were racially segregated. While the population of Cleveland was stagnant, the city's suburban areas increased, with a primarily White population. As historian Leonard Moore notes, Black Clevelanders faced four major challenges: housing discrimination, police brutality, inequities in public education funding, and employment. Coupled with the phenomenon of "White flight" from the city that led to a mass exodus of people and resources from the city, practices like redlining and racial covenants prevented Black residents from moving into the "Heights": Cleveland Heights, Garfield Heights, and Maple Heights. As a result, they were relegated to the central core near Lake Erie and the east side of the city. Due to the poor conditions of many of these living spaces, African Americans in these communities wrote to city leadership to improve their environments, conducted rent strikes for resolutions, and, in rare cases, used armed violence. Police brutality was everywhere in Black neighborhoods around Cleveland. Citizens experienced illegal searches, assaults, and harassment. There was also a lack of Black police officers the Cleveland Police Department. While African Americans made up nearly a third of the population of the city, they accounted for only about 4 percent of police officers.[10]

For the masses of African Americans in Cleveland, employment opportunities were often limited to government jobs, usually with maintenance work, sanitation, and various unskilled positions. Across the city, Black folks also owned and operated their own businesses in food and beverage, barbering and hairstyling, funeral services, automotive services, and cleaning services, among others. When it came to the private sector, the limitations were more rigid. Some businesses used vague job descriptions to mask their unwillingness to hire Black folks, while others printed their racial preferences in job ads. Many companies tried to avoid integrated workforces for fear of possible race wars. Companies, labor unions, and hiring agencies also relied on racial stereotypes, like laziness and susceptibility to being late for work, as reasons to discriminate against potential African American employees.[11]

In the area of public education, African American youth experienced overcrowding in many underfunded schools. Segregated education was par for the course, as Cleveland public school administrators refused to embrace busing despite protests from Black parents. There were myriad other problems in Cleveland: high pupil-to-teacher ratio, decrepit buildings, teachers without credentials, and old curricula that failed to center the experiences of Black youth. For example, in the fall of 1963, the school board decided to relieve overcrowding by building more schools in the all-Black Hazeldell community. The United Freedom Movement, a group of Black activists who focused on the civil rights of Black Clevelanders, along with the Hazeldell Parents Association, interpreted this move as a way of ensuring segregated education. According to historian Leonard Moore, this marked the first time the Black community in Cleveland organized around an issue in front of White politicians in the city. This move demonstrated that African Americans were no longer going to be quiet about issues dear to them.[12]

By 1964, the civil rights movement had achieved several successes but had not ended the economic inequalities African Americans faced. The franchise was accessible to more people, yet thousands of Black folks were threatened and imprisoned for their defiance of Jim Crow. Many White employers disapproved of their Black employees' activism and threatened to fire them from their jobs, and countless Black citizens were murdered for their involvement. Also, African American communities, homes, and businesses were routinely attacked as a means of intimidation to thwart the drive to end segregation and ensure White people maintained political power through the means of regionalization. Nonviolent protest was a strategy that had been utilized throughout the 1960s and even beforehand. Numerous civil rights organizations, including the Congress of Racial Equality (CORE), the SCLC, and the Student Nonviolent Coordinating Committee (SNCC), were ardent proponents of its tenets. Nonviolence was a hallmark technique of the movement and was used primarily to appeal to the sensibilities of the White masses. Many civil rights leaders believed this method was the best approach for African Americans to gain full citizenship rights, particularly with access to public facilities, educational institutions, and voting. Nonviolence successfully reached specific goals, such as the passage of the 1964 Civil Rights Act and the 1965 Voting Rights Act. However, not all Black community members agreed it was the best method for bringing about the change needed in American society.[13]

The Black freedom struggle shaped various facets of life for African Americans: the political, economic, religious, social, and even the athletic realm. John Wooten had several conversations with King. When the SCLC leader would come to Cleveland, he would often pick him up from the airport and drive him around. For example, in 1966, Wooten told King, "What you are doing, we are in full support. But I cannot let people spit on me, and drag me, and not fight. Therefore, I do not want to hurt the movement, so we are going to go this way." Wooten wanted to go the route of economic development. He contended, "We were not going to protest and march and all those things because at that time the protest was supposed to be non-violent and don't hit back and people could spit on you and pour water on you, and you were supposed to just keep going."[14]

While nonviolence was a tenet King promoted, he was also cautious about investing in capitalism as a means of liberation. King warned in his book *Where Do We Go from Here*, "We must honestly admit that capitalism has often left a gulf between superfluous wealth and abject poverty, has created conditions permitting necessities to be taken from the many to give luxuries to the few." He added, "The profit motive, when it is the sole basis of an economic system, encourages a cutthroat competition and selfish ambition that inspire men to be more I-centered than thou-centered." For King, capitalism would not benefit the whole, only a few. Jim Brown and members of the NIEU felt otherwise.[15]

Seeds Planted in Los Angeles

In January 1964, Jim Brown was in Los Angeles, California, for the Pro Bowl. While there, he was introduced to John Daniels, a Black businessman in the city. They discussed the need for an organization to "help Negroes help themselves." From his initial meeting, Brown remembers that Daniels was "entrepreneurial, a go get 'em kind of guy" whose energy he liked. Daniels, who was born and raised in Gary, Indiana, attended Butler University. After college, he wrote songs for artists signed to Capitol Records. His experiences with the record label served as his introduction to how businesses operated in the entertainment industry. The two men discussed different concepts for businesses, along with an organization that addressed Black economics on a national level, "an idea that was in the minds of a lot of bright people." Daniels wanted to garner Brown's financial support for *Elegant*, a fashion magazine that catered to African Americans. Brown was intrigued by Daniel's pitch and provided the seed money for the publication primarily to help with printing costs. The magazine folded later that year for financial reasons, as it could not rival top Black publications *Ebony* and *Jet*. Despite the failure, he and Daniels continued to collaborate.[16]

Brown told *Sports Illustrated* writer Tex Maule, "In my travels around the country with the Browns and when I worked for Pepsi-cola [*sic*], I ran into that situation a lot. I helped personally whenever I could, but it was too big a project for one man to handle." Brown was referring to the number of Black people who often came to him seeking his financial help with business ideas. He continued, "So I got the idea of forming an organization that would provide financing and technical help for Negroes." John Wooten remembered, "Jim was just so besieged with people begging him to loan them money to get started in business that he had to start turning many of them down no matter how worthwhile the idea." He added, "Jim being the kind of guy he is, this really bothered him. So he was the moving force in getting a bunch of us together."[17]

With the money he had been saving from playing in the NFL, Jim Brown had the financial resources to help Daniels but was unable to put up what was needed to keep the magazine afloat. Intrigued by their discussions, the two men continued to stay in contact with each other over the years. Busy schedules with football and filming on Brown's end limited their interactions. However, by 1965, the two identified people they believed could play critical roles in helping them realize their ideas. Daniels introduced Maggie Hathaway to Brown. The *Chicago Defender* described her as a "glamorous actress of stage and screen" who was "attractive and very exotic." Maggie Mae Hathaway was a native of Campti, Louisiana, and had several roles in films from 1939 to 1945, the most notable of which was in *One Dark Night* (1939). She was also active in the civil rights movement, bringing the fight for "freedom, justice, and equality" to professional golf. In 1952, the Professional Golfers' Association (PGA) refused to admit African Americans to play in their larger tournaments, even if they were members. She supported the careers of Black men Teddy Rhodes and Charlie Sifford to gain entry into the PGA. Furthermore, most professional White golfers had corporate sponsorships, but Black PGA members struggled to find backing. Together Hathaway and Brown provided financial support to Ray Botts and Pete Brown, two African American men who were members of the PGA. Her activism and Daniels's business acumen had inspired Brown. The trio explored a new organization featuring Black athletes that would focus on social, political, and economic issues. With Daniels's and Hathaway's connections in Los Angeles, and Brown's relationship with his Black teammates on the Browns, they were ready to capitalize on their social cache. Brown was looking to use the written word to set the stage.[18]

Getting Things Off His Chest

"All his life, Jim Brown has been running hard and saying little. He breaks his reserve in OFF MY CHEST, telling what it is like to come up against giant linemen who, game after game, are out to destroy him," Doubleday & Company's blurb read. Published before the 1964 season, this quote sensationalized Brown's experiences for potential readers. The description continued, "He speaks out—bluntly—about his relations with former Cleveland coach Paul Brown and with the men he plays with and against." Doubleday made explicit efforts to inform readers that Brown's book would take on a tone that had not been seen before: "He attacks the advertising business for its treatment of Negro athletes . . . forcefully expresses his positive views about race relations in general . . . and tells how it feels to sign autographs in a hotel lobby and then be turned out of its dining room." Before its publication, fans of the Browns, specifically White supporters, felt ambivalence toward Brown. They knew their team would not have the success it had enjoyed without him. However, his outspokenness on racial matters, his support of the Black Nationalist organization Nation of Islam (NOI), and his relationship with vocal proponents of the NOI, Malcolm X, and Muhammad Ali upset supporters.[19]

Brown's descriptions of Malcolm X and the NOI fueled the charges of militancy. He mentioned that many White authorities defined the NOI as "extremists" and the equivalent of the White terrorist organization, the Ku Klux Klan (KKK). Brown countered this view. For him, they were not as radical as some believed and were not in the same category as the KKK. Brown argued, "They don't stalk into the night and burn crosses and terrorize people and flog them . . . they preach against drinking, against smoking, against adultery. . . . The Muslims preach neatness, cleanliness, and courtesy. Where is the parallel between them and the Ku Klux Klan?" He added that the beliefs of the NOI were "not one iota different" from those of Black people at "the lowest economic class to the business and professional level." Brown's support of the NOI was not received well by Browns fans, and he was met with physical threats against his life.[20]

In September 1964, Brown appeared on *The Mike Douglas Show* to promote the book. Before he arrived, Forest Fraser, the producer of the show, received a bomb threat from a White woman. She told Fraser if Brown discussed any of "the things that have been in the papers . . . we are going to bomb his home." Police were dispatched to the station and surveyed Brown's home on the east side of Cleveland. Despite the danger, he appeared on the show without harm. Fraser asked Brown about his interactions with the NOI. He replied, "I am not one of the Muslims, yet I'm all for them because we Negroes need every possible element going for us. The more commotion, the better." Many civil rights strategists used disorder to get their demands heard, often playing off more radical groups and their ideals.[21]

Off My Chest was a precursor of Jim Brown's involvement in the Black freedom struggle, an issue on which he had been largely absent from before the memoir's publication. In fact Stan Isaacs, a *Newsday* columnist, noted in 1964 that Brown was "indifferent about social injustices to the less fortunate; that he was content with the world because he himself had made it big." The argument was "he had been like most successful black pro athletes, so silent publicly on the matter of race that he was almost regarded as an 'Uncle Thomas'—a successful Negro who was happy to get along with the white establishment." By 1964, however, there was no debate about where Brown stood. As evidenced by *Off My Chest*, many of the Black Cleveland Browns players did not embrace deference to White people. By 1964, with the civil rights movement in full swing, a fair number of Black male professional athletes refused to kowtow to White citizens.[22]

In Brown's opinion, the NFL wanted "nice guy blacks, humble blacks, just-glad-to-be-there blacks, lower-pay, work-hard, say-the-sky-was-blue, the-sun-was-shining blacks. Blacks who wouldn't rock the status quo." One of the long-held expectations was that African American players would be grateful for the opportunity to play in the NFL. The Browns did not have such "Blacks." As he recalled, "My leadership with the Cleveland Browns, was based on me being an African American man that believed in freedom, equality, and justice, and that I was an adamant fighter against discrimination and racism." Brown added, "If you were an African American player coming to the Cleveland Browns, for the most part, you were going to be a part of that. We controlled our own territory, we wore suits and ties, we carried our business papers with us; we presented ourselves a certain way." Controlling the narrative was important from his vantage point. He noted, "We had a very classier approach of representing ourselves. That was very important to us. If you came in as a rookie, you didn't come in and try to change the culture, in most cases you would join the culture." There was an expectation of respect players exuded, regardless of one's race on the team. However, Black players abided by these notions of representation to avoid the stereotyping that accompanied Blackness.[23]

From the vantage point of Black Browns players, to help prevent racial animus in Cleveland, they gave considerable attention to their presentation on and off the field. They embodied what John Wooten called a "seriousness" in their public demeanor since "most of us had a college education and were graduates. I felt that pushed us to a different level in how we carried ourselves. If you saw pictures of us back then at a home game or on the road, we were always coat and tie, attaché cases." He added, "That was the way we went about business. We did that for a reason because we wanted to show to the public that we weren't just a bunch of football players, scalawag type of guys. That we were college-educated men." They were conscious of their appearance and often projected a stern demeanor in public. There was an element of respectability politics at play for them. They made every effort not to be the laughing buffoon or "happy-go-lucky-negro" type. They were in a category of their own. In a "talented tenth" fashion, they saw themselves as representatives of African Americans, and rightfully so. While many White fans were unwilling to give the same encouragement and support to African American players on and off the field, there was a different sentiment among Black people. As Walter Beach remembered, "the Black community loved us!" Their admiration was because of their relationship with Browns players who lived in the same neighborhoods. There was a connection to other African

Americans for these men and a confident expectation that came with their status as professional athletes.[24]

Winning Championships Does Not End Racism

For the 1964 season, the Browns had a 10–3–1 record. After they won the Eastern Conference championship against the New York Giants, 52–20, the Browns earned the chance to play in the 1964 NFL championship game against the Baltimore Colts. The teams played before 79,544 people, the second-largest crowd for a championship game. The Browns had not won a championship in ten years, and players and fans alike were yearning for a victory. Now more than ever, Jim Brown deemed it necessary to remind his teammates not to get caught up in the game's hype. He mentioned, "We were very serious about our profession, and there was no fooling around . . . no dancing in the end zone." He continued, "We were standing on our image, our education, and on our future." During the nationally televised game, Sidney Williams made "silly faces" toward a camera that panned on him. His actions caught the ire of Jim Brown. He severely chastised Williams for the act. Brown told Williams, "We're on a mission here, we're being scrutinized, and we carry ourselves in a certain way. We're not clowns, shuffling, or uneducated. We're together, we play hard, and we want to be treated like professionals. So don't make faces on national TV!" In Brown's view, Williams's antics spotlighted him and took attention away from the team. It also reinforced negative stereotypes about Black athletes as buffoons. Despite the showboating, Brown and Williams lost no love between each other as the underdog Browns defeated the Baltimore Colts 27–0, led by Jim Brown's 114 rushing yards. After the game Brown told reporters, "It's the biggest thrill of my career. . . . I have had better days as an individual, but this is the most satisfying of all." Brown later received the Hickok Belt, a $10,000 diamond-studded award that honored the professional athlete of the year.[25]

Black players on the Browns knew their accomplishments on the field did not make them immune to racism. They recognized African Americans throughout the city grappled with inequities in housing and education. At the same time, police brutality was constant, and many did not have enough money to live as comfortably as they would have liked. Jim Brown also faced discrimination when he first arrived in Cleveland. For example, an all-White community denied him access to an apartment. Brown had no desire to be a civil rights pioneer around housing. All he wanted was a place near the Cleveland Browns practice facilities for him and his wife, Sue, and their three kids: Kevin, Kim, and Jim Jr. One place he knew to avoid was "Little Italy," a hub of Italian Americans on the east side of the city where there had been reports of assaults on African Americans. Brown was aware of what life would be once the touchdowns ended and he was no longer within the confines of Cleveland Municipal Stadium. He was aware of race relations off the football field. "I could have scored twenty touchdowns Sunday afternoon; if I walked through Little Italy that evening, I'd have been jumped. I'd have no 32 on my back, all they'd see was black." A Black man in Little Italy, and many other White sections of Cleveland after working hours, was considered a prime target for a racial assault.[26]

While integration was a significant goal of the civil rights era, some of the Black players on the Browns were not concerned about the acceptance of their White teammates outside of the locker room. They were cordial but were mindful of their objective of winning games. Thus, a player's race was of no concern on game day. The primary goal for each team member was to fulfill his duty at his position and ensure the team's success. Jim Brown noted, "America loved my performance, yet I couldn't check into certain hotels, drink from any water fountain when I was thirsty." He added, "I didn't want to give up football, did not want to close my eyes. I tried to find a way I could live with the contradiction, still feel decently about myself. I accepted trophies, [but] never displayed them in my home." Brown continued, "I liked the cheers, didn't allow them to fool me. I never forgot who I was, and from where I came. Throughout my career I'd drive to the bleakest neighborhoods in Cleveland, spend time with the lowliest brothers." The Browns running back spent much of his time in Black communities like Hough and Glenville, the areas he wanted to help most. Brown remembered, "On the football field they wanted me to be brave. Wanted me to take the ball when we were all backed up, our own one-yard-line, carry us out of there, where we could be safe. Away from football, they wanted me to be another guy. They wanted me to be docile." While he noticed the inherent contradiction, he asked, "How could I have the courage to run that hard, then be so weak off the field that I'd succumb to inequity?" For Jim Brown and other Black athletes, the intersection of race, politics, and athletics became apparent, and thus, they decided to join in the struggle for freedom, justice, and equality.[27]

In the March 8, 1965, issue of *Sports Illustrated*, Pepsi ran a full-page color ad featuring Jim Brown. Harvey C. Russell, a Black man who served as vice president of Pepsi-Cola Company Inc., had chosen him for this promo because of the relationship they formed in their work with the soft drink company. Russell believed the time was ripe for African Americans to be a key element of advertisements put out by the company. The caption under the picture read, "10,882 yards for Cleveland . . . 168,427 miles for Pepsi." Various outlets used Pepsi's ads over time, but Brown's feature was only published once. Bottlers were furious the soft drink company would use a Black man for "the white media." Before this spread, there was no outcry from the public over Brown's role as spokesperson for the soft drink company. Brown had served as an assistant to Russell and promoted the Pepsi brand in numerous meetings. His position allowed him to learn about the business world. He rode the trucks that delivered the bottled soft drinks, was among the workers in the bottling plants, and, during the offseason, studied with their advertising agency. Brown also learned about "special markets," which Russell explained meant Black communities. For Pepsi and other major corporations, "these markets had the needs as every other market, but there was no full department." In Russell's view, Brown was prime to sell to that area, while he was not ready to be a pitchman for White markets.[28]

By the summer of 1965, Brown had begun conversations with Wooten, Beach, and others Black teammates about forming a group that addressed social inequities in America. What formed from the extensive dialogue was the NIEU. The union made it clear to define itself before others could lump it with other civil rights and nationalist groups. NIEU members did not "seek a separate economy for Negroes or any other minority group, only full participation in the productive phases of the existing American economy." They formed an organization around their collective political consciousness. It was their goal to question notions of Black economic inequality. They developed a purpose of uplifting African Americans to promote business development and eradicate social problems in the United States. These men recognized this was not an easy feat but understood racial discrimination did not cease because they won an NFL championship or had their feats praised in newspapers.

For them, creating the NIEU and joining in the Black freedom struggle was a means to overcome racial oppression. Thus, there was no need to choose between "the movement" and athletics; they could do both.[29]

Two years after their initial meeting, in January 1966, Jim Brown and John Daniels opened Maverick's Flat, a nightclub and restaurant in the Crenshaw area of Los Angeles. After a few months of business, it "was the hottest club in Los Angeles . . . [and] attracted people from all over." The club was "the West Coast version of New York's famed Apollo Theater." This establishment was different from other after-hours spots in the city. An element of good, clean fun enticed people to visit as Maverick's lacked security, had no drink minimum, and did not serve alcohol. One of the club's early draws was the group The Temptations, whom Brown and Daniels invited to serve as entertainment for patrons. As Brown remembered, the members were "in school during the day, and performing in the club at night." Maverick's success was a significant development and was the small victory for Brown after the failed venture with Daniels and *Elegant*. Brown saw with the necessary planning, financial capital, and promotional support, he could help develop businesses.[30]

Jim Brown was arguably considered the best running back in the NFL as a member of the Cleveland Browns. In 1966, after his role in *Rio Conchos*, his career as a professional actor was in its infancy. So, he was dabbling in areas outside of football that provided him other financial opportunities. Brown and Daniels had plans to fashion Crenshaw Boulevard in Los Angeles into something akin to Las Vegas's Sunset Strip. They saw it as an effort to bring an array of Black-owned enterprises that provided services to Black people. They recruited other African Americans to assist in the membership drive. For Brown, the partnership with Daniels was simple: his business acumen and network in Los Angeles would benefit the organization. The expectation was for them to help existing Black businesses prosper but also "help the ghetto Negro . . . because as athletes we can reach them."

Building up Cleveland

While Brown was making headway in Los Angeles with John Daniels and Maggie Hathaway, he also began to introduce the NIEU's concepts to his Black teammates on the Cleveland Browns, in particular John Wooten, Jim Shorter, Walter Beach, and Sidney Williams. Their lived experiences did not leave them oblivious to the harsh realities of being African American, as the city of Cleveland was no stranger to racial injustices. As a result, they agreed with Brown that economic development was a strategy they were willing to support through the NIEU. Jim Brown noted, "I was making choices on how I wanted to contribute to a movement, and economic development was a major part of it. We were talking about 'Green power' and not 'Black power.' Business was totally necessary to get any kind of freedom, equality, and justice." The reference to "green power" alluded to the adoption of Black capitalism. Its acceptance among African Americans was not. Many prominent Black leaders espoused the philosophy, including Booker T. Washington and Marcus Garvey. They promoted a form of autonomy and self-reliance among African Americans in which they controlled the economic institutions within their own communities, like banks and insurance companies. These entities would serve as the economic foundation for Black businesses. Even in the 1930s, African Americans in Cleveland were focused on improving their economic plight. For example, the Future Outlook League, spearheaded by John O. Holly, was an early advocate of African Americans not supporting businesses where they could not be employed. In the context of the 1960s, Brown continued to devise a strategy of encouraging Black folks to embrace self-help, pride, and self-respect. Coupled with buying into the American economic system of capitalism to better one's lot in life, the early philosophy of the NIEU had a bootstrap ethic.[31]

According to Kwame Ture and Charles Hamilton, Black Power was a "call for black people in this country to unite, to recognize their heritage, to build a sense of community. It is a call for black people to begin to define their own goals, to lead their own organizations and to support those organizations." They concluded, "It is a call to reject the racist institutions and values of this society." For Black Power to work, there had to be unity among African Americans before they could "operate effectively from a bargaining position of strength in a pluralistic society." At its core, the strategy was dependent on a premise that was difficult to achieve.[32] The NIEU took on a pluralist strategy with their work. They were cognizant of the realities of a society that was based on race and socioeconomic status.[33]

Beyond economic empowerment, Jim Brown and many of his Black teammates knew the city's racial climate well and had their hands on the pulse of the Black community. They knew they were not willing to adhere to the call for nonviolence, a strategy made popular by organizations like CORE, SCLC, and SNCC. For them to do so contradicted the violent nature of their profession, a sport predicated on violence. CORE, SCLC, and SNCC embraced tenets of nonaggression as a means of moral persuasion to challenge institutionalized racism and inequities across the United States but also put pressure on White elected officials (including those who were segregationists) to uphold the law. While Brown, Wooten, and many others recognized the usefulness of the strategy, they agreed they would not be part of any efforts where they could not defend themselves if attacked by White counterprotesters. Wooten recalled, "We knew that was not in our nature to let that happen to us, so we didn't get involved in any of the marches. But we did feel we needed to be men fighting for . . . civil rights." Many Black Browns players actively discussed their thoughts and positions on the trajectory of the Black freedom struggle. After collective reflection, they recognized nonviolent marches were not a tenet they could support with the NIEU. Instead, they decided to promote economic prosperity in Black communities, a mission that they believed Black professional athletes and businessmen in cities across the United States would endorse. From these discussions, they moved forward with launching the group.[34]

In February 1966, the Los Angeles office of the NIEU opened while preparations were made to establish the headquarters in Cleveland the following month. Such a move fulfilled Brown's goal of Black professional athletes being the face and voice of the organization. As such, John Wooten and Jim Shorter began to build relationships with some of the entrepreneurs and politicians in Cleveland to gain their financial support and business acumen to help bolster the NIEU's presence and achieve greater buy-in from potential members and supporters. Wooten and Shorter attended numerous meetings to develop strategies for the union, keeping Brown informed of the happenings while he was away filming either in Los Angeles or overseas. For example, they participated in the inaugural Domestic Commerce In-Office Seminar hosted by the US Department of Commerce in March 1966 to discuss best practices to secure capital from business executives, a crucial step for the union.[35]

On Monday, March 7, 1966, the Cleveland headquarters of the NIEU officially opened with a celebration of over eight thousand people in attendance.

Dick Gregory, a comedian and civil rights activist, flew in from New York to show his support. John Daniels, who was present for the opening, gave remarks. He told those in attendance, "The name of the game is green. We recognize that for the Negro to become a potent economic force, we must endeavor to use our monies collectively to promote business and industry." Brown added the organization was "rallying the 'new-breed' which we believe represents the beginning of the Negro's ascension to true economic respect as a group." Daniels and Brown used the opening to promote business development for African Americans, old and young, to improve their lives. Religious and civic leaders also invited NIEU brass to come and speak to their parishioners. Being a professional athlete provided certain benefits and expectations, and many community folks wanted to attach themselves to the work of the union. For example, in February 1966, in a move to encourage his congregants to join, Reverend C. T. Nelson of Greater Friendship Baptist Church pronounced his membership in the NIEU and accepted his membership card during the Sunday service. Connecting to religious organizations was one of the ways the NIEU garnered support in Black Cleveland communities.[36]

At the time of the NIEU's founding, the concept of Black Power was still in its infancy, but the idea was popularized in 1966 by Willie Ricks (later known as Mukasa Dada) and Stokely Carmichael (later known as Kwame Ture). Both were members of the SNCC. With the call for human and civil rights and the push for Black Power as this period's hallmark, the NIEU faced the dilemma of how it wanted to contribute to this moment. In addition to fighting for civil and voting rights, there were efforts to end discriminatory hiring practices, inadequate housing, police brutality and neglect, and poor schooling opportunities.

On Wednesday, March 16, John Wooten met with the Lee-Harvard Community Association (LHCA), a Black civic organization, to form a partnership. The LHCA was founded in 1961 by Black residents from the Lee and Harvard neighborhoods on the east side of Cleveland. The group's goal was to ensure adequate quality of life, education opportunities, municipal services, and business support. The meeting with LHCA allowed union leadership to find out from Black Clevelanders how the union could serve their social, political, and economic interests. The LHCA encouraged all members to buy individual memberships with the union.

While its organizers reached out to religious and community groups, the NIEU also sought the help of political figures. In April, the union connected with Granville Bradley, a Black lawyer from the city who was the Democratic nominee for Cleveland's Twentieth Congressional District. Identified by the *Call and Post* as "being the best qualified candidate and offering the greatest new hope for Cleveland to send a Negro to Congress," Bradley promised to aid the NIEU if elected. With this endorsement, the union began putting its weight behind political campaigns. Unfortunately, Bradley failed to defeat incumbent Michael Aloysius Feighan, who, Bradley argued, failed to show "any concern or sympathy with the Negro's fight for first-class citizenship, dignity and equal opportunity." Most notably, Feighan called both John F. Kennedy and Eleanor Roosevelt "nigger lover[s]" with ties to communism.[37]

On May 31, 1966, the NIEU was incorporated as a nonprofit organization registered in Ohio, California, and Washington, DC, despite not officially opening an office there until 1968. With the national headquarters established in Cleveland, a strategic move since most of the executive board members lived in northeast Ohio, Jim Brown served as president. Bobby Mitchell of the Washington Redskins was a board member and a liaison in DC for a future chapter in that area. John Wooten was selected as executive director and vice president because Brown knew "Woots" was committed to helping other Black folks and possessed the "ability to get along with people." Wooten also "had the ability to call people that we didn't know, [and] setup meetings," a skill that stemmed from his earlier meetings with businessmen and politicians around the city. These attributes were necessary, as the Carlsbad native would be the key liaison for Brown's connection to the Cleveland community. Walter Beach helped orchestrate community outreach programs. This role ended up benefiting him in the long run because it became a key component of his work with the city when he was done playing in the NFL.[38]

A strong connection was developed between Black members of the Cleveland Browns and African American professionals in the community. For example, Sidney Williams and Jim Shorter were responsible for the youth development programs. While Shorter left the Browns in 1963 (he played with the Washington Redskins from 1964 to 1967), he was still essential to the union's operations in Cleveland. His role was to "channel the interest of youngsters into business." One way was to look to a program created at Howard

University to mold a project for Cleveland youth. Shorter told Dave Brady of the *Washington Post* in March 1966, "We hope to set up scholarships for students who do not have the means to continue their education. We would put them in business courses at regular colleges or in business schools because not every candidate would be qualified for college." Many Black adolescents in Cleveland were not privy to the employment opportunities they could take advantage of once they graduated from high school, a lack of preparation that spoke to the lack of direction provided by guidance counselors at Cleveland city schools. The union wanted to give Black youth the skills to decide how best to approach their postsecondary life.[39]

The NIEU made sure to connect business and political leaders in Cleveland. Arnold Pinkney, an attendee of Western Reserve's law school, served as treasurer. He had a long history of economic success in Cleveland as president of Pinkney-Perry Insurance. In this capacity of the company, he served as financial adviser to many Black men on the Cleveland Browns. Pinkney was also very involved in Cleveland's social and political scene with roles as a trustee for the Urban League and the Phillis Wheatley Association and vice president of the Cleveland NAACP. He also made sure the NIEU related to who could be deemed the "right people" for organizing programming efforts and funding. Pinkney understood the internal workings of the various political factions in the city, and the union's navigation of such hierarchies was critical to its success. Carl Stokes, who was a state representative and mayor hopeful, served as secretary and legal adviser to strengthen the Cleveland core of Brown, Wooten, Beach, and Sidney Williams. To get on board with the NIEU, he and Brown had talked for a couple of hours as it took some convincing for Stokes to warm to the idea. Stokes recognized that the platform Brown brought to the equation was a key factor in his decision to become involved. He noted to a Cleveland reporter, "If you or I, or almost anyone else, were running this thing, I'd say it wouldn't get off the ground. But, with Brown, it's got a good chance. Negroes have immense respect for him." Much like Pinkney, Stokes was a welcome and needed addition. He also understood Cleveland's political and social workings, especially across racial lines. John O. Holly, the founder of the Future Outlook League, mentored Stokes. This Black organization, founded in the 1930s, focused on business development and job opportunities for African Americans in the city. When Stokes entered his bid for mayor of

Cleveland in 1967, he introduced the organization to the city at large. He also resigned from his position with the NIEU. He continued to have a close relationship with the organization, serving as counsel when needed and connecting it to others across the city and nation who could be of help.[40]

The Ultimatum

As the union solidified its operations in Cleveland, Jim Brown contemplated continuing his professional football career. Earlier that year, in February 1966, several news media outlets began circulating stories that the upcoming NFL season would be Jim Brown's last, as he had one year left on his contract with the Browns. With no discussions between Brown and Browns owner Art Modell about a new one, it was evident to many that the end would be near for the Browns running back. During this time, Brown also began receiving more acting roles. In May 1966, he began filming *The Dirty Dozen* in London, England. This was his second film of a three-movie contract with Paramount Pictures. This created a problem for Browns management and coaches. Jim Brown's filming schedule conflicted with the team's training camp. By the end of spring, Paramount had about three months left of recording. Based on that time frame, Brown would come into the season a month after it began. Art Modell gave him an ultimatum to report by July 17, writing a press release on June 16 that stated none of the team's veterans—including Jim Brown—"were granted permission to report late to our training camp at Hiram College. Should Jim fail to report to Hiram at the check-in deadline, Sunday, July 17, then I will have no alternative to suspend him without pay." Modell added, "I recognize the complex problems of the motion picture business, having spent several years in the industry." He noted he had a duty to be fair to the coaches, players, and "most important of all, our many faithful fans" and had to abide by the deadline set forth.[41]

Jim Brown wanted to return to play for the Browns that fall but could not determine when filming would be completed, and the Georgia native was not particularly thrilled with Modell's intimidation tactic. As a result, Brown decided to retire from the NFL. A day before the announcement, Brown called Wooten from England. He wanted to let him know he retired so members of the Browns would receive the news from him first, not through the press. Wooten remembered, "Jim's departure shocked me. I knew that [he] was not intending to retire, but he got into a thing with Art Modell. And Art will be the first to tell you he made a horrible mistake. He put an article in the paper that if Jim did not report on time, he would fine him." Brown saw Modell's move as a sign of disrespect since he was the team's best player. Wooten also noticed Modell's strategy "really, really irritated Jim. He felt that he had stood up for Modell when they fired Paul Brown, and in helping Art overcome that, and now Art was treating him as a commoner."[42]

Jim Brown wrote a letter to Modell dated July 5 that began, "Dear Art . . . I am writing to inform you that in the next few days, I will be announcing my retirement from Football. This decision is final and is made only because of the future that I desire for myself, my family, and if not to sound corny, my race." Brown added, "I am very sorry that I did not have the information to give you earlier, for one of my great concerns was to try in every way to work things out so that I could play an additional year." He later stated before cameras on the movie set, "You must realize that your organization will make money and will remain successful whether I am there or not. The Cleveland Browns are an Institution that will stand for a long, long time." Brown concluded his press conference by telling Modell, "I am taking on a few very interesting projects. I have many problems to solve at this time and I am sure you know a lot of them, so if we weigh the situation properly the 'Browns' have really nothing to lose, but Jim Brown has a lot to lose."[43]

From the set of his movie, he read a letter, "I am leaving the Browns with an attitude of friendliness and cooperation. Once I return to Cleveland, I'll do everything I can do to help the Browns—other than playing." He continued, "My ambition right now is to devote as much time as possible to the national Negro industrial and economic union project, which stresses full participation of Negroes in the main stream [sic] of the American economy." Numerous media reports questioned Brown's decision and hinted that Brown would come back and play that year. It was seen as a matter where cooler heads would prevail, and the player and team owner could work out an agreement. Yet Wooten knew otherwise because "when [Brown] made up his mind, I knew him well enough not to waste time trying to talk him out of it." Brown left football without any regrets in a diplomatic moment of what could be deemed self-determination. His decision allowed him to focus on his acting career and work with the NIEU. Modell's ploy to pressure him into playing backfired. On July 9, Brown made his retirement official. Brown left as the NFL's Most Valuable Player (MVP) and the league's all-time leader in career rushing yards with 12,312.[44]

Assessing his nine years in professional football and recognizing his greatness with the pantheon greats of the game, Brown noted, "My first year in the NFL I led the league in rushing. My last year I was MVP. Bench that motherfucker." While recognizing that his on-field exploits provided him much social capital, Brown knew what happened to NFL stars who played beyond their prime. In the NFL, and all professional sports, once an athlete could no longer perform optimally, teams usually got rid of them, going with younger talent. Considering that many professional football players' careers did not reach three years, Brown's nine-year career was a standout on duration alone, but it was also singular because he was able to dictate it mostly on his own terms. Throughout his professional football career, Brown had prepared for life after the game; he was aware of the occupational hazards that accompanied football, and he knew his career would not last forever. He made connections to secure his financial security. Brown noted, "I had a consulting contract, an addendum to my playing contract, which ran for three more years. I had deferred payments coming for five more years. Straight out of football, I earned more than I did in it. And no one tried to bust my head." Brown was aware of the physical toll and the impact football had on one's quality of life. In his autobiography *Out of Bounds*, he said, "A man might love the game, but the game loves no one. The game will use what he has, discard him. The shit isn't personal. Game needs new blood. A ninety-year-old woman can't be on the cover of *Playboy*. A washed-up athlete can't play football."[45]

The Misery of Black Life

After Jim Brown's retirement from the NFL, the Cleveland offices of the NIEU continued their organizing efforts. Racial unrest in the Hough area forced the embryonic organization to reassess its focus. Of the nearly seventy thousand people who made up the Hough community, 90 percent were Black. Coupled with a predominantly White police department and White-owned businesses, racial tensions in Hough were high. The Hough area was considered a "northern cesspool of misery." It was an economically poor community saturated with White business owners who charged high prices in grocery stores and high rent for tenements infested with roaches and rats. There was a high crime rate and many single-parent homes. NIEU members were aware of the realities in Hough, as many had worked in the public schools there during the offseason as far back as 1960. Specifically, John Wooten, Walter Beach, Jim Shorter, and John Brown, an offensive lineman with the Browns, were teachers at Addison Junior High School. On a visit to a student's home, Brown said, "I got sick. I saw five people in one room, in filth. I had to go back to my supervisor for a reorientation lecture." The harsh realities of life in the Hough community were not lost on NIEU members. As members of the Cleveland Browns and Black men working in the community, they were given a certain respect among many residents, which inspired openness to the NIEU's agenda.[46]

The story of Sababa Akili, a student at Addison Junior High School in 1960, exemplifies how members of the NIEU were able to impact youth. Addison was located at 1725 East Seventy-Ninth Street. Akili remembered the school was "rowdy" and "buck wild." If any of the youth were to misbehave, he noted a "group of brutes" would "terrorize" the students. These brutes were the school security officers, who could implement corporal punishment. For example, if kids were late to class, they would gather all the students, take them into the auditorium, and paddle them. This was done to implement discipline and encourage student punctuality, but in reality, it only inspired the students' deep-seated disdain, leading many to drop out of school. Akili noted many of his friends would "go to jail for either car theft, robbery . . . some of them would get killed. It was that kind of atmosphere in the community." For example, a teenage friend of his, James Ford, was shot in the head and killed in the parking lot of an "after-hours spot." The violence on the streets often found its way into the school. There were many fights among the youth and, in some cases, between students and school administrators: one of the principals of Addison was "knocked out" by a student.[47]

By the eighth grade, many Hough youth had given up on school and dropped out. Akili mentioned they saw attending classes as a "trick" because the things they were taught did not match their reality. For young Hough residents, they did not know of the opportunities beyond their community, and many had no aspirations for better lives. On Wooten and Shorter's first day, one of Akili's classmates said, "Hey, man, they got some Cleveland Browns players teaching in the school." Akili asked, "Well, do they have any paddles?"

From his point of view, if the football players were going to implement the same strategies as the brutes, the fact that they were famous athletes would not change much. However, Wooten and Shorter wanted to understand the realities of the students, so "they talked to everyone" and dealt with "them like they were human beings." Wooten served as Akili's social studies teacher, as the previous instructor had died earlier in the school year. As a young pupil, Akili had gained the reputation of being a lollygagger. He had no interest in putting in the time required for success. When the Browns offensive lineman scheduled a paper on mental illness, he had meager expectations for Akili. Wooten assumed Akili would turn in an essay that addressed the basics, covering the different levels that affect humans. Instead, he received a paper that explored the rationale of IQ level as a way to assess human intelligence.[48]

Shocked by what he read, Wooten, joined by Shorter, told Akili he had not expected to see the material he covered and was encouraged to see him produce a high-quality assignment. Wooten told him, "I looked at your grades. You should be an A, B student. What's with all these Ds and Fs you getting?" Akili responded, "Man, this stuff is boring! Stuff in this school and the life that we live don't match up." Wooten told him, "You can do better." From that meeting, Wooten began exposing Akili to the world outside of Hough. He provided him a job cutting his lawn and those of Browns players Jim Brown and Bobby Mitchell and his brother-in-law Arnold Pinkney. The work introduced Akili to Black middle-class families who lived in Kinsman and Shaker Heights. Akili's relationship with Wooten set him on the "right track." He admitted, "With the mind that I had, I would have been one of the sickest criminals in America or locked up forever." Wooten's time at Addison led to a lifelong friendship between the two even as Akili transitioned to East High School and later helped form Afro Set in Cleveland. Wooten's interactions with Akili were also a precursor to the work the union would do combating poverty by providing job programs for young adolescents. The relationship between Akili and Wooten is an example of the relationship Black members of the Cleveland Browns developed with their community. However, there were issues outside of the schools that created great discord among Cleveland residents.[49]

Job opportunities were an important issue for Black Clevelanders. The lack of good-paying opportunities for African Americans was considered a significant reason for the rise in violence in many major urban cities in the United States. Throughout the first half of the twentieth century, Cleveland served as a significant industrial hub. But by the mid-1960s, those job prospects began to decline. In the summer of 1963, African Americans made up 18 percent of the labor force, while 45 percent of Black youth under the age of twenty-one were unemployed. As a result, there were significant economic disparities between White and Black households in the city. On average, White families brought in $2,500 more than Black households. Such a discrepancy in wealth is revealed in the facts that 66 percent of people in predominantly Black communities like Central, Hough, and Glenville were on welfare and more than 75 percent of dependent children received federal aid. There were other factors at play leading to economic inequities. One businessman from the Cleveland area argued that White folks "don't want to work next to" Black people. White employees of companies did not have to complain about having Black coworkers, as many businesses and their senior administrators were not comfortable with a Black labor force. Thus, companies capitalized on this xenophobia to justify not hiring Black workers. These issues became a focus for the NIEU.[50]

The Aftermath of Hough

The fallout from the Hough riots could have negatively affected the efforts of the Cleveland NIEU office. Instead, union members used the incident to position themselves to be part of improving the political and economic inequalities in Black neighborhoods. They used their social clout as professional athletes to call on city politicians and businessmen to begin solving the problems from which the earlier violence stemmed. Using the press was one strategic move. John Wooten told Hal Lebovitz of the *Cleveland Plain Dealer* that Black people in Cleveland needed representatives willing to associate "with them and [talk] their language, a leader who they will listen to. Somebody who will go in the barbershops, get haircuts with them; go into the pool rooms, onto the playgrounds; somebody they can come to with their problems." He continued, "I know this won't make me popular with some of our elected officials, but it's the truth. The masses don't have leaders to identify with and communicate with."[51]

Wooten knew the pulse of the Black community because he lived among other Black folks. He knew they wanted leaders and representatives with whom they had a relationship. The NIEU, from Wooten's view, had people who were willing to serve in leadership roles. He told Lebovitz, "Cleveland was lulled into a feeling [the riots] couldn't happen here because we had so many Negro officials. Cleveland is a good city. With the right kind of leadership it wouldn't have happened here. Maybe now it will wake up and be a better one." How Beach, Brown, and Wooten responded to the aftermath of Hough placed them in an essential political conversation on the Black community at the time. Their sentiments resonated with Hough residents and residents throughout the greater Cleveland area. As executive director, Wooten became a spokesman for the group, articulating the union's position on issues in different public venues along with Jim Brown. For the University of Colorado graduate, it was about the formation of alliances and relationships that would "bring about unity through racial pride, a unity that [was] created by a coming together and doing things for ourselves . . . [and] to give money to help build up Negro communities. The Jews, Italians, and Irish have done this. Negroes have to do it, too."[52]

For the NIEU, the focus during the summer of 1966 was developing connections and building rapport. By the winter the focus shifted to fundraising. That December, Jim Brown set a goal of raising $10 million so the organization would not "have to go to the SBA [Small Business Administration] for help" because they believed "we can help people on our own" and because going through the SBA meant the SBA could dictate how the union was able to use any federal funds it received. Brown operated under the belief that if enough people donated to the union, its financial objective would be easily reached, even with such an ambitious goal. African Americans were financially committed to numerous organizations throughout the country, like the NAACP and the National Urban League, not to mention the local entities, like churches and community relations boards, that were also supported by Black dollars. Jim Brown noted, "We're not in competition with anyone; we're not worried about who's in the forefront. We just want Negroes to participate in the economy of the country so they can stand on their own feet and won't have to beg anybody to give them a little of this and a little of that. What could be more dignified than that?" Brown made these statements to put to rest any claims he wanted to create a separate economy. Because of Brown's friendship with boxer Muhammad Ali, many writers assumed he was a member of the NOI. The union and NOI had similar goals: focusing on business development and opportunities for African Americans, without a reliance on White financial institutions.[53]

The call for green power was like the demands made regarding school desegregation, voting rights, and protection from White vigilantism. From Brown's view, promoting Black capitalism was essential to the fight for freedom, justice, and equality. He used his retirement tribute scheduled for Sunday, January 29, 1967, to promote the NIEU and bid farewell to the Browns. Brown received a Western Union telegram from Martin Luther King Jr. It read, "My heart warmed with [the] example you are setting for our nation. To express athletic powers is noble but to show an example of superior manhood is devine [sic]. For too long our great heroes have settled for glory of crowd applause without looking into pressing needs of our disinherited brothers." He added, "Negro Industrial and Economoic Union speaks to our most pressing needs." King saw the value of the NIEU and noted he would like to send Jesse Jackson to meet with him to discuss SCLC's plans in Chicago and how the union could help. Brown's athletic prowess on the football field garnered the attention of many, and King recognized that fact. King's memo was an expression of gratitude about Brown's creation of the NIEU, so the SCLC leader wanted to extend an olive branch to him and the union on behalf of his group, as he recognized the utility of such a relationship between both organizations.[54]

King's letter demonstrated that Jim Brown could reach the masses because of his exploits with the Cleveland Browns. Between that time and 1964, the Browns fielded dominant teams while yielding the highest number of Black players in the league. The fact they had a player like Jim Brown, a league MVP, placed him in great company with football fans. He also built a reputation as a "race man" for not being shy about publicly addressing racist practices. When the time came to celebrate the end of his professional football career, an event titled Farewell Day, it was no surprise that thousands came out to recognize him. Cleveland Browns football embodied the social fabric of the city, and in a calculated move, he used the moment to address the inequalities in American society and in Cleveland in particular.[55]

Brown's speech at Farewell Day drew the attention of an FBI informant. Federal documents center on the retirement celebration, Brown's film *Dark of the Sun* in Jamaica, and the charges that were brought against him by an eighteen-year-old, Brenda Ayres, who filed suit against him in 1965 for assault and battery in a motel room as well as for paternity of her child. He was eventually acquitted of the charges. Reviewing the FBI's observations through its Counterintelligence Program (COINTELPRO) reveals that federal officials tried to find ways to undermine Brown and the NIEU's efforts. COINTELPRO was designed to "neutralize" Black Nationalist organizations, including the four the bureau recognized as "hate groups." The union was not identified as one of these four, on which the FBI had permission to conduct surveillance, but the NIEU was watched.[56]

As countless African Americans had been physically threatened, harmed, or killed in the fight for civil rights, Jim Brown appealed for the use of free enterprise over violence to achieve equality as something all people, "black, white, bigot, liberal," could agree on. While Black Power was considered "a good rallying cry, Brown believed the term failed to be defined by the people using it. From his point of view, African Americans had "taken it and twisted it into something that is very sensational, but nothing else. It has been a crutch for many people who did not have a program." Ricks (Dada) and Carmichael (Ture) with SNCC and the Lowndes County Freedom Organization used the slogan as a call for political power through the vote. The Black Panther Party saw the phrase as a method to end police brutality and gain community control. Martin Luther King Jr. and SCLC viewed the phrase as the death of any future gains within the movement.[57] On top of the lack of agreement on the term's meaning among Black activists, White people's view of the term was often based on misinformation and laced with disdain and fear.

NIEU membership was not restricted to only Black people. Brown argued that White people could join the organization if they had its interests in mind. On a personal level, it demonstrated that he was not against working with White folks. He was keen on the realities of their role alongside Black people. He noted, "Yet the inclusion of whites was not integration, that was just including people. Your reference point can't be something that's not true. You can't make excuses for things. So, when you try to bus people and superficial things, it doesn't work." The answer was simple for Brown. He argued that governments should "just give people their rights, or if you're cheating them, make up for it. Level the playing field. Open up the opportunities that you were denying people at the same time you were taxing them." In essence, local and state governments and the federal government were failing the people they were supposed to be protecting. He called on reinvesting money that had yet to be utilized for Black communities. Brown made it an objective not to promote Black Nationalist sentiments, but he was also no fan of racial integration. For him, the latter was not the answer to the inequalities Black people faced. He believed the best solution was providing equal access to financial resources and institutions and creating economic opportunities for those disenfranchised for many centuries.[58]

More than forty years after his retirement, Brown revealed, "I bought into the concept that I pay my taxes I would have representation. I'm an American citizen. I deserve the rights of every other American citizen. I don't have to discuss someone liking me or not liking me. All I want is my rights. That keeps out all the weak arguments and discussions." He continued, "I'm of African descent. I don't believe in integration. It is important to be very definitive in your position and your position should be one that is correct. And the correct position is discrimination is wrong, and those who practice it are wrong. What you got to do is wrench your freedom out of the hands of these sick people." What Brown and others knew in the 1960s (and in retrospect) was moral suasion was not conducive to a group of people who lacked the moral capacity to consider African Americans as equals. This paradigm of White supremacy prevented an overwhelming number of Black citizens from enjoying the liberties granted by the American Constitution. To a large degree, the greatest need was for the federal government to protect the rights of Black people, members of the taxpaying citizenry.[59]

By the summer of 1967, the NIEU had concluded its first year. It was a small victory as the group began to garner national attention but was far from fulfilling its mission of supporting Black businesses on the grand scale they expected. As the union continued its efforts to grow its membership and form chapters in cities across the United States, some of its core members became involved in a significant demonstration of solidarity with Muhammad Ali. He was known as the heavyweight boxing champion of the world, a recognition given by the World Boxing Association and World Boxing Council.

However, his refusal to enlist with the US Selective Services and the threat of jail time jeopardized his professional boxing career. This decision put Main Bout Inc., a management group he helped form with Jim Brown, in limbo. As a result, John Wooten, at Brown's encouragement, contacted several high-profile members of the NIEU to convene for a meeting with Ali. Ali's decision about participating in the Vietnam War greatly affected the union's efforts as a national debate ensued, changing how Americans viewed the intersection of race, religion, sports, and civil rights.

2

The Ali Draft Summit

On the Sunday afternoon of June 4, 1967, a meeting convened at the NIEU headquarters in Cleveland. Facing jail time, Muhammad Ali, heavyweight champion, devout member of the Nation of Islam (NOI), and financial contributor to the NIEU, had reached a crossroads. The public debate about his religious beliefs was at its peak, putting his boxing career in jeopardy. Brown called for NIEU members to meet with Ali to discuss his position on the Vietnam War and the US military draft. The *Chicago Tribune* described the meeting as the "nation's top Negro athletes" trying "to try to convince him to accept induction into the army." The *Washington Post* noted that Brown and the group would "try to make Ali see the light." Numerous media outlets referred to this meeting as the Ali Draft Summit.[1]

At the center of the summit stood three men who epitomized Black athletic activism in the 1960s: Muhammad Ali, Jim Brown, and Bill Russell. These men, the "holy athletic trinity" of the Black freedom struggle, were arguably the best in their athletic professions (boxing, football, and basketball, respectively) and were outspoken about the social and racial injustices in the United States. Accompanying the trinity were eight others: Curtis McClinton (Kansas City

Chiefs); Willie Davis (Green Bay Packers); Walter Beach III, Sidney Williams, and John Wooten (Cleveland Browns); and Jim Shorter and Bobby Mitchell (Washington Redskins). Lew Alcindor (later known as Kareem Abdul-Jabbar), a basketball player at the University of California, Los Angeles (UCLA), was the only college athlete present. Carl B. Stokes, a state representative at the time and former legal adviser for the NIEU, was preparing for his bid as mayor of the city of Cleveland. Lorenzo Ashley, a Glenville native who attended Indiana University on a football scholarship, was also there. Although he tried out with the Browns, he had a short career in the Canadian Football League, and stayed connected to many of the guys in Cleveland. Contemplating the issue, NIEU members gathered at the summit to decide whether they would support "the champ."[2]

Examining a series of personal and professional obstacles involving Muhammad Ali helps us understand the summit's significance and the NIEU's work. This chapter explores the development of Ali's racial and political consciousness about his religious beliefs as a member of the NOI. It also focuses on his friendship with Jim Brown and how it played out in the development of Main Bout Inc., a business venture designed to create job opportunities for African Americans in sports. At the time of the summit, Main Bout was the first Black company to promote and televise professional boxing matches, and Ali's refusal to enter the military was causing some instability for Brown's brainchild. The NIEU and Main Bout had to address their brotherhood with Ali and the financial ramifications of his decision.

"The Greatest"

Cassius Marcellus Clay Sr. and Odessa O'Grady Clay's first child, Cassius Marcellus Clay Jr., was born on Saturday, January 17, 1942, in Louisville, Kentucky. He and his younger brother, Rudolph, were reared in Baptist teachings where "turning the other cheek" was not an option. For example, when a young Cassius had his bicycle stolen by a kid in his neighborhood, he was encouraged to get it back, even if he had to fight for it. This incident marked the beginning of his pugilist training. He recounted, "I reported it to the neighborhood branch of a police youth program. I saw a lot of boys boxing in the gym there, and I've been at it ever since. Never did get my bike back, though." He joined the Columbia Gym located at 824 South Fourth Street.

There, he met other young boxers and soon developed a fondness for the sport, participating in the Louisville Police Athletic League, organized by Joe Martin, a Louisville police officer. Under Martin's guidance, Clay won numerous Golden Glove titles at the state and national levels. Such feats allowed him to represent the United States at the 1960 Olympic Games in Rome, Italy. A successful showing there was a recipe for a lucrative professional career in boxing.[3]

Turning professional on October 26, 1960, Clay grappled with the realities of athletic stardom under Jim Crow. He entrusted his career to the Louisville Sponsoring Group (LSG), a collection of White businessmen from his hometown who felt their alignment would "be good for Louisville, good for boxing, and good for Cassius." Led by distillery executive William Faversham, the eleven members were aged twenty-five to seventy, and of them, ten were millionaires. They signed Clay for $10,000 to handle all his financial matters, "pointing out to [him] how much money he's earned, what the expenses are, how much is being taken out for taxes, and so on." They hired Angelo Dundee, considered "a topflight professional," as his trainer to ensure a successful beginning. Over the next two years, Clay won his first ten bouts, seven by knockout or technical knockout.[4]

In 1962, he moved to Miami, Florida, to live and train. While there, he became involved with the NOI. Knowing what his link to the religious organization could mean for their fighter, LSG members encouraged him to remain silent about his involvement. They felt any public connection of Clay to the NOI would hurt him (and them) financially. It was their perception that the NOI's rhetoric of White people as "blue-eyed devils" would not be beneficial to his boxing career. Despite his management group's warning, Clay was enamored of the NOI's rhetoric and continued to attend meetings at Mosque No. 29 in Miami. He also enjoyed numerous conversations with Ishmael Sabakhan, minister of the Miami mosque and Clay's first teacher of the NOI philosophy. The young pugilist's interest got the attention of the Chicago headquarters. Elijah Muhammad reminded his ministers their purpose was "to make converts, not to fool around with fighters." The NOI leader felt they should not concern themselves with frivolous activities, especially sports. Despite failing to receive Muhammad's endorsement, Clay continued to relate to the religion's teachings, finding the group especially appealing for its open contestation of racism in America. Furthermore, the Louisville native admired the discipline exhibited by their stoic demeanor, pristine attire, pork-free diet, and rhetoric that called for the unification of Black people through their brand of Islam.[5]

The NOI became particularly influential in Clay's life after he discovered minister Malcolm X, whose powerful oratory and charismatic sermons delivered from soapboxes along the streets of Harlem brought new members and supporters to the NOI. X verbally defied White supremacy and its proponents, whom he referred to as "blue-eyed devils." Over the next several years, Clay developed a relationship with X, and they formed a friendship and strong bond. Together, they discussed religion, politics, and the role of Black people in American society. Clay admired X, often referring to him as his "big brother." He invited X to Miami while he trained for his match against Sonny Liston, scheduled for February 25, 1964. While X dealt with internal matters over his comments about the death of President John F. Kennedy, Clay had another problem. In January, he had taken a preintroduction military qualifying exam. He passed the physical portion of the test with no difficulty. On the mental fitness section, he scored in the sixteenth percentile, below the minimum qualification for military service, thereby reclassifying him from 1-A status (based on his 1963 results) to 1-Y: "available for military service, but qualified only in case of war or national emergency." Based on these new results, military service was not a consideration for him.[6]

As the match with Liston drew closer, the NOI distanced itself from Clay because of a widely held belief within the organization that Clay would lose to the heavily favored Liston. Behind closed doors, the relationship between Clay and LSG was also becoming strained. As word got out about Clay's growing friendship with the minister, Bill MacDonald, the lead promoter with the group, wanted Clay to publicly reject his connection to the Black Muslims and Malcolm X. Clay swore to MacDonald, "I'm not a Black Muslim any more than you are." When Malcolm X, while under suspension from the NOI for his remarks about the assassination of Kennedy, visited the boxer's training facilities, creating a frenzy among sponsors and members of the media, MacDonald threatened Clay that LSG would find another boxer to replace him on the card if he did not issue the public rejection. When asked his opinion about the matter, Malcolm X encouraged Clay to refuse. Harold Conrad, the publicist for LSG, proposed a compromise: X would leave town to ease the tensions. Both sides agreed, but the minister could return to attend the fight without any questioning from sponsors.[7]

Before X retreated, Jim Brown visited him and Clay. It was the first time Brown sat down with both men. Brown admitted his time with the two greatly influenced his activism and outlook on American society. He stated, "I was increasingly perceived as a militant. [In spending] time with Malcolm X, [I] made no attempt to hide that fact, and Malcolm made many people nervous." When Malcolm X spoke publicly, he addressed the inequalities he saw in America with a particular popular fervor. He did not go out of his way to make the harsh realities so many experienced seem pleasant. His honesty is what many adored about him. Brown added, "Malcolm and I spoke a lot that week. I found him brilliant and reasonable, and I would leave our talks exhilarated." Malcolm X was the closest to a hero that Jim Brown had. The rhetoric X espoused fit the ideology and beliefs Brown fostered.[8]

According to Brown, the NOI minister "represented the kind of manhood I wanted to represent. . . . You come here and slap me, you gone get slapped back twice as hard." The Cleveland Browns captain was intrigued by X's social consciousness; he "spoke of economics and voting rights and political power [and] questioned the goals of the integration movement." Brown, Clay, and X asked themselves, "Did black folks really want to sit down next to white people on the toilet? Was that a goal for black people?" These conversations intrigued Brown and helped influence his role in the Black freedom struggle. He opposed racial inequities in the NFL but believed finding a feasible way to engage in social issues off the field was necessary. Brown left Clay and X asking, "How I'm gone be a warrior on the football field, and not stand up?" He found his answer that night.[9]

There was also a civil rights component to the Liston-Clay fight. While Clay was preparing for the backlash of his affiliation with the NOI, Sonny Liston had a vested interest in the match aside from winning that garnered little attention. While Liston was not actively participating in the Black freedom struggle, he challenged segregation. According to historian Michael Ezra, Liston ensured the locations showing the closed-circuit telecasts of his fights were not segregated. Due to Louisiana state law, two theaters could not show the fight in New Orleans. Although public memory has linked Liston to organized crime, he did have a racial consciousness and connection to the Black freedom struggle.[10]

On the night of the fight, a record 355 locations in Canada and the United States aired Clay's seventh-round technical knockout. The Louisville native was now heavyweight champion. Elijah Muhammad and the NOI reversed course and embraced the new champion. After the upset victory, Clay and Brown were supposed to attend a postfight party with hundreds of people at the Fontainebleau Hotel. However, Clay wanted to retreat to the Hampton House, a Black-owned motel, for a gathering hosted by Malcolm X. Clay was away from the festivities, providing him and Brown the opportunity to talk. The Browns running back remembered, "For the next two hours, he told me about Elijah Muhammad and the Nation of Islam. He told me about the Mother Ship, how it came out of the sky, gave birth to all the little ships." Brown would have preferred taking part in the celebration in Clay's honor than listen to NOI ideology and so found the new champion's choice of topic odd; however, Clay also told Brown a big surprise: his friendship with Malcolm X had to end.[11]

On Wednesday, February 26, 1964, the day following his victory over Liston, Clay announced at a press conference that he was a member of the NOI and was now going by the name Cassius X. On March 6, he took the name Muhammad Ali, given to him by Elijah Muhammad. Even though he requested to be called by his new name, very few people complied. Muhammad Ali had become the symbol of the NOI, replacing Malcolm X. In the days after Ali received his new name, Malcolm X left the NOI and formed Muslim Mosque Inc. and the Organization of Afro-American Unity. In May 1964, Malcolm X and Muhammad Ali both visited Ghana separately, but crossed paths in Accra, the capital city. The former minister gave him a telegram. It read, "Because a billion of our people in Africa, Arabia and Asia love you blindly, you must now be forever aware of your tremendous responsibilities to them. You must never say or do anything that will permit your enemies to distort the beautiful image you have here among our people." When Ali was asked about Malcolm, he said, "Man, did you get a look at him? Dressed in that funny white robe and wearing a beard and walking with that cane that looked like a prophet's stick? Man, he gone. He's gone so far out he's out completely." Ali's remarks about Malcolm X demonstrated the lengths to which the two had grown apart. Ali added, "Doesn't that just go to show . . . that [Elijah] is the most powerful? Nobody listens to that Malcolm any more [sic]." These sentiments had a greater impact than the Louisville native recognized then.[12]

On Friday, April 3, 1964, Malcolm X visited Cleveland's Cory United Methodist Church. The Congress of Racial Equality had invited him to Cleveland. His connection with them and Cory United illustrated the growth of liberation theology among Black Christians and Malcolm X's broadening of his political philosophy beyond the constraints of the NOI. His speech "Ballot or the Bullet" was given before three thousand attendees and garnered much attention for its poignant position that civil rights organizations needed to consider the utility of voting and armed struggle regarding advancing the Black freedom struggle. Many civil rights leaders questioned X's call for violence, arguing it would hurt the cause. Others saw it as a rational conclusion that had been quietly uttered in Black communities for over a century. In all, X's words were prophetic; the following four years brought much violence and rioting across the United States, along with the death of two pillars of the movement: X and Martin Luther King, Jr.[13]

Vietnam and Main Bout

Muhammad Ali's contract with LSG expired in October 1965, and he signed with Jim Brown's new management company, Main Bout. The group's core consisted of Brown, Herbert Muhammad, John Ali, Michael Malitz, and Bob Arum. Herbert Muhammad was the son of Elijah Muhammad and a close confidant of Ali on Elijah's behalf. John Ali was the national secretary for the NOI and served as leading management keeping the religious organization tied to the boxer's financial and legal dealings. Malitz was a television producer, and Arum was a lawyer. Before joining Main Bout, they were members of Lester M. Malitz Inc., a closed-circuit television group. They brought numerous technical and promotional insights to the company. Jim Brown brought members of the NIEU into the company's operations for advertising. John Wooten served on the promotional staff, and several other men (Jim Shorter, Sidney Williams, Walter Beach, and Brady Keys of the Pittsburgh Steelers) developed relationships with theaters nationwide to show fights.[14]

Religion and race were key factors in this new outlook on managing Ali. Main Bout was considered a "Muslim takeover" by many news outlets because of the NOI's involvement in the company. Over the five years Ali was managed by the LSG, there had been no discussion of White millionaires exploiting or mishandling him. However, numerous newspapers printed negative stories about Main Bout. To set the record straight, Jim Brown argued, "This is not a religious thing, it is a business project. I have no objection at all to working with Muslims. No more objection than I did to playing football in Texas for the first time, where I had no idea how I would be treated. I deal with all people—even if I don't agree with them." For Brown, it was all about green power and the ability of African Americans to get into the realm of professional sports as more than just athletes. White professional athletes dominated athletic competitions, from the training staff to the team's owner. The presence of Black athletes in positions of economic power was not the norm. Professional sports mirrored American life, and if African Americans were going to be in positions of leadership in one of the most lucrative career spaces, then in the minds of many White people, it meant a restructuring of American society. Main Bout was "an unlikely consortium" but represented the possibilities for African Americans as sports agents. Robert Lipsyte of the *New York Times* saw what others feared when he wrote, "Boxing may soon have a wholly new hierarchy. Only the fighters will be the same." Main Bout, with Ali, was historically significant because, for the first time, African Americans were a part of the decision-making with promotion and telecasts, two forms of profitability in professional boxing.[15]

Despite the group being Brown's idea, Herbert Muhammad was not initially accepting of Jim Brown's role. The NOI wanted complete control over Ali's career without any intermediaries. Muhammad may also have hesitated because of Brown's relationship with Malcolm X. However, Arum and Malitz supported Brown's role. They came to Brown's defense, telling the NOI leader's son, "Herbert, look! This guy has value. He knows all the athletes. He knows the people that can promote these fights, televise them. And he's the guy who put us together in the first place!" There was an agreement that Brown would receive 10 percent. As for Muhammad Ali, it was hard to accept the idea of Main Bout, especially with disapproval from the NOI regarding Brown's role. Brown mentioned, "It took great pains to convince him this association would be in his best interest and the best interests of the Negro people." Despite Herbert Muhammad's early reservations regarding Brown's role, he eventually conceded, but his father instructed him to safeguard Ali from "a crooked business."[16]

While the NOI's involvement in Muhammad Ali's affairs received significant attention, military service for Ali continued to loom. On February 17, 1966, he was informed of his reclassification and told by the Louisville draft board he would be called for the United States military. As a result, Ali's lawyers prepared his appeals. An NOI member who was involved in Ali's personal affairs told Jim Brown that "they wouldn't mind him going into the service, but they couldn't tell [Ali] that." While Ali believed his fate was "in the hands of Allah," Herbert Muhammad and NOI leaders wanted alternatives for him.[17]

Ali said he would serve in the military if it protected African Americans' civil rights. Such a proposition in his mind guaranteed he would never serve in the country's military. He told reporters, "If I thought going to war would bring freedom and equality to twenty-two million of my people, they wouldn't have to draft me. I'd join tomorrow. But I either have to obey the laws of the land or the law of Allah. I have nothing to lose by standing up and following my beliefs. We've been in jail for four hundred years." Ali's statements demonstrated how his political and social consciousness was connected to the struggles of other African Americans. Many Black people did not make the same decision as the heavyweight champion because jail was not an option for the average citizen. Ultimately, Ali believed refusing to serve was for the greater good of Black folks and the best way to obtain freedom and equality.[18]

Muhammad Ali and Jim Brown had formed a stronger bond in the wake of the official announcement of the formation of Main Bout. Their history of exceptional athletic feats and a racial consciousness they were not afraid to share publicly allowed for such a relationship. In his autobiography *Out of Bounds*, Brown discussed the numerous trips the two took to Black communities in New York and Philadelphia during the 1960s. Brown noted "We would go to barber shops, shoe stores, barbeque places, Ali would shadow box and tell jokes, put me in a headlock, brag how he could whip my ass. We'd sit around, just talk to people." They were fully aware of the cache being professional athletes afforded them and consciously tried to stay connected to other Black people. The camaraderie provided Ali and Brown with a genuine friendship where they could support each other through good and challenging times.[19]

In an interview with reporters on February 20, 1966, one journalist asked Ali why he did not feel obligated to enlist in the military. The champion responded, "You want me to give up all this love, America? You want me to do what the white man say and go fight a war against some people I don't know nothing about—get some freedom for some other people when my own people can't get theirs here?" Ali's antiwar sentiments gained ground across the nation. Growing numbers of Americans questioned the US role in Vietnam with mass protests. Some people argued the United States needed to address domestic affairs like poverty and race relations rather than focus on war; others centered their arguments on foreign policy and did not believe the United States should impose its will on other nations.[20]

Jim Brown used his public persona to help deter some of the negative press Muhammad Ali received by holding up a mirror to the country. Brown told reporters there needed to be some concern given to "juries in the South that make a mockery out of our court system or a murderer acquitted in the South and writing a magazine article about how he did it. Such injustices are more important to the future of our country than the draft status of Muhammad Ali—or, if you prefer, Cassius Clay." Brown additionally used the argument of freedom of religion by asking, "What do you do with a man's belief?" He replied, "You leave it alone." Over the next few months, numerous flights were canceled, including Ali's first fight with Main Bout against Ernie Terrell. Despite what others may or may not have articulated at the time, this was mainly due to the NOI's involvement.[21]

Brad Pye Jr., a writer for the *Los Angeles Sentinel*, provided an assessment of the cancellations. He remarked, "Unsavory characters of all kinds, except ones of color, have been permitted to stage all sorts of title fights. Yet, when Negroes stand to share a big swag of the loot, virtually every politician and alleged do-gooder puts the knock on the Clay-Terrell match." Whether it was the connection to the Black Muslims or Black male athletes getting a financial cut in professional boxing, Ali's stance against Vietnam did not help matters. The friendship between Muhammad Ali and Jim Brown was unsettling for some. There was an expectation that Brown, a former service-man himself, would encourage Ali to enlist.[22]

In March 1966, Brown told reporters at a press conference held at NIEU headquarters, "Cassius and I are friends, but he never has tried to influence me toward the Muslim religion. I'd be less of a man if I tried to run away from him now." He added, "The things he's saying do not appeal to me but my association with the champion has nothing to do with the NIEU. In business, you must deal with many kinds of people. . . . The NIEU is a beautiful thing. I'd hate to see anyone trying to destroy it. I believe in this with all my heart." Appealing to reason, he finished by contending, "It can open up many doors for the Negro people. All I'm asking is that the truth about it be told. There are no secrets."[23]

Ali refused a proposal from his legal team, led by H. C. Covington and Quinnan Hodges, to enlist in the army to continue his boxing career. This did not deter Main Bout's effort to finally orchestrate its first fight and the closed-circuit, theater-TV production of the fight with George Chuvalo in Toronto. They were aware of what the opportunity presented. Brown noted, "[Black people] have always been the gladiators in the ring, the men who were throwing the punches and getting a pretty good share of the money, but not the share of the money we would get with closed-circuit TV or network TV."[24]

Jim Brown scheduled a meeting with Democratic representative Adam Clayton Powell Jr. from Harlem, New York, to address the cancellations. He was joined by NIEU members Cookie Gilchrist of the Denver Broncos; Willie Wood of the Green Bay Packers; Walter Beach III and John Wooten of the Browns; and Bobby Mitchell, Jim Snowden, and Lonnie Sanders of the Washington Redskins. Powell, who served as the House Labor and Education Committee chair, was also a pastor of the Abyssinian Baptist Church in Harlem and had developed a reputation for challenging racial injustices. Brown wanted Powell to examine if "organized forces" had treated the Ali-Terrell fight unfairly. The Harlem representative met with President Lyndon B. Johnson at the White House to address the matter. Powell concluded that the Civil Rights Act was violated when their meeting ended. Union members and Powell held a press conference at the Rayburn Building. Powell said, "This is a violation of Federal employment practice regulations. My lawyers tell me it may be a violation of the anti-trust law . . . the anti-black trust law." The NIEU refused to accept the argument that Ali's "unpatriotic" remarks were the reason for the push to stop the fight. They believed race and the money they were bound to earn were motivating factors. Brown argued, "The bout [had] been booted around because Main Bout Inc. has the TV rights. For the first time Negroes own stock in closed circuit TV and will be in on some of the big money." Unapologetic at this point in the process, Brown recognized the racism of "organized forces" who sought to end the company's operation.[25]

Powell agreed the problems Main Bout encountered were due to the racial composition the group. He also concluded Muhammad Ali's affiliation with the NOI was a major issue because, he pointed out, there had not been "the slightest scintilla of criticism against Gene Fullmer when he was fighting. He is a Mormon, and no Negro can hold office in their religion." When asked if Ali was anti-American, Powell replied, "No, he is a pacifist and so am I. I don't think there is any thing [sic] glorious about the war in Vietnam or any other war." With these remarks, Powell put his political career on the line to support Ali and the union's business efforts as well as promote an antiwar stance. During the press conference, Powell also addressed the racial inequities in the NFL. He asked, "When are the Redskins—and all the other professional football, baseball, and basketball teams who have been making all that money off the black backs of our athletes—going to integrate off the field? Edward Bennet [sic] Williams is my good friend, but when are the Redskins going to have their band, the Redskinettes, and the front office integrated." The points were poignant, with three Black members from the team in attendance supporting Powell's statements.[26]

Main Bout had its first fight on Monday, November 14, 1966, in the Astrodome in Houston, Texas. It was more than a year after Ali signed with the company. Cleveland "Big Cat" Williams faced Ali with the winner of the fight scheduled to face Ernie Terrell the following January. With over one hundred theaters showing the event, Main Bout was also able to show the match at a few historically Black colleges and universities, in particular Southern University, Grambling State University, and Tennessee State University. The early predictions for this fight did not consider this an easy win for Ali. Sonny Liston called Williams the "toughest puncher he ever faced." Despite the doubters and legal woes surrounding his military service refusal, Ali defeated Williams in the third round, earning his fifth title defense.[27]

Ali's fight with Ernie Terrell was planned for Monday, February 6, 1967, in Houston. Main Bout partnered with Astrodome Championship Enterprises

Inc., to handle the closed-circuit distribution and satellite orders. While Brown and company organized the business aspects of the fight, Ali went before the draft board six days before the match. His lawyers had 3,810 signatures on a petition and forty-two affidavits to support his claim he was a Black Muslim minister. The appeal was denied. While Ali's opposition to the war was not unique, his refusal to serve in the military was highly significant. He was one of the world's most notable athletes and risked his livelihood to demonstrate his discontent with American foreign and domestic policies on religious grounds. Despite the legal matters, Ali won his match over Ernie Terrell at the Astrodome by a unanimous decision in fifteen rounds. On Wednesday, March 22, 1967, Muhammad Ali fought Zora Folley at Madison Square Garden in New York. Ali knocked him out in the seventh round, successfully defending his heavyweight boxing title. It was his ninth defense of the championship and twenty-ninth straight victory. Five days later, Ali's April 11 induction was postponed: Hayden Covington, one of his attorneys, had his records transferred from his hometown of Louisville to Houston so that the champion's legal residence would be Texas, which allowed them more time to prepare for an appeal.[28]

The issue of Vietnam continued to loom not only for Ali but for members of the NIEU as well. In March 1967, West Coast executive director of the union Richard "Dick" Bass embarked on a seventeen-day "handshaking trip" to Vietnam. He was joined by Don Meredith, quarterback of the Dallas Cowboys and the league's 1966 Player of the Year, and Larry Wilson, a defensive back with the St. Louis Cardinals. Upon returning, Bass assessed, "I don't know why we're fighting over there, and most of the Negroes don't want to be over there. They count the days until their time is up and they can leave Vietnam alive." While the trip was deemed a goodwill mission to increase soldier morale, Bass saw the effort differently. His time in Vietnam allowed him to see the conditions of Black combatants on the frontlines. Knowing there would be those who would criticize his comments, Bass added, "Being in the spotlight is like walking a tightrope. You also lose your identity. People don't think of me as Dick Bass: they think of me as Dick Bass, the football player." This was contrary to the belief athletes were expected "to be one-dimensional quasi-cartoon characters." Due to their careers as professional athletes, the humanity of many Black males was in many ways dismissed. Outside of athletic competition, they were not encouraged to voice their concerns about social, political, or economic issues, even when those matters involved the sports they played professionally. Bass demonstrated that many other athletes, aside from Muhammad Ali and Jim Brown, were aware of the problems presented by pro-America war propaganda, but they never lost sight of their commitment to the Black freedom struggle.[29]

Muhammad Ali continued to hold steadfast to his beliefs. By late April, his lawyers had changed their approach and offered him an opportunity to join the National Guard. Accepting induction would have been an "easy way out" for Ali, but he continued to adhere to his principles. Engaging in any military effort, whether it involved picking up a gun or fighting exhibition matches, was not going to happen. The proposal stated if Ali were to enlist with the National Guard, he would not have to fight in combat but would serve as a goodwill ambassador. Joe Louis, a former African American heavyweight boxing champion of the 1940s, received the same deal during World War II. Louis adorned military flyers in full army gear, holding a Springfield M1903, with the phrase, "We're going to do our part . . . and we'll win because we're on God's side." Louis exhibited the mold of what American athletes were expected to be: Christians and supporters of the war effort. Muhammad Ali was the antithesis of this sentiment.[30]

Despite numerous appeals, on Friday, April 28, 1967, Ali reported to the Houston Induction Center. Rumors circulated that he would give up his citizenship to become a religious expatriate and reside in Egypt. Ali arrived at the US Armed Forces Examining and Entrance Station on San Jacinto Street, where he underwent physical and mental aptitude examinations. He also told officials to call him by his Muslim name, not Cassius Clay, and ensure it was on his paperwork. They called his name when the time came for his oath of induction. Ali, stoic-faced, refused to step forward. As a result, a new trial date was set for him.[31]

While Ali's actions were embraced by many anti–Vietnam War supporters, the New York State Athletic Commission felt his refusal was "detrimental" to the best interests of boxing. The *Cleveland Press* posted an anonymous column that read, "When the man who is presumed to be the best prizefighter in the world refuses to put on a uniform and fight, he abdicates whatever laurels he has had—regardless of any official action." The writer added that Ali was "in no way resembling the attractive boy who won the Olympic boxing championship in 1960." The article concluded that Ali had "permitted himself to be brainwashed out of an opportunity given few young men: to be an idol, a symbol of prowess and manhood. It is a pity."[32]

Fortunately, many influential folks understood the boxer's position and dilemma and were willing to support him publicly. Two examples were high-profile civil rights leaders: Martin Luther King Jr. and Bayard Rustin. On Sunday, April 30, 1967, King spoke about Muhammad Ali's courage from the pulpit of Ebenezer Baptist Church: "Every young man in this country who believes that this war is abominable and unjust should file as a conscientious objector. He is giving up even fame. He is giving up millions of dollars to stand up for what his conscience tells him is right." King's comments served as a microcosm of his position on Vietnam. At this time, he began shaping his antiwar views on the US involvement in Southeast Asia.[33]

Bayard Rustin, a civil rights activist who played a pivotal role in the Black freedom struggle as a key organizer of the March on Washington in 1963, defended Ali in an article for the *New York Amsterdam News*. He encouraged people not to pay so much attention to the NOI's teachings when thinking about the political implications of the boxer's decision. Instead, they should consider Ali's right as an American citizen to seek deferment from the draft. Rustin argued, "In the case of Ali and the Muslims, the authorities seem to be insisting on the right to make their own determinations." Appealing to citizenship rights, he noted, "The constitution clearly warns against any official establishment of religion, but it would seem that by now insisting on the right to determine what is or isn't a legitimate minister, or what is or isn't a legitimate religion, the authorities are taking a clear position concerning the establishment of religion." The teachings of the NOI might not have been popular, Rustin argued, but Black Muslims' religious liberty was protected by the Constitution.[34]

Reaching the Summit

Muhammad Ali publicly demonstrated his religious commitment on Sunday, June 4, 1967. With his original court date of June 5 moved to June 19, the timing of this meeting was critical. Ali was given several options to avoid jail time. According to Herbert Muhammad, the federal government was willing to let

Ali serve in the Special Services, a move that would have allowed him to keep his championship titles and livelihood as a boxer. Muhammad, recognizing the opportunity to keep Ali out of jail and continue making money fighting, reached out to Jim Brown to persuade Ali to accept the new proposal. Since the NOI opposed military service, Brown was shocked by the proposition. Ali would neither have to fight on the front lines nor wear a uniform. The only expectation was for him to participate in some exhibition fights on military bases. This would not prevent him from continuing his professional boxing career. With this knowledge, Bob Arum contacted Brown to see if Ali would be willing to take the deal. Brown made an effort to convince Ali. He told Brown, "Man, you know I believe in my religion. My religion says I'm not supposed to get in any wars and fight. I don't want any deals. I don't plan to fight nobody that hasn't done nothing to me, and I'm not goin' in any damn service."[35]

Jim Brown recognized the magnitude of his friend's dilemma and wanted to develop a strategy to build support for him. He contacted John Wooten and told him, "Call the guys to get them to come to Cleveland for a meeting with the champ." As he went through his Rolodex, Wooten remembered, "Not one guy I called said, 'Who's going to pay the fare?' All they said was 'When and where?' They were there to hear Ali out and determine what support, if any, they wanted to provide him." He realized Ali needed public support from other professional athletes—specifically NIEU members, since they were all connected to Ali on personal and business levels—in case he chose not to enlist. In his autobiography *Out of Bounds*, Brown mentioned, "I wanted Ali to sit down with these athletes, explain his declaration. I knew Ali would need support, broader than what he had. By having a community of famous black athletes behind him, it would show the press, the public, Ali was backed by more than just the Muslims." Brown's sentiments demonstrated he recognized Muhammad Ali had the right to refuse entry into the military. If men who served in the armed forces were willing to defend him, others would as well. With the press conference called for Sunday, Wooten called everyone to meet at Jim Brown's Cleveland home to hash out Ali's stance on Saturday night. It was the culmination of some of the most influential Black athletes.[36]

Bill Russell was a prominent figure in the NBA who had received numerous accolades from the media for his athletic achievements, winning nine

NBA championships with the Boston Celtics by 1967. At the time of the meeting, Russell was a player-coach with the Boston Celtics, serving as the league's first Black head coach. He also had a reputation for challenging the racism engrained in American society on and off the basketball court, which garnered him the nickname "Felton X." Russell once stated, "There can be no neutrals in the battle for human rights. If you are for the status quo, then you are against the rights of man, because you are afraid to rock the boat. Well, I've rocked the boat. The black-white issue in America is perhaps the fault of a white mass which has kept the blacks down." He noted, "But to segregate oneself and become totally black is as wrong as the problem itself and will certainly not work toward a solution." Russell also fought for equal rights in the city where he played. Boston has been deemed a center of American liberation through the lore of the American Revolution. It was also a racial battleground. In May 1963, Russell led a three-mile march from Roxbury to Boston Common. There, ten thousand people gathered to support the busing of Black children to White schools as a means of garnering support for equal access to education. This gathering was a counter to the massive protests initiated by White Bostonians who were against the integration of schools in the city. Russell also had business interests in the city. For example, he owned Slades Bar & Grill in the Roxbury community. Russell's connectedness was unique. Numerous professional athletes, specifically Black athletes, were unafraid to address the inequities in American society. Interestingly, college athletes were also following suit.[37]

During his sophomore year, Ferdinand Lewis Alcindor and the UCLA Bruins won the NCAA championship (the first of seven straight titles for the school), and he also received Player of the Year and All-American honors. Wooten reached out to Alcindor and, on his "own dime," ensured he was in attendance. Ali was one of the college star's heroes. Years later, the Harlem native recollected, "He was in trouble, and he was someone I wanted to help because he made me feel good about being an African-American. I had the opportunity to see him do his thing [as an athlete and someone with a social conscience], and when he needed help, it just felt right to lend some support." Thus, showing support for Ali was an easy decision for Alcindor.[38]

Jeff Prugh, a writer for the *Los Angeles Times*, interviewed Alcindor and concluded he was not fixated on only playing professional basketball but was more concerned about developing an understanding of what responsibilities he would hold in American society. Prugh mentioned, "He is searching for answers about the role of his race in the world around him, a search that has been most recently manifested in the classes he has taken at school (Islamic and African history) and book he has read ('Malcolm X Speaks')." He added that Alcindor "is searching too, for his personal place in life. He wants to be known as something more than a man with a two-handed stuff shot and a 30-point average. He wants recognition as a whole person." Brown and Ali were fans of the young basketball star, who had turned twenty on April 16, and loved what he was doing with his work in the community. His presence symbolized a "passing of the torch" for Black professional athletes who were unafraid to face the realities of inequality on and off the field. The social consciousness of Black athletes was embodied in this meeting space.[39]

During the meeting, Bill Russell asked Ali whether his actions were in the best interests of furthering the cause for African Americans. Ali answered Russell, "I'm doing what I have to do. . . . I appreciate you fellows wanting to help and your friendship. But I have had the best legal minds in the country working for me, and they have shown me all the options and alternatives I could use if I wanted to go in." He continued, "Things like going in to be an ambulance driver, or a chaplain, or a truck driver. Or joining and saying I would not kill. I could do any of those things, or I can go to jail. . . . Well, I *know* what I must do. My fate is in the hands of Allah, and Allah will take care of me." He concluded, "If I walk out of this room and get killed today, it will be Allah's doing and I will accept it. I'm not worried. In my first teachings I was told we would all be tested by Allah. This may be my test."[40]

While Ali interpreted his experiences as a spiritual trial brought forth by Allah, it was his association with the NOI that incited animosity. His beliefs led many in the press to cast him as an un-American villain. Many Black athletes did not separate themselves from the harsh realities of the 1960s. They were willing to go so far as to put their social cache and, in some cases, their jobs on the line to support a friend amid a sociopolitical firestorm. Alcindor suffered no repercussions from UCLA for his presence at the meeting; the school had a long history of supporting its students' involvement in civil rights issues.

However, the young basketball star had not yet been public about his interest in Islam; thus, his support was a sign of solidarity with Ali.[41]

John Wooten remembered "everybody grilling [Ali] and came to the conclusion he was a Muslim minister and conscientious objector, and we could support his right not to step forward. We wanted to hear from his mouth what this whole thing was." Players like Wooten, Davis, and McClinton wanted to understand why Ali would jeopardize his career and livelihood, not to mention the possibility of facing a five-year jail sentence. They also proposed that Ali accept the offer to perform exhibition fights for the troops. This solution guaranteed he did not have to fight on the battlefields of Vietnam. The group wanted him to understand his options. It was a foregone conclusion that the court's decision would not favor him. They adjourned late that night with Ali still refusing to enlist. They agreed to end the conversation and continue the next day at the NIEU headquarters for one last meeting.[42]

The Sunday meeting began at 3:00 p.m. Going into the meeting, the attendees discussed how best to address Ali's refusal to enlist while also expressing their support for him. There was a growing concern about whether Ali was genuinely resisting on religious grounds. Since many of the men did not know him as intimately as Brown, there was a lot of catching up to be had between the men. The meeting began with an onslaught of questions and scenarios to Ali. Brown remembered, "Ali started preaching! He delivered a sermon on the Mother Ship, Elijah, the Nation of Islam. Despite the tension outside, it was funny as hell." He added, "Ali was in there with some of the top black athletes in America, whose intent was moderation and balance. But Ali was such a dazzling speaker; he damn near converted a few into the Nation of Islam. Guys were nodding their heads, going Hmmmm."[43]

While NIEU members held a solid commitment to the Black freedom struggle, they also had a connection to military service, as many of them were or had been in the US armed forces in some fashion. Jim Brown was in the ROTC during his freshman year at Syracuse University. Upon graduation, he became a second lieutenant and completed basic training in Tuskegee, Alabama. John Wooten completed his military obligation in 1960, during the offseason of his second year with the Cleveland Browns. Jim Shorter served in a reserve unit. Bobby Mitchell served with the 354th General Hospital

Unit in 1962 in Washington, DC. By 1967, Mitchell had been classified 5-A, a ranking reserved for those over thirty-one. Bill Russell, who did not serve in the military, participated in several goodwill missions overseas for the federal government and represented the country in the 1956 Summer Olympic Games. Willie Davis participated in similar trips in 1966. He visited servicemen and wounded soldiers in Vietnam with Johnny Unitas of the Baltimore Colts, Sam Huff of the Redskins, and Frank Gifford, formerly of the New York Giants. Walter Beach III had the most extensive time in the military, serving four years in the US Air Force as a cryptographic operator deciphering coded messages.[44]

Sidney Williams did six months of active duty in Fort Knox, Kentucky, and Fort Leonard, Missouri. At the time of the summit, he was in the army reserve. Curtis McClinton Jr. also served in the US military at McConnell Air Force Base in Wichita, Kansas. Once a month, he went to the reserve and practiced his military specialty. For McClinton, "Being in the military [was] real. Whether you in active duty or reserves, your ass is on the line." During the meeting McClinton made a plea to Ali. He told him, "Hey, man, all you'd do is get a uniform and you'd be boxing at all the bases around the country . . . Your presence on military bases gives that motivation to military men . . . that we recognize them and give them respect." After World War II, Carl Stokes was discharged as a private and received the Victory Medal. The men in attendance fully understood the seriousness of the armed forces, and after engaging Muhammad Ali on numerous issues for a few hours, they understood his position better. Ali concluded, "Well I know what I must do. . . . My fate is in the hands of Allah, and Allah will take care of me. If I walk out of this room today and get killed today, it will be Allah's doing and I will accept it." He added, "I'm not worried. In my first teachings I was told we would all be tested by Allah. This may be my test."[45]

As the meeting adjourned around 6:00 p.m., the group exited. Jim Brown and Ali led the way as "flash bulbs went off like a lightening [sic] bug convention." Outside of the office, supporters from the United Black Youth, Draft Resisters Union, the Committee Against War and Fascism, and the Cleveland Committee to End the War in Vietnam joined in chanting "Hell, no—We won't go." Brown and Ali sat down at the press conference table, accompanied by Bill Russell and Lew Alcindor. The other members stood behind the four. Brown opened, "The announcement made by the press that we met to discuss

Muhammad Ali's switch on the draft was an erroneous statement. . . . We wanted to get to the source of the situation the champion is in." He continued, "The long discussion we had with Muhammad Ali convinced us that the champion is sincere in his heart about his religious beliefs." Brown added, "We are satisfied, and we part as honest and good friends." Muhammad Ali declared, "I was invited by my friend Jim Brown to discuss the situation with the top athletes you see here today." He echoed Brown's reference to the assumptions of the meeting. Ali said, "The statements printed in the press regarding my visit here at the headquarters of the NIEU is false." He added, "All we did was talk about the black man's problems. We're all buddies, friends—what we call soul brothers." Brown and Ali made it an objective to let the media know the speculation about the gathering was wrong but obscure the specific details. There were no hard feelings among the men at the meeting. While the discussions were "heated," the love and respect the men had in the room for each other did not subside afterward.[46]

A reporter asked Ali about his draft status and if he had any plans to rescind his earlier decision, to which Ali replied, "I have no comment." Bill Russell followed, "Muhammad Ali is my friend. . . . The things he had gone through have made him a lonely man." Bobby Mitchell added, "As long as Muhammad Ali is sincere, we are with him. We can't tell him to go into the Army or not. We understand there are many problems involved." Like many of the union members present, Mitchell reiterated that Ali made his stance specifically on the grounds of his religious beliefs, which was his right as an American citizen, and he was grateful none of those in the meeting room tried to change his position. Brown ended the press conference by telling the "forty to fifty" members of the press gathered at the union office that all the athletes present, including him, "were of other faiths and beliefs."[47]

As Carl Stokes left the union headquarters, a crowd dominated by Black Cleveland residents blocked the sidewalk leading to the union office. They continued chanting, "We won't go! We won't go!" Stokes told the media, "This racial situation is becoming a serious thing. It is becoming more evident every day, not only in Cleveland, but over the entire nation." The war in Vietnam, the rebellions over economic disparities, and the denial of civil rights to African Americans by White supremacists loomed large. These issues had become the focal point of political discussions throughout the nation. Brigman

Owens, a defensive back for the Washington Redskins and the regional director for the Washington, DC, chapter of the union, supported the position of the members present as he saw Ali's decision as him simply "standing up for his rights." As a member of the National Guard, Owens understood the commitment of the boxer and the other athletes present. The presence of the NIEU was gratifying to Owens. He remembered, "We were standing by [Ali] not allowing him to be isolated. That was a risky thing at that time for athletes. There was no question in my mind that you had to support him. Those were his beliefs." Ali made sure to let reporters know he was not worried about finding fights. He said he had half a dozen offers to fight outside of the United States. Although Brown tried to correct the previous day's headlines, their press release for the summit stated, "The purpose of this meeting will be to discuss Muhammad Ali's entering military service." To the group's credit, there was no language about convincing or encouraging him to enlist.[48]

Even as Brown and Ali identified the flawed reports about the call for the meeting, reporters continued to harp on NIEU's failure to convince Muhammad Ali to enlist. The next day, headlines read, "Athletes Fail to Sway Clay" and "Clay Spurns 'Join Army' Plea." These types of captions illustrate the liberties reporters took with headlines. Addressing the false accounts in newspapers, Wooten stated, "They got it wrong. We took the position that we were not there to talk him into enlisting. We were there to support him not enlisting, or not stepping forward." He added, "That's different from what our goals and intentions were. If you don't step forward, you can be imprisoned. Our position was that we wanted to support him, and why he wasn't stepping forward."[49]

Some of the men in attendance, like Willie Davis and Bobby Mitchell, wanted to persuade Ali to accept the call for the draft. "But after about 15 minutes of being there, I'm saying to myself, 'No way is this guy going to change his mind,'" Davis reflected. Willie Davis had all intentions of changing Ali's mind as he believed it was the boxer's civic duty to serve in the military and his rationale not to do so was "unpatriotic." Mitchell noted Ali "convinced all of us, even someone like me, who was suspicious. We weren't easy on him. We wanted Ali to understand what he was getting himself into. He convinced us that he was." In all, the main objective for the men in attendance was to hear from Ali rather than from other sources. They wanted to understand why the boxing champion objected to joining the US military when his options would not require him to engage in combat. As the press conference neared an end, Ali was asked how he felt about losing his title. He quipped, "Ratings don't mean a thing. The people know who's the champ. Ninety per cent of the white people and 100 per cent of the Negroes and all of Asia, Africa and Europe."[50]

While Bill Russell addressed his support for Ali at the press conference following the summit, he wrote an article for the June 19, 1967, *Sports Illustrated* issue titled "I Am Not Worried about Ali." In this piece, Russell addressed the misrepresented reports, calling them a "return to McCarthyism in this country that the papers slant and distort the news until it is almost impossible to determine the truth." Russell believed the reason Ali received so much hate from others was because of his connection to the NOI. The focus of Russell's article supported the idea that American citizens had the right to religious freedom. Thus, Russell's vouching for Ali was confirmation that the NBA's most notable player agreed Ali had the right not to enlist in the military. Muhammad Ali still had his detractors in 1967. Members of the Veterans of Foreign Wars (VFW) of New York, who were critical of Ali before, continued to address their anger in a *New York Amsterdam News* column. Tired of the support the African American paper provided the boxer, they stated, "Clay is not black, he's yellow. Why don't you have the courage to say this, it will cheer up all the wonderful Negro soldiers who are fighting and dying while Muhummed [*sic*] Ali is getting rich by being a slacker in the country which gave him everything." The VFW's tone was problematic. First, the comments assumed they understood the realities of African American soldiers. Second, he was referenced as "yellow" for not wanting to serve in the military, suggesting he was less of a man for not wanting to fight in the war.[51]

Sidney Williams was aware of how certain interest groups, like the VFW, tried to utilize Black voices for their gain. From what he remembered a large majority of the American population could not fathom why Ali did not enlist in the army. The belief was all American males should want to serve their country in some capacity. Williams noted, "They resented the fact that here is this big celebrity they cannot control. He's not going to go into the military so they can use him as a tool of the government. He really believed in being a Muslim. They thought he was playing a game, but he was into the religion." Curtis McClinton shared similar sentiments. He mentioned, "We were respecting the judgment and actions of Muhammad Ali and his decision predicated on his religion. That was not a deviant to the norm and the morays to our society over a period of time." McClinton continued, "Our position was we not only honored that judgment of [him] and his religion predicated on the fact there had been others who over a period of time that did not serve on religion. Our position was to acknowledge that."[52]

Despite his religious leanings, Ali was a figure of pride for many Black males, especially those who played professional sports. Los Angeles Rams defensive end Deacon Jones recognized the transformative power of Ali. He explained in an interview, "Muhammad Ali was a favorite idol of mine. I had so much respect for him. Not for just his boxing, although you got to admire that, but what he did lifted our race up more than any athlete or anybody else that I have ever known." Abner Haynes, who played running back for the Kansas City Chiefs from 1960 to 1964 also had Ali in high regard. The boxing champion "was like a breath of fresh air for us." He noted, "We hadn't seen a brother that was for that time, that out there. What I mean by that is he was confident. . . . You can't have a lot of confidence living in segregation. And it's hard to have confidence when you do not have no power."[53]

While many Black athletes and attendees of the summit knew Ali's stance was not popular, they recognized that many nationwide would view the decision to support him unfavorably. Yet, they held the principle that Ali could make his own decision. According to Walter Beach, everyone in attendance "agreed with him. We were not afraid of losing our jobs or losing the respect from people who [did] not respect you anyway." Beach's assessment demonstrates that through collective effort, they were not coerced into a stance by media pressure or requests from the management of their respective teams. Fortunately, none of the men suffered any immediate consequence for their positions. However, there may have been an economic impact. According to Bob Arum, the meeting attendees were to "become the chief closed-circuit exhibitors of Ali's fights all over the United States. . . . Each of them would get a particular region, and they would make a nice chunk of change every time Ali fought." Despite the money forfeited because Ali refused to enlist, union members supported him throughout a difficult time. Yet, his battle with military service did not end when the summit's press conference adjourned.[54]

At Muhammad Ali's trial on June 19, after twenty minutes of deliberations, he was found guilty of draft evasion, violating US selective service laws. At Ali's request, the sentencing was not delayed and was given shortly after the jury's decision. When Judge Joe Ingraham asked him if he wanted to speak to soften his sentence, he replied, "No, sir." The judge sentenced Ali to five years in prison and a $10,000 fine, a particularly harsh sentencing considering the average sentence for draft dodging was eighteen months. However, the former champ was released on bail pending an appeal. He also had his passport confiscated, which prevented him from being able to compete internationally. Since no boxing commission in the United States granted him a license to fight, Muhammad Ali had to take a hiatus from professional boxing. By 1969, Ali had been suspended, too, from the NOI. Historian Claude Clegg III contends this dismissal was mainly for financial reasons. Ali's refusal to enlist had become costly on many levels, as he had to cover lawyer fees and alimony payments to his ex-wife. Numerous boxing commissions also prevented Ali from finding worthy opponents to produce lucrative fights. Since he was no longer bringing in revenue from boxing, his significant monetary contributions to the NOI dwindled, so the NOI distanced itself from Ali, putting him in a more significant financial predicament.[55] Muhammad Ali lectured nationwide to meet his financial needs, discussing his experiences at colleges and universities, and went into a business venture with a group of men to form the Champ Burger Corporation.

As for Main Bout Inc., it no longer existed in its original form. Jim Brown, along with Arum and Malitz, formed Sports Action Inc. Brown also supported him financially, as Ali needed. Despite being suspended from the NOI and stripped of his title, Ali continued to hold to his religious convictions. It took three years for the US Supreme Court to throw out Ali's draft conviction. Ali noted in June 1970 that his legal fees totaled $2 million. Being able to compete again would help him pay off his debts. Ali's refusal to serve in the military was costly, but he was willing to endure whatever penalties it incurred to ensure he was committed to his religious beliefs. His stance against the war became essential to the Black freedom struggle and the human rights campaign of the 1960s and 1970s. Ali confronted long-held notions of patriotism and what it meant to be a US citizen, along with the role of athletes and their connection to social and political issues in the United States. The creation of Main Bout and the problems it encountered demonstrated that although many pundits argued politics and sports should not mix, they were, in fact, part and parcel. Jonathan Eig contends that, "With closed-circuit deals, some of the athletes would double or triple their annual income, and they would continue to make money from their franchises long after their athletic careers ended." Ali's refusal to accept Johnson's deal on religious principle marked the end of Main Bout.

By 1970, the union had increased its efforts to accomplish the organization's objectives on a larger scale. This was evident with Muhammad Ali's return to professional boxing. The group continued to be instrumental in showing his fights and keeping control of the ancillary rights. The union's involvement with Muhammad Ali was just one aspect of the their involvement in the movement for equality in the professional sports ranks.[56]

Following the Ali Draft Summit, many members of the union challenged the NFL's bureaucratic structures demanding new contracts with their teams. This was largely due to broader concerns around equitable treatment, fair pay, and the provision of health benefits once their playing careers were over. As pro sports expanded in the late 1960s and early 1970s, Black athletes increasingly used their platforms to fight for racial justice, economic equality, and institutional reform. There was a true challenge to the expectation laid for Black athletes to stay away from matters that pertained to social change.

3

Challenging the National Football League

In the summer of 1967, Black players in the NFL set off alarms across the league with a record number of player holdouts. Clem Daniels, an All-Pro running back with the Oakland Raiders and supporter of the NIEU, had a dispute with team management over his contract. He was offered a $2,000 increase, which he interpreted as "tokenism and a personal insult by the Raiders to his dignity as an athlete and a man." Six Black players with the San Diego Chargers had contractual issues with the team. All-Pro defensive backs Leslie "Speedy" Duncan and Kenny Graham, running back Gene Foster, linebacker Frank Buncom, tight end Willie Frazier, and defensive end James "Jim" Griffin held out after walking out of training camp. Chargers head coach and general manager Sid Gillman fined them $1,000 each for their failure to report and enacted a fine of $100 per practice session. They did not report for training camp until they got new contracts.[1]

The Cleveland Browns had a set of player holdouts. Sidney Williams, John Wooten, running back Leroy Kelly, defensive back Mike Howell, and offensive lineman John Brown wanted to negotiate with Art Modell over their salaries and respective roles with the Browns. As a collective, they decided they would not show up for team meetings or practices until their new contract agreements were met. Their decision to act as a collective was unprecedented and obviously surprised management. This tactic illustrated these men's consciousness regarding the value of their labor to the Browns. They wanted what they deemed to be fair compensation. Generally, the average player's career was short, and often, the contracts of Black athletes were not guaranteed. It was in their best interest to get as much money as possible while they were playing.[2]

Management for the Washington Redskins had players holding out, some of whom were NIEU members as well. Bobby Mitchell, a former teammate and good friend of the Browns holdouts, signed a three-year contract with the Redskins worth $110,000. Having finished sixth in the NFL in total receptions, he was rewarded for his stellar play. However, his fellow NIEU members Jim Shorter and Brig Owens had not agreed to terms with the team. They were part of a group of seven players opting for new contracts that guaranteed them more money in Washington. Such actions by African American players in the NFL put many owners on notice. Across the league, team managers believed the pay holdouts were protests about equality, which had become a hallmark of the Black freedom struggle.[3]

By the beginning of the 1967 season, professional football attendance in the NFL and American Football League (AFL) had risen 13 and 17 percent, respectively. This was mainly due to the creation in 1967 of the Super Bowl, which began as an annual matchup between the top team in the AFL and the NFL that year. The AFL had formed out of the NFL's denial of Lamar Hunt, founder of the Kansas City Chiefs. He created a league whose teams were worthy of rivalries with their NFL counterparts in San Diego, Oakland, Buffalo, New York, Houston, Boston, Denver, and Dallas (later Kansas City). To capitalize on the economic growth available by the 1960s, both leagues agreed to come under the banner of the NFL and split into two conferences, the National and the American. Their popularity led Columbia Broadcasting

System (CBS) to pay $20 million for the right to broadcast their games and $2 million to show the Super Bowl. The NFL saw a rise in revenue, and the players were aware of the salary increases many of their teammates were given. There was a long-held belief among players that they needed to be compensated fairly. They knew the league was growing as a staple of American entertainment and experienced an unheralded prosperity compared to previous years. As a result, many athletes demonstrated their "discontent over salaries" and the power owners and coaches tried to wield over them. From 1966 to 1970, Black athletes affiliated with the NIEU made headway challenging the power structure of the NFL. There was a restructuring of labor across the league. There were individual and collective efforts through the players' union, the National Football League Players Association (NFLPA). By the early 1970s, the NFLPA had begun to push for concessions after a decade-long struggle with the NFL. John Mackey and Brig Owens, two members of the DC chapter of the Black Economic Union (BEU), formerly the NIEU, played critical roles in the union's leadership. They helped lead the challenge of the NFL's control over its players. BEU members confronted NFL management to contest the hierarchical structure of the league. They promoted Black business development within Black communities and fought for better economic opportunities for themselves as professional athletes.[4]

Building on the civil rights and Black Power movements, Black athletes saw themselves as participants in a struggle for freedom, justice, and equality. They knew the merits of the sporting world were short lived and fleeting. Thus, there was a major motivation to capitalize on the financial opportunities that playing professional sports provided. Players also discussed their earnings with each other. Salary negotiations exposed the institutionalized racism that existed in the NFL. Contract negotiations were shaped by a player's race, athletic ability, and management's perception of their value to the team. Black players who played critical roles in their team's successes were often paid less than White teammates who were on equal or lesser footing. Members of the BEU, influenced by the civil rights and Black Power movements, took ownership of their professional athletic careers and challenged the reserve rules where teams had full control over the labor of athletes dictating where they could provide their labor. This reality had dictated much of professional sports throughout the twentieth century.

Blackballed

During the 1966 season, on a plane ride back to Cleveland after a game against the Los Angeles Rams, Walter Beach settled into his seat and pulled out Elijah Muhammad's book *Message to the Black Man*. Muhammad was Nation of Islam (NOI) leader who espoused that White people were the enemy of Black people. He also proclaimed White Americans were the reason for the lack of progress Black people had made toward racial equality in the United States. The NOI leader's proposed solution to ending their "wickedness" was through war. As he was reading, Beach's book caught the attention of Art Modell. According to Beach, the Browns owner suggested to him on the plane that he not read the book. Beach responded, "You have to be joking. A man can't tell another man what to read. I'm under contract to play football, but don't ever think you can tell me what to read." He added his reading "was not one of the things [he] was going to give up for football." Modell countered and asked him if he was a member of the NOI, to which Beach replied, "I've read the Torah too, but that doesn't make me a Jew." While Beach may have made a salient point to Modell and illustrated his right to spend his spare time as he chose, his actions came with dire consequences. He noted, "From that point on, I had a lot of difficulty in football." Although Art Modell was likely not comfortable with Beach's choice in literature, his suggestion to put down the book was probably made to ensure that Beach's White Browns teammates, several from southern states, did not see the defensive back's reading material, out of concern that any resulting drama would harm the cohesion of the team. It would be a defining moment for the Pontiac native.[5]

Hal Lebovitz of the *Plain Dealer* interviewed Beach, John Wooten, and John Brown that summer about the Hough riots. Beach argued that Cleveland lawmakers should have spent more money to help eradicate the prevalent poverty-related problems in the Hough community. He admitted he "sympathize[d] with the residents of Hough, knowing their discontent and the causes." When Modell read the feature, he told Beach to "concern himself more with football and less with commentary on social problems." Beach believed his views regarding the social and economic problems that influenced the Hough riots had been enough for Modell to begin arranging his departure from the Cleveland Browns and the NFL altogether. He was right, but any actions against him would not be delivered immediately. Despite Modell's disapproval of Walter Beach's public sociopolitical commentaries and his reading material, he finished the 1966 season as a member of the Cleveland Browns. The following summer, on Friday, July 7, 1967, just two days before the start of training camp, the team placed Beach on waivers. Bernie Parrish, a defensive back for the Browns, saw this move as Modell's way of addressing Beach's refusal "to bow to illegal and degrading rules." Being cut from a team was the reality for many professional football players in the NFL, and for those who chose not to comply with the team's demands, it was another issue. By NFL guidelines, the waiver process allowed any other NFL team to claim Beach, but they had to agree to take on the remainder of the contract he signed with the Browns. If no club signed him after ten days, he would become a free agent and be able to sign with whatever team he liked without interference from his former squad. The New Orleans Saints, then an expansion team in the NFL, were interested in him and claimed rights to Beach. However, the Browns blocked his ability to go to the Saints, by retracting his name from the waiver list, an illegal move. Art Modell then informed Beach he would be put back on waivers on Wednesday, July 19.[6]

No teams were interested in signing Beach after he was cut by the Browns. He wrote letters and made telephone calls to all sixteen teams in the NFL, but none responded. A few days after the Browns officially waived Beach, he received a letter from New Orleans Saints head coach Tom Fears. After opening the letter with pleasantries, Fears told Beach, "I want to thank you for advising us of your availability and there is little doubt in my mind that you could make our club. After much thought and deliberation, I have decided to go with what we have and try to develop our younger boys." Despite the Saints' initial waiver claim, Fears alluded that Beach's thirty-four-year age was the reason the Saints would not sign him. Yet Beach had a proven record of competing against players much younger than him, even after having recovered from bleeding ulcers the previous season.[7]

Unable to find a team, Beach moved on from the NFL under the belief he had been blackballed from the league. In hindsight, Beach felt that the issues over his reading material and his sentiments regarding the Hough riots and the social conditions in Cleveland were part of a "series of racially oriented incidents . . . [that] incurred the displeasure" of Art Modell. On the other hand,

Modell simply did not want any friction between the team's players. From his point of view, his goal was to put the team in the best position to compete for an NFL championship, and having Beach on the squad jeopardized that goal. With Jim Brown no longer with the Cleveland Browns and unable to vouch for Beach to stay on the team, the Pontiac native was easily expendable. His age and what Browns management deemed a "rebellious nature" jeopardized his spot on the team. Walter Beach was not without work long; Carl Stokes added him to his staff that summer to help with his campaign to become mayor of Cleveland. Stokes won the election that November, becoming the first Black person to be mayor of a major city in the United States. Beach was appointed coordinator for the mayor's Council on Youth Opportunity. This position allowed him to work in Cleveland communities and help push the programs of the union. While his professional football career ended, he was not done dealing with the NFL.[8]

"The Group"

On Saturday, July 22, 1967, training camp for the Browns opened an hour southeast of Cleveland at Hiram College. John Brown, Mike Howell, Leroy Kelly, Sidney Williams, and John Wooten did not report. Carl Stokes, who served as the men's lawyer, sent a telegram to Art Modell that day on behalf. It read, "These men have advised me to inform you that they will not report to training camp until a conclusion has been reached on their contracts. I'll be glad to meet with you at your earliest convenience." The same day, Modell responded to the letter at his press conference, telling reporters, "I regret the actions of the five Browns players and Carl Stokes. However, I will not be intimidated by any person or group of individuals." He added, "There is no place for actions such as this in professional sports." Stokes called Modell that evening. After exchanging pleasantries, he told him, "All five players have said that if one of them is traded to another club in the National Football League that the remaining four also must be traded." The Browns players' actions were unprecedented: before 1967, many players often represented themselves and handled their financial matters individually with team ownership, but these five players had opted to do so collectively and through a representative. Based on Modell's comments in response, he believed Brown, Howell, Kelly, Williams, and Wooten had violated their contracts. To put pressure on the five holdouts, Modell publicly stated their refusal to report warranted fines, suspensions, and trades to other teams, an outright dismissal of their request to be sent to one team.[9]

Confused by the players' demands, Modell told reporters, "I am rather proud of my treatment, in all areas, of our players. . . . The Browns record over the years regarding the treatment of Negro players speaks for itself." He added, "Early in the club's history, the Browns paved the way for the mass influx of the Negro athlete into sports. In recent seasons under my ownership, they have composed almost one-third of our squad—more than any other team in the NFL." The Browns owner played on the team's history and efforts with integrating the NFL during the 1940s and 1950s, none of which were part of his tenure as owner. There was an unspoken gentlemen's agreement to not sign Black players in the league from 1933 to 1946. Stokes was annoyed by Modell's sentiments. He stated "I am dumbfounded by Art Modell's response. There is nothing racial about the position of the players. None of them is alleging racial discrimination." He added, "Their response is based solely on the fact that they have not been offered the amount of money that they feel their services are worth." While Modell believed the player's issues were over race, the real matter was twofold: financial compensation and equal opportunity for playing time. Stokes told reporters, "I regard Mr. Modell's characterization of this as a racial issue as being irresponsible and out of keeping with the respect in which I formerly held him." Although none of the players had stated anything about being mistreated by the team because they were Black, Modell brought up race as a tactic to use the team's favorable treatment of Black athletes to his advantage.[10]

Art Modell believed the players had "no basis for negotiations, period," especially not John Wooten. The offensive lineman had signed a two-year contract before the 1966 season, and Modell expected him to honor the contract he signed. By Monday, July 24, the Browns management informed the holdouts it would issue a fine of $100 for every day they were not in camp. Modell also gave the group four stipulations before he would consider negotiations: Wooten's contract talks would cease since he was signed through the 1967 season; Sidney Williams's contract would focus only on financial negotiations, and the coaches would determine his playing time; all contracts of the players were to be handled individually, and once agreements were made, they would sign and report to camp; and the "all for one, one for all" provision would cease.[11]

On Thursday, July 27, from the Metro-Goldwyn-Meyer movie set for his film *Ice Station Zebra*, Jim Brown chimed in on the situation. He felt Art Modell was "completely off base in telling the press what the Cleveland Browns have done for Negro players." He stated the actions of the five Browns were purely economical, and they were "not concerned with charitable contributions made to them on the basis of race." For example, Brown discussed Mike Howell's annual salary. Howell was a starting defensive back for the team and was paid $16,000. In 1966, he was second in the NFL for total number of interceptions. To end his holdout, the team proposed a $3,000 increase. Brown argued that what Howell received was not equal to other players at his position around the league or fair for his level of play. To illustrate this point, Brown compared Howell to another player on the Browns whose name he did not reveal. The player received a raise and bonus of $11,000, nearly three times more than what the Browns offered Howell. Brown concluded that the proposed pay "by modern day standards [was] not a first class raise." The former gridiron star also discussed the other players who were holding out. He mentioned that the $15,000 salary John Brown received as a starter on the offensive line was "low by any standard."[12]

Jim Brown had a history of maximizing negotiations with the Browns front office. In the summer of 1960, he signed a two-year contract worth $50,000, which Paul Brown considered was "in line with being the best running back in the history of the game." Brown led the NFL in rushing since he was drafted and after three years of play, he tallied the most rushing yards in a season, most rushing yards in a game, and tied the record for touchdowns. By the summer of 1960, his career yardage put him fifth all-time in league history. The $65,000 salary he was paid in his last year with the Browns was the result of several renegotiations with Modell, to which the Browns owner begrudgingly conceded. As the team's best player, he requested more money when he felt it was due, and when he felt like Modell and the coaching staff did not value him as he saw fit, he used the Cleveland and national press to put stories out that he was threatening to quit the game if he was not paid commensurate with his talents.[13]

In the case of his ex-teammates, Brown understood their issues. Despite being away from the game with much of his attention on movie roles and NIEU efforts, he was still aware of players' financial matters and was willing to speak on their behalf. As a retired player, Jim Brown had nothing to lose. On the other hand, his former teammates and friends had much to consider. The *New York Times* labeled John Wooten the "ringleader" of the holdout and "a long-time [*sic*] disciple of Jim Brown." Despite the negative media assessments, he was steadfast in his desire to renegotiate his contract because of what he believed was an "outstanding season."[14]

His other teammates sought similar results. Leroy Kelly earned $20,000 as the starting running back for the 1966 season, the team's first without Jim Brown. Underlying Kelly's negotiation was a $45,000 difference between his pay and what Brown earned in his last year with the team. Kelly amassed over 1,500 total yards, scored sixteen touchdowns, was the second-leading rusher in the NFL, and was selected to the All-Pro First Team and the Pro Bowl. Kelly was compared to Jim Brown, and Brown noticed the outstanding season of the Morgan State graduate. He told reporters Kelly was "not even close to making the salary that average untried rookies [were] guaranteed." In addition to providing public support for his former teammates and union members, Brown also questioned the power dynamics within the NFL. He rhetorically asked, "Should the owners be complete dictators in salary negotiations? Is it wrong to have legal representation when dealing with legal problems?" He added, "And should untested rookies receive greater salaries than proven veterans—or should Clinton Jones (a rookie) make more money than Leroy Kelly?" Brown posed valid points, and many issues he raised were the topics of conversations among NFL veterans. They believed first-year players, who had yet to play an NFL game, should not make more money than them. It was a matter the league and its players would deliberate for the next forty years. The dilemma with the five Black Cleveland Browns players was not the only time that summer that African American players made headlines over their contracts.[15]

In Cleveland, the fines for the five Browns players had reached $1,100 by August 1. Team management and coaches wanted to reach a resolution, but only two of the five demands had been met. Sidney Williams, dissatisfied with the lack of commitment from his coaches for playing time, told Browns management he no longer wanted to play for the team. As Williams remembered, Modell and the coaches were "stumped, could not believe it . . . startled." They tried to convince him to stay, but he told them they were unfair about his playing time and refused to change his stance. The linebacker left Modell no option but to trade him. The Browns sent the rights to Williams to the New York Giants, who "anxiously" awaited his services. Shortly after arriving for camp, he was released by the team and later signed with the Redskins. John Brown, one of the team's starting offensive linemen, was traded to the Pittsburgh Steelers who were "enthusiastic" to get him in exchange for draft picks. The Browns communicated with other teams about trading for Leroy Kelly and John Wooten. Mike Howell decided to report to the Browns after his two-week obligation with the National Guard.[16]

Modell refused to negotiate. He told reporters at a press conference, "If I give in to them, I'm dead. I may lose the battle, but I don't intend to lose the war." By "war," Modell meant the "preservation of the practice of negotiating individually with each athlete and keeping his salary confidential to avoid comparisons." Confidentiality and negotiation practices were among the main issues the five Browns wanted to address. Carl Stokes called the makeup of players' contracts in the NFL a form of "peonage" and suggested legal action against Modell. Stokes and many others believed that keeping players' pay private benefited only team owners. The secrecy prohibited players from determining their value in relationship to their peers across the league. Most importantly, owners across the NFL had their fingers crossed that Modell would not give in to the players' demands. Doing so, would have created a "domino effect" across the league.[17]

On Monday, August 7, 1967, after several discussions between Browns management and Stokes, Kelly and Wooten agreed to end their holdouts and report to camp. Kelly was presented with a new contract from Art Modell but decided not to sign it, playing under his rookie contract. While his refusal to sign the offer resulted in the loss of 10 percent of his salary for the year, it allowed him to become a free agent the following year. This move permitted him to sign with any team of his choosing, or he could re-sign with the Browns for what he expected to be a more lucrative contract. Modell was surprised by Kelly's decision. He noted, "We shook hands on the deal. I am puzzled and mystified by this. . . . [He] called and said the contract we had agreed on was not acceptable and that he also wanted a different level of negotiations for next year." As for John Wooten, he did not get a new deal. He returned to camp in Hiram and played the final year of his two-year contract.[18]

In the aftermath of the holdout, "The Group" helped bring the negotiating power of athletes to the forefront of the labor discussion in the NFL. While their demands were unmet, they demonstrated that Black athletes could obtain better economic opportunities. As the *Cleveland Call and Post* affirmed, "Since the merger of the two leagues [NFL and AFL] . . . the players having no bargaining position and having to play at any figure that management sets is equally ridiculous." Fortunately for the players, their understanding of this point helped usher in a new era of player's rights with the solidifying of a union the following season. They were unaware that those who questioned the NFL structure were considered "a threat" by management. As a result, NFL officials "did everything in its power to discredit those who challenged the system." The actions of the five Browns players were only the beginning of problems with the league for two from that group: John Wooten and Sidney Williams.[19]

Whiteballed

The issue of financial compensation was at the heart of the matter for the five holdout Black players in 1967. They believed it was essential to confront injustices on or off the field. In July 1968, John Wooten and teammate Ross Fichtner, a White defensive back with the Browns, got into a public dispute that led to both men being traded from the team. That summer, Fichtner, who had been with the team since 1960, did not invite any of his Black teammates to a golf tournament held at the Country Club of Ashland, although the previous year, he had invited the whole team. According to reports about the 1967 gathering, the Black invitees from the Browns—Walter Johnson, Leroy Kelly, Jim Shorter, Sidney Williams, and Wooten—"stuck by themselves and did not seem to enjoy the occasion." Organizers of the event felt the players were disinterested because they failed to engage with many of the event's White guests. In addition, there was an issue over an alleged unpaid bill at the golf pro shop by a Black member of the team. John Wooten felt because he had won the tournament, the White organizers found reasons not to invite them back, for fear of losing to a Black man again.[20]

The following year, 1968, officials at the Country Club of Ashland encouraged Fichtner to refrain from sending invitations to the African American players. Wooten, the lone Black player who frequented the establishment, was understandably offended. He reached out to Fichtner to gain an understanding of the situation. Wooten told Fichtner his actions were wrong, "and for him to get on the phone and say I'm not going to invite the black players because one or two, whoever did not pay their pro shop bill" disappointed him. Wooten requested Fichtner present the alleged bill as proof of the grievance, but one was never presented. Fichtner told Wooten, "I didn't discriminate against anyone as far as this situation is concerned. It is not a Cleveland Browns promotion . . . it is the Country Club of Ashland." To take race out of the situation, Fichtner also told his teammate some White team members were not invited to the tournament at the request of the club. According to Fichtner, the limitations placed on the number of invites were a reflection of the golf club's exclusivity. While Fichtner was correct to remind Wooten the gathering was not the work of the Browns team, he failed to understand the implications of the club's decision for his Black teammates.[21]

Wooten believed Fichtner was being racist, and the Browns lineman was not shy about discussing the ordeal as the situation garnered national press. On July 23, Art Modell was in no mood for distractions in a second consecutive offseason because of racial issues. He released Fichtner and Wooten before training camp after no teams were willing to trade for the two and considered the move "in the best interests of both the club and the players." Both men were devastated; finding a team before the start of the season was difficult because teams had already decided which players to invite to fill their rosters, and clubs were cautious about signing players labeled troublemakers. It was the belief around the league that these types of players created a toxic environment and were detrimental to team culture. Wooten's history and link to Jim Brown, coupled with his affiliation with the NIEU and other civil rights and Black Power advocates, did not help eradicate his "racial militant" label.[22]

William Wallace, a writer for the *New York Times*, opined, "Pro football's off-the-field problems with its players are not over so long as John Wooten, the former star guard for the Browns, continues to brood and plot in Cleveland." Wallace referenced Wooten's dispute with Fichtner, quoting the lineman: "We black Browns are after the hide of this white Brown." Wooten vehemently denied making the statement. He said, "It is absolutely untrue. What does it mean? That we were going to get together and beat up Fichtner. I don't know what it means. . . . I would not deny any man the right to make a living at his job. I am for total justice for everybody." Wallace never addressed Wooten's rebuttal, but he did acknowledge Wooten was "a proven performer." Wallace was also suspicious of the fact that no NFL team had an interest in Wooten, while Ross Fichtner was able to sign with the New Orleans Saints shortly after clearing waivers. The *New York Times* writer suggested Wooten take legal action on "charges of conspiracy and restraint of trade." The NFL held a conspiracy hearing two years later, in 1970, at which several players were called before a grand jury to discuss player and management relations linked to antitrust violations.[23]

Reflecting on the golf tournament more than forty years after it happened, Wooten had no regrets. He said, "The situation with Ross Fichtner was something I would do tomorrow morning. That is something that I could not have lived with myself if I had not done it." Despite his release from the Browns, it was clear he felt strongly about challenging his teammate on the ramifications after so much time had passed since their incident. The golfing matter damaged Wooten's reputation with league officials, hurting his chances to sign with another team. The harm done was not fully understood until he threatened the league with a lawsuit. This led to a meeting with Alvin "Pete" Rozelle, the NFL's commissioner, who hastily encouraged him not to move forward until they could discuss the matter in person. They decided to meet on August 3, 1968, in Canton, Ohio, for the Hall of Fame enshrinement ceremonies. They talked for over two hours about the lack of interest from teams. Rozelle told Wooten that several clubs were scared to sign him, fearing that racial incidents would escalate on their squads or, in a more extreme view, that there would be a Black takeover of the NFL.[24]

With racial tensions high throughout the country, Wooten was informed league owners "thought we were trying to band together to create our own union and strike. That the Black players would band together with the [Black] Economic Union, and then collectively strike." Rozelle also told him, "You all are trying to take over the NFL." Wooten laughed at the commissioner's revelations, saying, "This is ridiculous." He thought to himself, how could they come to such a conclusion when "they had never read one single statement from anybody in our organization, meetings, talks or anything else, that said anything about collectively banding together to strike against the NFL." He asked Rozelle, "Well, what gave you that idea?" The commissioner responded, "Look at how you are dressed!" Wooten was wearing a dashiki.[25]

While the idea of a Black takeover was never a thought for Wooten or union members in the NFL, team owners were aware of the involvement of Black players in the freedom movement. Their engagement at this level scared many owners around the league. As a result, they made attempts to keep any potential troublemakers off their teams. The number of players, especially Black athletes, who participated in holdouts from 1967 to 1968 was unprecedented. These challenges can be attributed to the growing consciousness among many African Americans influenced by the demands of the civil rights and Black Power movements. So while they were influenced by the social and political elements of the time, they had no intention of taking over the NFL or starting their own league.

What started as a by-product of a handful of athletes wanting better compensation became a league-wide issue. It resulted in a change in how ownership conducted contract negotiations. Before, owners consulted directly with each player, with a "take it or leave it" approach. Teams had control over player movement as they owned their rights. Thus, players left a team if they were traded or released. As a result of the holdouts, players began to utilize agents and lawyers to help advocate and protect them from signing contracts that were not in their best financial interests. NIEU members played an integral part in strengthening players' negotiating power and control over their careers.

NFL owners and league officials' perception of the NIEU was not optimistic. Many Black athletes associated with the organization were notable NFL, NBA, and Major League Baseball (MLB) players. League officials mistook their promotion of Black economic development as an espousal of Black Nationalism. Their involvement with Muhammad Ali and Arthur Ashe, one of professional tennis's best competitors, caused great alarm. There was a fear the recent holdouts were the sign of a Black coup of the NFL that would lead into other areas of the sporting world. While coaches and team owners never openly criticized the NIEU or the organization's work, teams made assumptions about the group based primarily on their involvement with the Black freedom struggle. A "guilty by association" label was placed on Wooten.

However, he continued to stand on principle with his challenge toward Fichtner despite it costing him his job with the Browns. The move also impacted the social and political relationships he had formed in Cleveland, affecting his work with the NIEU.[26]

Following his meeting with Pete Rozelle, Wooten discussed joining the Los Angeles Rams and Philadelphia Eagles; however, a contract never materialized from those conversations. On Monday, August 12, 1968, he signed with the Washington Redskins for $35,000, joining Bobby Mitchell and some of the other DC chapter NIEU members who were on the squad. This was considered an excellent move for Wooten for a couple of reasons. Otto Graham, a former Cleveland Browns great, was the head coach and used an offensive game plan like the Browns did. This made Wooten's transition to the field more manageable even though he and Graham were not on the best terms. The Black players on the Redskins also helped him adjust to being in DC. It was an example of how African American players built a community among themselves.[27]

Just as the chaos ended for John Wooten, Sidney Williams hoped to escape the drama he left in Cleveland. However, it followed him to Washington that summer. In 1966, Williams played the entire year with the Browns but had to "fight for playing time" after Johnny Brewer transitioned to defense. The club's move dumbfounded Williams. In an interview, he explained, "The linebacker position is delicate. It's damn near like quarterback. With a linebacker you have to cover someone out of the backfield, deal with that tight end on your head, fight him off. There is so much you have to do." In his opinion, it was impossible for a player, Brewer in this case, to play tight end for the entirety of his career and then change to linebacker. Williams added, "You cannot be converted from offense to defense to play that position. They did back in the twenties and thirties, but at this time, you were specializing in a position." Despite the demotion, Williams went through the year with a "good attitude." He did what he felt was for the best of the team. Interestingly he was told by Brown's management "he [was] as best or better than any linebacker on the team," yet that acknowledgment was not sufficient for him. He was aware that several other Black teammates and players around the NFL had been told the same and were never promoted to the starting position or outright denied the opportunity to play. Williams wanted the meritocracy of sports to be embraced by Browns coaches. However, Art Modell and his position coach refused to make any promises. If he was not given a fair chance to showcase his talents, Williams wanted the Browns to trade him, and in the end, that's what happened.[28]

As a member of the Redskins in 1967, he earned considerable playing time for a few games at linebacker. After that season ended, he scheduled a meeting with Otto Graham to begin discussing renegotiating an extension on his contract with the team since he had a year remaining. After sitting down and exchanging pleasantries, Graham began the conversation with questions about Jim Brown, asking if the former Browns running back had any personal problems with him. The Redskins coach had taken offense to some critical comments Brown made about him in his 1964 book *Off My Chest*. He wanted to see if Williams had any insight on the matter. Graham had criticized Brown when he was a member of the Cleveland Browns. He once told reporters Modell should have traded the running back for his lack of effort on pass-blocking plays, a critique that belied his Hall of Fame career. Williams responded, "Hey man I didn't come in here to talk about Jim Brown, I came here to talk about my contract." Graham was befuddled by Williams's lack of interest in discussing Brown. He believed if the linebacker wanted to discuss money, he expected Williams to at least amuse him. The meeting ended abruptly, and the renegotiation never happened.[29]

When Williams arrived for training camp the following season, he noticed he could not please his coaches. He remembered, "I could be inches off, and what I was doing was wrong." Washington released him a few days before the first game. The Southern University grad's refusal to defer to his coach led to his dismissal from the team. Fortunately for Williams, he signed with the Baltimore Colts, where the team won the NFL championship and played in Super Bowl III, a loss to the AFL champion New York Jets. Williams's move to Baltimore kept him employed and in contact with the union's members and programs in nearby Washington, DC. That same month, Arnold Pinkney, a board member and legal adviser of the NIEU, met with Art Modell to discuss hiring African Americans for executive positions with the team. He argued, "Somehow, whenever the Browns hire a secretary, she is always white. . . . Somehow, no Negro is even considered for an executive position in the Browns organization." His concerns were valid and raised a critical question: Were African Americans only good enough to be players but not serve in other roles in the NFL and professional sports overall? Pinkney's meeting with the Browns owner was a precursor for the fight to increase the numbers of Black employees in upper-level management jobs in the NFL. Little did Pinkney know that the struggle for representation between players and owners would remain for future generations.[30]

Representation and the NFLPA

Black NFL players soon became involved in the creation of a labor union. The result was the NFLPA. The union had been two separate entities, with the AFL and NFL each having an organization to represent the players. In 1968, the two associations became one after the AFL and NFL merged. Two members of the NIEU—John Mackey, a tight end with the Baltimore Colts, and Brigman Owens, a defensive back with the Washington Redskins—were pivotal to the NFLPA's challenging the power of NFL owners and the financial structure of the league. The work of Mackey and Owens represents the complexities of Black athlete identity. They also saw themselves involved in the struggle for Black freedom. Mackey and Owens were keenly aware of those who came before them and, ambitiously, were hopeful of improving the lives of future generations who played in the NFL.

John Mackey was born September 24, 1941, in Freeport, New York. He remembered, "If your parents saw me doing something wrong, they'd kick my butt and then tell my parents and they would thank them and then they would kick it. . . . It was that kind of thing, you couldn't be disrespectful." Mackey's father was a Baptist minister, Reverend Walter Mackey, and his mother, Marnack, grew up in a large family as one of ten children (one sister and eight brothers). His parents were keen on John doing his best and excelling at whatever he did, but never at the expense of losing his sense of self. As a teenager, he marveled at playing football, and his mother gave him approval to play starting his sophomore year at Hempstead High School. Mackey eventually earned a scholarship to play at Syracuse University as a running back. He wanted to wear number 44 because it was the number of his idol Jim Brown. However, Ernie Davis, the team's leading rusher at the time, had already claimed the number. Refusing to be a backup to Davis, Mackey switched positions and found a new number, 88. He believed he "was twice as good as number 44." Mackey was a proud player and wanted coaches to know he was second to none. His Syracuse football number eventually became synonymous with his professional football career.[31]

At six-foot-two and deemed a "rock-hard 250 pounds" during his time at Syracuse, Mackey had an illustrious career playing tight end. Known to be light on his feet, he was given the nickname "Twinkle Toes Mackey" by his future wife, Sylvia, and her friends. Upon graduating in 1963, he held the school record for receiving yards in a run-oriented offense that predominated in college football. Head coach Ben Schwartzwalder told reporters the Freeport, New York, native was "our best football player." He noted, "If some folks haven't heard too much about John right now, they'll hear more next year when he steps into the professional ranks." Before turning pro, he was selected to play in the annual game between the College All-Stars and the NFL champion Green Bay Packers, coached by legendary coach Vince Lombardi. After a good showing in the game, where the collegians beat the pros 20–17, Mackey was provided a couple of opportunities to play professionally. The Baltimore Colts of the NFL drafted him in the second round, and the New York Jets of the AFL selected him in the fifth round of their draft. Mackey chose to sign with the Colts and began one of the most remarkable careers for a man who "revolutionized" the tight end position.[32]

By the summer of 1966, Mackey had played three years and had been chosen to play in two Pro Bowls. He was one of the league's best players and wanted to be compensated as such. He and teammate Jimmy Orr left camp after they failed to agree to the terms of their contracts with the team. The two eventually signed their contracts, begrudgingly, before the start of training camp. However, their brief departure impacted their relationship with team management, who did not appreciate the negotiation ploy, especially team owner Carroll Rosenbloom. It led team officials to declare, "Never again will the Colts negotiate with a player who walks out of training camp." Mackey was aware of his abilities and value to the Colts. This was evident in his selection to the Pro Bowl the following two seasons, in 1967 and 1968. In his first six years with the team, Mackey earned All-Pro honors three times and was selected to the annual Pro Bowl five times. While he continued to garner numerous accolades for his feats on the field, he and many other players, regardless of racial background, could not ignore their lack of economic power.[33]

By 1968, the American Football League Players Association and NFLPA sought to align and form one union with central leadership. As a collective, they agreed Mackey was the best person to represent them since, until this agreement, "the Association was little more than a social club dependent on lawyers to do the brainwork." When players negotiated with team owners, legal aids were not allowed in the room. This irritated players like Brigman "Brig" Owens, a defensive back with the Washington Redskins. Therefore, players had "to caucus and go to the hallway and talk to our attorneys, then come back in and make our demands." He was troubled by the back and forth and the fact that "the lawyers would cite all these different cases. I didn't know what the heck they were talking about." Owens began going to the law library and did his research to "figure out what the hell they were talking about." He had an epiphany and concluded, "These guys are not that damn smart." He recognized the lawyers knew how to utilize cases to their advantage as the "law [was] all about precedence." Owens decided to enter law school at Antioch College's satellite campus in the nation's capital. He knew if he wanted to get the best contract for himself, he could not depend on Redskins leadership or someone else.[34]

Brig Owens came into the NFL as a former quarterback from the University of Cincinnati. The school was one of only a few who recruited him to play quarterback since many White football coaches deemed Black players unfit to play the position. Interestingly, he was able to catch the attention of several colleges on name recognition alone. One school was Brigham Young University (BYU). With a name like "Brigman," Owens thought the school sent him recruiting materials because they believed he was a Mormon. Owens's assumption was proven correct when one of the coaches visited his high school and thereafter, BYU stopped recruiting him. Other schools who recruited him were concerned about not Owens's race but his position on the field. They wanted him to play running back, wide receiver, or defensive back. Cincinnati was the only school that allowed him to play the position he loved.[35]

By 1963, Owens had demonstrated great athletic ability at Cincinnati as a triple-threat quarterback (he could pass, run, and punt). In 1964, he led the school to ten victories, the most in its history at the time, and garnered the attention of many NFL scouts. However, the teams considering him wanted him to play something other than quarterback. For example, in 1965, the

Dallas Cowboys drafted him in the seventh round, and he spent his first year with the team on defense with the practice squad. Owens noted, "I never played defensive back before, never tackled anyone." Aware of the restraints on African Americans playing the quarterback position, Owens knew if he wanted to play professionally, he needed to adjust to defense. In Dallas, Owens was also awakened to the financial realities of professional football. He saw "a lot of veteran players leave, some crying. I realized it was really a business."[36]

NFL players had to battle the "numbers game" during training camp. Teams brought in more than sixty guys with only forty roster spots. Hence, players were easily replaceable, especially Black players who were on teams that implemented racial quotas. Owens's experiences with the Cowboys helped him understand his career in the NFL was not guaranteed. Fortunately, he played well on the practice squad, and the following year, Washington traded for him to play defensive back. Owens noted, "This was the best thing that ever happened to me." The move to DC put him among people who would play essential roles in his life.[37]

While playing in Washington, Brig Owens became involved with the NIEU through Bobby Mitchell and became involved with the NFLPA through his relationship with John Mackey. More on his work with the NIEU is detailed in chapter 4. When it came to player engagement, Owens remembered, "I was one who used to complain about getting things done on time." One day, Mackey approached him and said, "We need to have you come help us with the [players'] union. We need some support and your time." Owens countered, "I don't have that kind of time. I'm going to finish up law school." Mackey lashed back, "You little ass, you always complaining, let's make it right. Give me a year." A year turned into five and a half years, during which Owens served as the player representative for Washington and a member of the negotiating committee that bargained on behalf of all players.[38]

Serving as a player representative required a significant commitment from players. Aside from worrying about their play on the field, "a lot of energy was focused on negotiations and organizing" the team. It was believed among players that "anybody who was a rep put their career on the line"; it was that person's role to maintain unity within the team when dealing with player demands, as any breakdown in negotiations could do severe damage to a team. Despite these responsibilities, Owens never considered setting aside this role. Fortunately, Washington had coaches and team officials who were former players and understood many of the issues players raised. Even so, there was some resistance when Owens wanted to attend law school. While Owens's coaches supported his role with the NFLPA, they did not want him to attend law school, as a show of power over the players. "I remember George Allen, when he heard I was going to law school, he got pretty upset because I was one of his captains. He said, 'I need you to call the signals, need your leadership. . . . I need your attention with the Redskins.'" Owens told him, "Law school already got my money. It's nonrefundable." Allen countered, "Well, I will give you your money back." Owens told his coach, "My mom always said, 'If you start something you have to finish it.'" As a result of his failure to comply with his coach's demands, he was benched for two weeks. He would give hand signals for play calls. After dealing with pressure from other players, Allen gave Owens his starting role back.[39]

With most occupations, workers can leave their jobs freely and seek a position with a competitor if a position is available. Since the 1940s, NFL labor had been organized through a reserve system the owners created. This arrangement is composed of five parts: (1) the choice of which teams selected players, (2) the length of players contracts, (3) control over player discipline, (4) the ability to determine all disagreements between players and management, and (5) the reservation to trade or waive players as they saw fit. The foundation for the league's reserve system was the annual draft. Each year, college seniors (underclassmen could play in the Canadian Football League) made up a pool of players from which teams decided who they wanted on their squads. Those who made themselves available through the draft were utterly powerless over which teams selected them, although they were not obligated to play for the club that selected them. They had the right to sit out the year. The team that selected the player also could trade him to another club. From the players' perspective, this system created the need for a union that combated the inequities in the relationship between owners and players.[40]

In professional football, players were limited in where they could work. If he did not like his employer, a player was not allowed to leave without suffering some penalty. In terms of compensation, players' options were to accept the pay presented to them by team management, hold out in hopes of a better offer, or not play at all. And in terms of job security, if coaches or ownership had requests for players, especially those who were not "stars," it was in the players' best interest to oblige them if they wanted to keep their roster spot. There were no rules or entities in place to protect athletes.

On Tuesday, June 9, 1970, the NFLPA went before the National Labor Relations Board in Minneapolis, Minnesota. John Mackey filed a petition to break the NFL's refusal to recognize the group as the representative entity for all players. The owners argued they would do so if the player's association waived the right to negotiate the minimum salary players received for exhibition games "forever." Tex Schramm, president of the Dallas Cowboys and chair of the Player Relations Committee, argued that collective bargaining should not be an issue for players since an agreement was reached in 1968. But the NFLPA wanted to address the compensation given to rookies for preseason games, along with "increased benefits in the player pension plan, the working of the option clause in the player contract, improvement in fringe benefits such as training camp . . . as well as severance pay, and a larger share of product licensing for the association." The last grievance dealt with the power of league commissioner Pete Rozelle; he dictated player movement and team compensation at his discretion, limiting athletes' ability to choose where they played.[41]

John Mackey used Don Shula, his former coach with the Baltimore Colts, as an example of the issues surrounding players' freedoms in the league compared with those of coaches. Shula had left the Colts to serve as head coach, general manager, and stockholder of the Miami Dolphins; however, a player could not break his contract and sign with another team. In a statement issued to the press through association public relations director Tom Vance, Mackey asked, "If Shula can break a contract, if he can leave to better himself, why can't a player?" By July, the NFLPA agreed to hold out if it did not receive "a satisfactory contract package." One spokesman for the owners mentioned that the NFLPA's actions in response to Rozelle's power have "shocked the league and will leave deep scars." The unnamed source noted the players did not need to reduce the commissioner's power because the player's union denied him "the right to exercise some of the powers" that made him "the strongest of the sports commissioners."[42]

On Thursday, July 9, 1970, John Mackey sent letters to players informing them to report to camp only if they received further notice. The NFL countered by barring all veterans from training camp but requested all rookies to arrive as scheduled. Of the thirteen hundred veterans in the NFL, only seven men decided to attend camps. Over two weeks, players could not work out at the team facilities. Brig Owens was part of a contingent of twenty Washington players who attended "Camp Georgetown," where they held clandestine practices on the campus of nearby Georgetown University. Despite the players' requests for privacy, many from the media followed them. While players gathered across the league in their own de facto camps to prepare for the upcoming season, NFLPA leadership tried to reach an agreement with the owners. By the end of July, they agreed to the pay for preseason games and the commissioner's role but still needed to settle on the amount of money given for pension plans. The players also wanted better economic security for injured and retired players in the same fashion as other professional leagues like MLB and the National Hockey League, where players received health benefits once their playing careers were over.[43]

At a press conference on Friday, July 17, 1970, John Mackey told reporters, "Considering the violence of the sport we feel the owners should be ready and willing to pay benefits to those individuals who are injured during the performance of the sport." He believed the owners were not fair in the negotiations. Mackey argued they operated "in a manner similar to the way they negotiate individual contracts—accept our offer or retire from football." The NFL owners made every attempt to denigrate the leadership of the NFLPA, calling its proposals "ill-advised." They argued, "The demands by the players association are so unrealistic as to indicate they were formulated by a party or parties completely unfamiliar with the sport of professional football, its economics and its administration." They went so far as to compare them to Black Nationalists when they contended the NFLPA utilized "Black Panther tactics." Team representatives laughed off the owner's ploy characterizing them that way. Union leadership only wanted the best for its members.[44]

The earliest sign of the strike's end came on Thursday, July 23, 1970. The owners presented a proposal to the NFLPA that allowed the veterans of the Kansas City Chiefs to report to training camp to prepare for the College All-Star game. Since they were the reigning league champions, they were scheduled to play in the annual game against the future NFL stars. Many Chiefs players did not want to break ranks with the NFLPA and sought to continue their strike. However, the union allowed for the exhibition to take place. The lockout was official on Friday, July 31, and players across the league were united. It took a 5:00 a.m. meeting with eighty-seven players representing twenty-six teams (sixteen from the NFL and ten from the AFL) to reach an agreement. On Monday, August 3, the players and owners agreed to a four-year, $19 million deal for the pension plan; $1 million went to benefits for widows, maternity and dental plans, and disability. The NFLPA sought $26 million over four years, while club owners initially offered $18 million.[45]

The pension plan for retired players was the most critical component for the players in their new deal. The association wanted a proposal that compensated them adequately. This was based on the following premise: if a player received his benefits at age fifty-five, he received $8,280 if he played for five years, $16,560 for ten years, and $24,840 for fifteen years. Those who wanted their pension at sixty years of age received $12,540, $25,080, and $37,620 for the five, ten, and fifteen years of playing, respectively. At age sixty-five, the payout was $19,980, $39,960, and $59,940. Players who retired before 1959 were not factored into the plan. Team owners sought to keep more significant profits instead of spending more on retirement benefits. The biggest issue was the minimum number of years played. Football is not a profession where one can play for thirty years and retire well. Players rarely reached the minimum five years to earn a pension, and fifteen years in the NFL was very uncommon. According to the NFLPA, by 1970, only one in one thousand players played professionally for fifteen years, while one in five played for ten.[46]

Near the end of the summer of 1970, the NFLPA's push to become "the sole bargaining agent for the players" was becoming a reality. Mackey led the group and was considered "a poised and intelligent spokesman." Alan Miller, a former fullback with the Oakland Raiders, served as the legal counsel for the association. Jack Kemp and Jim Bakken, presidents of the AFLPA and NFLPA respectively, were also involved. This move set the appropriate backdrop for the many labor issues that plagued the league. During the 1970 season, a federal grand jury investigation was conducted to examine the NFL's labor practices. This probe included former Browns teammates Walter Beach and Bernie Parrish, among other NFL players. In their depositions, Beach and Parrish contended they were blacklisted from the league. Parrish was instrumental in organizing players in the 1960s as former vice president of the NFLPA when the league's owners did not officially recognize the players' union. He believed that Art Modell mistreated him during his tenure with the Browns. He told reporters present after the deposition that Modell pushed him out of the league unfairly because of Parrish's desire to galvanize players into addressing financial issues and how the league treated retired players. Modell brushed off Parrish's postinvestigation comments as a publicity stunt, stating, "Mr. Parrish can say anything he wants—and he will—to promote his book." Modell strategically deflected by suggesting that Parrish had selfish motives for his criticisms. That November, Parrish released *They Call It a Game*. In his book, Parrish argued that Art Modell used his power to force not only Beach and himself out of the NFL but also "all four of the 1964 championship game [defensive] backfield." Beach's time with the grand jury lasted three hours, during which he addressed many issues like the banishment of players, gambling, and racial discrimination.[47]

John Sample, a charter member of the NIEU and former member of the Baltimore Colts, Pittsburgh Steelers, Washington Redskins, and New York Jets, was also called before federal investigators. His first three years in professional football were with the Colts as a defensive back, where he won two league championships. After three years in Baltimore, he played the next two seasons with the Pittsburgh Steelers, where head coach Buddy Parker once told him, "Black ball players don't deserve as much money as white ball players." It was an unsettling comment but a harsh reality of how race shaped the thought processes of coaches and owners toward Black players. The conversation with Parker was one of numerous incidents Sample mentioned during the federal probe to illustrate the racist attitudes coaches held toward him. He asserted NFL owners conspired to send him to the AFL after the Washington Redskins released him in 1965. In the AFL, he played with the New York Jets for three years, from 1966 to 1968. During his tenure with the team, he argued he was forced to play while injured, and the team also "hurt his other business enterprises." This led him to file a $1 million lawsuit against the Jets. Sample addressed much of the infractions he encountered as a professional football player in his 1970 memoir, *Confessions of a Dirty Ballplayer*.[48]

When the probe ended, the NFL was cleared of any wrongdoing. Unsatisfied with the outcome, Walter Beach decided to take matters into his own hands. On Friday, May 28, 1971, Beach, now a law student at Yale University and no longer in Carl Stokes's cabinet, filed a suit against the NFL and the Cleveland Browns for conspiracy "to deny him a position 'because of his race' and political and racial views." He argued that the NFL engaged in a conspiracy to restrain trade, violating the Sherman Act and antitrust laws. He used the waiver claim with the New Orleans Saints in the summer of 1967 as evidence. Beach argued he was prohibited from joining the team after the Browns blocked the deal. He believed Modell had agreed with the other fifteen NFL clubs not to offer him a contract. The NFL also denied him his pension. The suit was not settled until 1975 when he was given his pension and back pay, dating to 1960 and his time with the Boston Patriots.[49]

Despite Beach's strivings for restitution, the NFLPA had gained excellent bargaining power with the owners by 1972. The players secured a larger share of the revenue from the league, increased pensions, and better health care coverage. These gains happened under the leadership of John Mackey, whose objective was to improve the economic conditions for players in the NFL. Interestingly, by the start of the 1972 season, there was speculation about whether he would retire from the NFL, as the Colts placed him on waivers on Wednesday, September 13, 1972. The San Diego Chargers claimed him four days later. According to Brig Owens, after a "hot negotiation session in Chicago, when John got back to Baltimore, 'he lost half a step,' so they say, and he went to San Diego and never played another down." This claim about his sudden loss of speed after the meeting demonstrated how power was wielded in the NFL.[50]

Whether or not the presumption was based out of spite, in San Diego, Mackey rarely practiced, and playing time in regular season games was sparse. Some players felt bad for Mackey, who revolutionized the tight end position. Pettis Norman, a Black player ahead of Mackey on the depth chart, would feign injuries so the Syracuse alum could get playing time. Thus, a player who was voted the best tight end for the All-Time NFL team in 1970, which spanned the league's first fifty years, was a nonfactor for any team's plans two years later. There was much debate within NFL circles about whether Mackey's decline directly resulted from the Colts and Chargers looking to get rid of the NFLPA leader or whether Father Time was tapping him on the shoulder. John Mackey retired from the NFL on Tuesday, July 24, 1973, at thirty-two. In his retirement, he became a sports agent, a career market that was yet untapped by

African Americans. As a result, Mackey resigned from his position as president of the NFLPA to avoid any conflict of interest since he was a representative of WMA Sports Inc., a subsidiary of William Morris Agency Inc. When he announced his retirement, he talked about his new endeavors away from the game. He told reporters, "My joining WMA Sports is in keeping with my objective of helping the athlete's career on and beyond the playing field. . . . I only wanted to play ten years and I am fortunate enough to be able to walk away from the game healthy." The Freeport, New York, native bowed out of the NFL gracefully.[51]

Players like John Wooten, Walter Beach, Sidney Williams, Brig Owens, and John Mackey checked the power structure of the NFL through the formation and recognition of the NFLPA, which gave athletes the right to challenge the league's labor system. Mackey noted, "The Union victory was important when you look back, but at the time I was just doing my job." He added, "Therefore, it's not something I look back at, other than at that particular time I did the thing that was right to do, based on the situation that was going on, because it was my job to do what was right for the players." The efforts for free agency set the stage for future generations of players to have a more significant say in where they provide their talents. By 1972, the work of the NFLPA had helped redistribute the revenue in the NFL. Yet even with these victories, the union's fight did not subside entirely; the issues the NFLPA addressed in the early 1970s continued to direct discussions about labor relations in the NFL throughout the twentieth century and well into the twenty-first.[52]

In short, the principles of financial empowerment never lost precedence in the thoughts and actions of members of the NIEU. These men gave much attention to the inequalities they faced in the sporting realm and dedicated themselves to economic justice. They focused on creating and improving Black businesses in their respective communities and acquiring funding for the organization to operate. The NIEU also created offices in New York, Kansas City, and Washington, DC. During that time, the organization developed several social projects to educate youth on how businesses operated to provide them with the belief they could create enterprises that would improve their communities. The NIEU set the stage for Black athlete activists through its work in Black communities as well as its assistance to Black business owners across the United States.

John Wooten (*left*) and Cleveland Browns defensive tackle Walter Johnson (*center*) in June 1968 at the NIEU offices.

John Wooten outside of the NIEU offices in June 1968.

In June 1968, Jim Shorter (*far right*), then a member of the Washington Redskins, served as assistant executive director. Here he is meeting with a couple of businessmen to discuss loan opportunities through the NIEU.

Members of the NIEU have a meeting about the Jim Brown Farewell Day for January 1967. *From left to right*: Cleveland Browns fullback Ernie Green, John Wooten, Walter Beach III, Cleveland Browns defensive end Bill Glass, Paul Hurd (commissioner of Public Hall, the Cleveland Convention Center, and Cleveland Municipal Stadium), and US senator Frank Lausche (former mayor of Cleveland and governor of Ohio).

On January 29, 1967, Jim Brown (*left*) and New York Giants linebacker Sam Huff (*right*) greet each other for Brown's retirement celebration at the Farewell Day sponsored by Browns owner Art Modell.

In April 1966, Jim Brown walks past the front of the NIEU offices at East 105th Street.

Jim Brown (*left*), John Wooten (*center*), and Jim Shorter (*right*) discuss NIEU matters at the Cleveland office.

In March 1968, Carl Stokes (second from left), mayor of Cleveland, visits the American Steel Fabricating Machinery Company, an organization the BEU helped provide funding. Also pictured are *from left to right*: Rollan Harris, the general manager; Nolan Williams, president; and Luke Kirksey, an employee operating an electric eye pantograph machine.

In the summer of 1965, Jim Brown and his wife, Sue, await the ruling in an assault trial filed by Brenda Ayres.

In October 1968, Jim Brown wore a suede outfit designed by New Breed, a company supported by the BEU, to the premiere of his movie *The Split*.

John Wooten (*center*) with the Williams brothers (Allen on left, Nolan on right) at the American Steel Fabricating and Machinery Company located at 2470 East Ninety-Third Street in Cleveland. The Williamses received a $3,000 loan from the NIEU in 1968.

The BEU initiated Project Vanguard in 1972, a housing development program for single-family homes. These are four of the initial eight on Keemar Court that were part of phase one, which included twenty-six buildings with a total of 312 units in 1974.

In August 1972, US president Richard Nixon (*left*) and Jim Brown (*right*) meet in the Oval Office of the White House. Nixon had been a fan of Brown's athletic exploits since 1961, and over that time, Brown had become a supporter of Nixon's political campaigns. (Richard Nixon Presidential Library and Museum)

John Wooten pictured in Arlington, Texas, with his first-place trophy from the 1967 Ashland Country Club in December 2024. (Author's Collection)

Curtis McClinton and his daughter Margo McClinton Stoglin pose in front of his case in the Hall of Honor at Arrowhead Stadium for the Kansas City Chiefs in January 2011. (Courtesy of Margo McClinton Stoglin)

4

In the Community

John Wooten made a national plea to the American business community in the June 1968 issue of *Nation's Business*. He was a featured columnist as part of a special report the journal was promoting for that month. Wooten titled his piece, "The Human Environment: Poverty—Before You Can Teach Them, You Have to Reach Them." He addressed unemployment in Black communities as well as the collaborations the NIEU had created with nonprofit organizations and local corporations around Cleveland. He also gave a telling solution for how the White business community could assist Black folks who were looking for jobs. Wooten asked, "How do you break down the barriers of distrust and hostility enough, so they'll at least try?" He answered, "You do it by talking their language. By going into their neighborhoods and using people they trust to talk them into trying, to give them confidence to take the big step and encouragement to stick with it when the going gets tough." However, before the readers, who he knew were primarily White people, got ahead of themselves, he assured them, "You can't do it. You're white. They won't listen to you. But organizations like ours can."[1]

Throughout the twentieth century, African Americans were denied the right to vote, due process, better education, job and housing prospects, and the freedom to move about as they saw fit. They did not sit idle and accept their fate; one tool they used to combat these inequalities was protest. By 1967, there had been hundreds of nonviolent demonstrations across the nation. In that year, members of the NIEU began to enact their programmatic efforts in Black communities across the country. They recognized these problems could not be solved by themselves alone and sought the support of the federal government. NIEU leadership wanted to become an economic force through the development of Black businesses. Providing jobs and financial aid to those enterprises was a significant move in developing the financial needs of African Americans across the country. The NIEU was able to capitalize on the racial dichotomy that existed between White businesses and Black labor. Such efforts helped address the rioting that took place in more than one hundred cities throughout the 1960s. While nonviolent direct action had been a key aspect of the movement at this time, the slow pace of progress had ignited many African Americans to challenge the disdain city officials and business leaders had presented. Largely because of the lack of economic commitment in urban communities around housing, education, and recreation, many cities across the United States experienced unrest.

While John Wooten was aware of the racial prejudice and poverty in his *Nation's Business* piece, he knew that if African Americans were to achieve freedom, justice, and equality, there needed to be greater contributions from White business. From 1967 to 1972, the NIEU's focus on green power was twofold: first, to create social programs that provided job opportunities and skill development for entrepreneurship, and second, to provide technical and financial assistance to Black businesses to aid in growth. Accepting the mission of training "productive citizens," the union created the Hough Progressive Youth Center (HPYC) and Project Job Interest and Motivation (JIM) in Cleveland, an acronym playing off Jim Brown's name. These initiatives addressed youth delinquency and unemployment. The NIEU also created a national program, Food First, which had the goal of finding a solution to poverty in communities across the country. As the Cleveland and Los Angeles offices grew in 1967, the organization opened branches in Kansas City, Missouri, Washington, DC, Oakland, and New York in 1968. During this time, the organization also changed its name to the Black Economic Union (BEU), reflecting the cultural changes in Black identity. This chapter explores how the organization's agenda for economic development was shaped by the advantages and limitations of Black capitalism. Komozi Woodard, a scholar activist, noted that economic development for Black communities "was another aspect of grassroots organizing, creating alternatives to poverty." There were many facets to Black capitalism. Many people who embraced the philosophy were "for the collective good of the people and others as exercises in self-interest and greed." The elements of green power walked a very thin line.[2]

Finding Their Place without the Drum Major

The year 1967 was crucial for the BEU. The organization wanted to create new programs to introduce Black youth to business concepts where they could see themselves as producers of goods and not simply consumers of commodities. For the union brass, inspiring children in areas where the living conditions did not encourage a positive outlook on life was important but no easy feat. In March 1967, the Cleveland chapter, in partnership with the Greater Cleveland Associated Foundation, created the HPYC. This initiative offered job training and employment opportunities for adolescents aged fourteen to eighteen. There were three objectives with the HPYC: to impart "self-respect and racial pride" by educating Black youth on their "heritage" and the place of African Americans in the history of the United States; to "raise the sights" of Black youth so they would desire to provide for themselves; and to expose participants to other African Americans "who represent accomplishment and success." This setup represented the BEU's efforts to be involved in the community. For the organization, it was one of the hallmark examples of how it could make a difference.[3]

The first initiative created was Project JIM. John Wooten sent Vice President Hubert Humphrey a proposal to get federal support for the effort. Two grassroots activists, Jim Hunter and Leroy Ervin, were critical to Project JIM. Hunter served as the public relations coordinator, and Ervin was the effort's manager. Hunter was instrumental in creating a credit union in the Hough area. Brown and Wooten looked to his business knowledge to pull Black residents "away from loan sharks." He and Ervin also had the skills to educate the youth about consumer behaviors, one of the tenets of Project JIM.[4]

In its first year, Project JIM provided work training and job opportunities for more than 130 Black male youth to strengthen their morale and self-image. It provided employment opportunities through a partnership with the Cleveland Board of Education's initiative Schools' Neighborhood Youth Corp (SNYC). On average, the program could find jobs for Project JIM participants where they worked thirty hours per week, earning at least $1.25 each hour, roughly $0.15 more than minimum wage. John Wooten, Leroy Kelly, Jim Shorter, and Sidney Williams taught courses on civic engagement, leadership styles, and democratic governance. There were also workshops on economic conflict resolution, courses on Black history, and discussions about the relationship between educational attainment and work opportunities. SNYC and HPYC also provided Black teens visits to businesses across the city to give them a sense of how companies operated. Many of the youth involved in the program had no exposure to working in corporate settings.[5]

Along with Project JIM, the BEU created the Future Businessmen's Club (FBC). A Lee-Harvard neighborhood gang called The Ponderosas was the direct beneficiary of the program. They comprised twenty Black males between the ages of fifteen and twenty, including six high school dropouts. The FBC's objective was to help provide leadership opportunities for those who believed there were none in their communities. Most of the members of The Ponderosas had criminal records, so finding work through legal means was difficult. As a result, the gang was part of a larger contingency of 450 Black youth the BEU helped find jobs that summer. Programs like Project JIM and the FBC were necessary during the summer of 1967 due to the large-scale rioting across the United States, particularly in major cities with large Black populations like Cleveland, Detroit, Newark, and Washington, DC. These demonstrations were mainly due to many African Americans' frustrations with police brutality and their dire economic conditions. With few quality jobs, poor living conditions, and a lack of political engagement from their elected representatives, many African Americans were disengaged with leaders in their communities. The work of the BEU was a critical component in combating such issues, especially as it pertained to Black youth.[6]

There were also influences from outside organizations in Cleveland. Throughout 1967, civil rights leader Martin Luther King Jr. visited the city to campaign for Carl Stokes's mayoral bid and to also help promote Operation Breadbasket, a protest effort inspired by Leon Sullivan, Alfred Dunston, and Joshua Licorish, three Black ministers from Philadelphia, Pennsylvania. The motive behind this campaign was to get companies with a considerable Black consumer base to hire more Black people in the company. If any of the targeted entities chose not to employ African Americans, Black consumers would take their business elsewhere. The overall goal was to address economic inequalities using the collective efforts of Black churches to create job opportunities. Operation Breadbasket was introduced in Atlanta and Chicago with moderate success, so the organization wanted to see what they could achieve in northeastern Ohio. To help spread the message of this initiative, King visited students at East Tech High School and Glenville High School. On Wednesday, April 26, 1967, King's speeches focused on building self-esteem, using nonviolence to achieve their civil rights goals, and having a sense of belonging in their communities.[7]

Considering the racial climate in Cleveland at this time, Operation Breadbasket had potential. However, it was less successful than many had hoped. King warned that if Cleveland officials did not address the poverty and economic issues in the city, there would be rioting that summer, as had been seen the previous year in Hough. If King's presence in the summer of 1967 garnered national attention for the concerns of many Black Clevelanders, the mayoral campaign of Carl Stokes kept that momentum going in the fall. At that time, no African American had been elected mayor of a major US city. Stokes's platform had four critical components: create more jobs for Black workers in the private sector, provide the unemployed a standard of living "compatible with health and dignity," offer better living conditions for residents in public housing, and improve standards and funding for public education.[8]

Carl Stokes won his mayoral bid on Wednesday, November 8, 1967. His election was heralded as the solution to the problems Cleveland and its Black citizens had been experiencing. Stokes knew that to the Black community his election represented triumph over past struggles, dreams fulfilled, and an optimistic future but that to the White business structure it meant something else. He noted, "Clearly, I was a 'safe' candidate. In the backs of their minds, those white men believed that if they put me out front they would be buying off the ghetto."[9]

Stokes worked arduously to obtain support from the federal government for the city to rebuild its infrastructure and provide job opportunities for the poor and unemployed. City officials wanted to support Stokes to make sure frustrations did not escalate into large-scale rebellions that were present in other urban areas across the nation. He was expected to make overnight changes that decades of racial oppression and strife had been unable to solve. Reflecting on the challenges he faced as a politician, he reminded people in his autobiography that "underneath all the high talk, the campaign promises, the idealist theories, politicians are mostly interested in perpetuating their privileged positions." He added, "No matter how well a man understands this, no matter how hard he is, if he fights for the have-nots he will find himself alienated from most of his fellows, and they will do their level best to wear him down, to break him."[10]

One of Stokes's most extraordinary tasks as mayor came less than six months into his first term, on Thursday, April 4, 1968. On that evening, Martin Luther King Jr. was pronounced dead after he received a gunshot to the head while standing on the balcony of the Lorraine Motel in Memphis, Tennessee. As news of King's death spread across the country, rioting ensued across the United States. Government officials tried their best to quell uprisings, but people were filled with rage over the death of a man they considered a savior. For instance, Chicago mayor Richard J. Daley harshly criticized policemen in his city for not shooting arsonists and looters. James Reston of the *New York Times* stated, "At this critical point, therefore, the leaders of every community—all of them, black and white, labor and management, educational and religious—will have to mobilize to deal with their local situation, whatever it is." BEU members, saddened by the death of a friend and inspirational figure, wanted to ensure the work they had done with the city youth was not in vain and answered the call to help calm the violence.[11]

In Cleveland, Stokes rode with his convoy throughout the city's neighborhoods, spending significant time in the Hough area, some nights until 3:00 a.m., talking to people to ensure they would stay calm. His objective was to keep citizens safe and prevent property damage. The last thing he wanted was another riot. Interestingly, Cleveland and Memphis were the only major cities that did not experience unrest. Stokes expressed his gratitude toward Cleveland citizens and their efforts. He told reporters, "I think that Cleveland has really done itself proud. . . . It has stood out among all of the cities in the United States in observing the tragedy that affected all America. It demonstrated a splendid coordinated, cooperative effort and attitude among all of our people."[12]

BEU members were pivotal players in keeping the peace. They assisted Stokes in Cleveland after the mayor reached out to John Wooten to contact other Black male professional athletes to help calm the tide of violence. They also did the same in other cities across the United States. Wooten, Walter Beach, Jim Brown, Curtis McClinton, Gale Sayers of the Chicago Bears, and Bill Russell of the Celtics were among thirty-five Black male professional athletes who were called on to help keep the peace in their respective communities. Wooten delivered a telegram to numerous organizations across the United States that read, "We feel in the last few days the rioting and looting that has taken place in this country has been totally wrong. We understand the frustration, and we understand the sorrow and shock." He added, "However, our move at this time has to be one of dignity and pride befitting a man that carried the torch of pride and love to all mankind . . . it is up to us to make real the plans he left with us. In a short while, the NIEU will have programs in your city that will most economically and socially meaningful to you." In a plea with his community, he said, "We don't want homeless people in your city. We don't want soup lines . . . don't be a part of making this kind of thing happen. Let us make this pledge that we will make our city and ourselves proud to have known and loved the Rev. Dr. Martin Luther King Jr."[13]

Jim Brown echoed Wooten's sentiments. He issued a statement: "We feel it is a tragedy when a man of peace and nonviolence is shot down in cold blood. . . . There will be a need for unity and hard work not only to get rid of the negative of our society." He continued, "We will join all Americans in not letting the great effort of Dr. Martin Luther King be in vain." Despite the plea for peace, many African Americans across the nation took to the streets with rage the following day. Over fifty-five thousand Army National Guard troops were deployed to major cities like Baltimore, Los Angeles, and Harlem and throughout the South in Georgia, Florida, and Mississippi. In Washington, DC, some of the Washington Redskins, like A. D. Whitfield and Brigman Owens, were called on as well since they were both members of US reserve units with the military. For Owens, King was a major influence. He remembered the Baptist minister saying, "A man dies a little if he refuses to take a stand." Owens recalled the smoke and planes that were part of the scene of the rioting in DC on April 5. He was eating at a restaurant on Howard University's campus and realized many people's frustrations would not go away overnight.[14]

Some companies were unaware of the threat that loomed because of King's killing. When Owens went to pick up his wife from work, her supervisor was unwilling to let her leave. He recalled, "I got the supervisor on the phone and told him, 'Under no uncertain terms, you better let her go, and for the safety of your employees, let them go home.'" A car ride home that usually took them twenty minutes lasted four hours. As they rode home, Owens remembered, "Everything was being torched, and they were doing it in their own neighborhoods, not realizing that they were torching some of their own businesses and support systems. I think people were angry and were damaging things indiscriminately for personal reasons."[15]

Unfortunately, businesses the BEU supported were also affected. Since some were already working from a deficit and did not have insurance or could not afford the costs, many were forced to close their doors for good. It took other businesses several years to recoup. The rioting across the nation was a series of demonstrations by African Americans who were furious over the violent killing of someone they revered, coupled with their displeasure with the order of society where African Americans were still denied full citizenship guaranteed to them through the Fourteenth and Fifteenth Amendments of the Constitution. The riots of 1968 led to White flight as White businesses left urban areas to avoid the financial downfall caused by the destruction. They took with them many African Americans' jobs. As a result, Black communities were significantly impacted, particularly the youth. The BEU felt its outreach was more important than ever.[16]

Sunday, November 17, 1968, was the day of the BEU's official name change. At a news conference, Jim Brown stated, "The Negro is dead and the black man is alive." There was a change in the consciousness of many African Americans and a more outward expression of racial pride. The following day, the group officially opened the union's Washington, DC, chapter. Bobby Mitchell, a critical component of the Washington Redskins team and aspiring figure in DC's political leadership, led a makeshift unit with limited funds and resources in the early years of the organization. However, by 1968, he participated in other ventures, particularly with Senator Robert F. Kennedy. The politician from New York asked Mitchell to join him in his efforts to get African Americans involved in their community and become a political force in their towns. Thus, other members of the Redskins organization and community members had to pick up the mantle of the branch.[17]

Arthur J. Mitchell, unrelated to Bobby Mitchell, led the Washington, DC, office and was instrumental in securing loans from banks in the area to help Black entrepreneurs. Brig Owens, who was encouraged by Bobby Mitchell to work with the organization, served as regional director. In their respective roles with the BEU, one of their primary objectives was to help negotiate loan paperwork with local banks. The union also conducted research projects that measured how businesses could improve. This was done so companies would know what they were doing well and what areas needed strengthening. DC BEU members also went into Black neighborhoods to gauge the interests of businessmen. A friend of Brig Owens, David Abramson, director of Abramson and Himelfarb Advertising Inc., accompanied Owens and other union members as they walked around DC neighborhoods and evaluated shops. When they came upon Black businesses, Owens explained, "We told them who we were, and did a survey in terms of how we could help them improve their business." They also took the opportunity to pose questions of their own. For example, if owners were having any problems, they asked questions like how long items were in display windows or how often they cleaned their storefront. In short, they "talked to them about better ways of doing business." Owens posed critical questions when visiting shops. He asked, "When you look at it, how do you improve the quality of the minority business environment? How do you improve the quality of the housing there? What can you do? Educating people how best to buy, maximize the dollar." For these enterprises, Owens wanted to show "how important it is to have your books in order, and not have a bunch of receipts in a box. The importance of establishing a relationship with a bank, getting to know people in a bank, so they know who you are when you come in. More than just someone going to the teller." The office also conducted programs that taught business owners about consumer education and management training. These classes were important because in 1968, Washington, DC, had 800,000 residents, and African Americans comprised 63 percent of that population. However, they were only

3 percent of the business community. This large discrepancy was a significant reason the BEU made it a primary objective to help existing businesses.[18]

By the summer of 1969 in Cleveland, Project JIM had expanded to be year-round, placing over four hundred Cleveland youth in jobs with White and Black businesses throughout the city. With this growth, there was the launch of four programs. The first was the World of Work, which focused on job placement and money management. Participants developed a budget and opened savings accounts for the money they earned from their jobs. Field trips to different businesses across Cleveland were also part of the agenda. This offered them the opportunity to see how companies functioned. The second, Future Businessmen's Club, placed young boys and girls in groups and helped them develop plans to form their own "profit-making business enterprises," allowing them to get firsthand experience in developing their ideas. The third program, Project MEN, an earlier initiative of the BEU, had grown into a mentorship program where over two hundred African American professionals allowed Project JIM participants to shadow them every week to help young people gain "interest and motivation." Hence, they pursued their careers of interest. In this phase, youth were present in business meetings and participated in the work of the respective offices. The last phase was the Scholarship Program. The union also provided financial assistance to high school graduates pursuing higher education degrees or attending trade school. These phases served as the blueprint for how the BEU structured its community activism and engagement. Although the program centered on providing employment opportunities, the program's evaluations illustrate that Project JIM lacked the oversight to ensure participants were getting to their jobs. While over the summer the teenagers fulfilled the requirements, once the school year began, many fell delinquent. This oversight hurt the union's relationship with many of its business partners; when the employees they were counting on did not show up, these businesses lost some of the goodwill that had been developed with the organization.[19]

Nixon, Black Power, and Black Capitalism

During the 1960s, the term *Black capitalism* had some ambiguity. According to historian William Van Deburg, some used it to refer to Black business owners who were "thoroughly co-opted and had become indistinguishable cogs in the monopoly capitalist machine." Others believed it referred to the "collective or cooperative accumulation of capital by and for the benefit of the black masses." At its core, Black capitalism was a concern for not only African Americans but also politicians. In 1968, a presidential candidate, Richard Nixon, made Black capitalism part of his campaign narrative. Nixon, former vice president to US president Dwight Eisenhower, focused on promoting free enterprise to support "minority business" as part of the "war on poverty." It was a strategic move on behalf of his election managers in their desire to get the Black vote. As vice president, Nixon had also worked with the National Association for the Advancement of Colored People (NAACP) as a member of the Committee on Government Contracts to end discrimination in that sector. He also helped lead efforts with the Civil Rights Act of 1957 and supported the Civil Rights Act of 1964 and the Voting Rights Act of 1965. Still, there was doubt among Black voters about whether Nixon was willing to give the financial resources to address the needs of Black communities. While the political objectives of African Americans in the first half of the 1960s focused extensively on voting rights, fair housing, and improvements in education, by the second half of the decade, African Americans were motivated to address poverty, job opportunities, and entrepreneurial endeavors.[20]

Nixon defined Black Power as Black capitalism. During a radio broadcast on April 25, 1968, Nixon explained the term and modified it for his own purposes. He said, "What most of the militants are asking is not separation, but to be included in—not as supplicants, but as owners, as entrepreneurs—to have a share of the wealth and a piece of the action. And this is precisely what the federal central target of the new approach ought to be." He added, "It ought to be oriented toward more black ownership, for from this can flow the rest—black pride, black jobs, black opportunity and yes black power, in the best, the constructive sense of that often misapplied term." Despite his public proclamations regarding the Black community, Nixon once argued African Americans were the "problem" with America and that they were not mentally fit to compete with White people. Despite these sentiments, he articulated a platform that projected Black economic development to grow African American support of the Republican Party. It was a strategic way to get buy-in from the business community in response to the riots that happened across the nation that spring. By November 1968, it worked out well as Nixon garnered a little less than 15 percent of the African American vote, enough to defeat Democratic nominee Hubert Humphrey and independent George Wallace.[21]

The historian Hugh Davis Graham noted that Nixon's attitudes toward economic equality and civil rights were "inconsistent and incoherent" with his political agenda. In 1969, he nominated two southern conservative judges, G. Harold Carswell and Clement F. Haynsworth, to the Supreme Court and recommended a constitutional amendment that prohibited busing students with the intent of racial balance. However, Nixon also signed amendments for voting rights and equal opportunity that led to the creation of affirmative action programs that provided African Americans opportunities to receive federal contracts and employment in public and private sectors. In March 1969, within the first few months of his presidency, Nixon named Maurice H. Stans secretary of commerce. Stans had previously worked in Eisenhower's cabinet and was a partner with the accounting firm Glore Forgan, William R. Staats & Company. Nixon also appointed him head of the Office of Minority Business Enterprise (OMBE). This federal agency was created under Nixon's Executive Order 11458 and focused exclusively on developing "minority" businesses. People of color who were supporters of Black capitalism were apprehensive about Stan's appointment because they believed he would not fully support Black business development. Several "liberal antipoverty circles" believed Stans was out of touch with the needs of the poor and people of color. As a result, they did not trust him to rule in favor of those who needed assistance. They argued that organizations and businesses that would apply for funds could be denied aid based on Stans own bias. Nixon claimed that would not be the case since his administration's purpose was to provide economic resources to "potentially successful persons who have not had access to it before."[22]

Despite the federal government's efforts, some African Americans were not enthusiastic about the government's support of Black business development. Andrew Brimmer, an economist who served on the Federal Reserve Board, was one of its most outspoken opponents. In a speech before the American Economic Association, he noted that African Americans had higher debt than White Americans. Thus, their ability to be viable consumers was not a substantial reality. He said, "Self-employment offers a poor economic future for colored people" because, as he saw it, "in the long run, the pursuit of black capitalism may retard economic advancement by discouraging many from the full participation in the national economy with its much broader range of challenges and opportunities." According to Brimmer, in 1969, Black people were 11 percent of the nation's population and constituted $35 billion of personal income. While this was roughly 6.5 percent of the total personal income for the United States, African Americans owned less than 2 percent of the household assets in the country. In all, Black Americans lacked economic resources in comparison to White citizens.[23]

There was considerable purchasing power among Black people, but they lacked the means to be producers on a grand scale. Thus, the best way to solve the "Negroes'" financial problems was to integrate them into White companies. From his view, Black workers could, at best, have jobs and learn how to operate their businesses after honing basic skills. However, his rationale that African Americans should not seek "self-employment" and go into business for themselves did not go over well with many Black leaders. James Foreman, a member of Student Nonviolent Coordinating Committee, considered Black people who saw capitalism as a solution for liberation as "Black power pimps." He argued, "The people must be educated to understand that any black man or Negro who is advocating a perpetuation of capitalism inside the United States is in fact seeking not only his ultimate destruction and death but is contributing to the continuous exploitation of black people all around the world." From Foreman's viewpoint, African Americans needed to think of ways to take control of the United States and not be happy with morsels that would not free them from the grasp of racism and poverty.[24]

To contest Brimmer's arguments, Jim Brown and seven other African American leaders formed an "ad-hoc federation of black entrepreneurs." For them, anyone talking negatively about Black capitalism hindered their efforts to gain federal support. They addressed the Black economist's comments in a press conference. They opined, "Where we differ with Governor Brimmer is his use of past performance of black-owned businesses to assess their potential. We contend that performances of black-owned businesses in the past is a result of the constraints and deprivation to which they have historically been subjected." They continued, "By projecting the future of black-controlled businesses on the basis of these results would be no different than drawing the conclusion that Black Americans cannot learn because they have performed poorly in a deprived educational environment." The coalition also sent President Nixon a telegram stating the time had come for the group to meet with him "at the earliest possible date" to address the direction of the federal programs geared toward minority business. One of the union's main issues with Nixon was his administration's lack of communication with them and its failure to consult with them about the agenda for the OMBE. They believed the idea of green power could be fulfilled by setting aside provisions from the government. The president also needed to increase the number of middle-class African Americans, an ideal he promoted during his campaign. Over four years, money designated for "minority businesses" increased from $75 million in 1969 to $2.6 billion in 1972, which benefited organizations like the BEU and its members, like Brady Keys, whose All-Pro Fried Chicken became one of the largest Black-owned fast-food chains in the 1970s before a merger with Kentucky Fried Chicken (KFC) thanks to the help of the BEU.[25]

The Fried Chicken Merger

Defensive backs in the NFL must have a high level of self-assurance, and Brady Keys was never short on confidence. By 1966, Keys had garnered a reputation as a staunch defender and was named an All-Pro and to the pro bowl team for that season. He was mindful of the reach he had as a professional athlete. In the 1960s, he was keenly mindful of the Black freedom struggle and saw the development of enterprises as a way to achieve equality. He remembered, "We needed to get together to bring about change. Jim, as big and powerful as he was, could not do it alone. Brady Keys, as big and powerful as he was, could not do it alone, but together could bring about change." He saw the BEU as an important organization and joined the group in 1966 after Jim Brown and John Wooten contacted him to see if he would be interested in the promotion of Muhammad Ali's fights under the banner of Main Bout in Pittsburgh. Since he had the necessary connections that would assist them, they felt Keys would be a welcomed addition. This business venture was the Texas native's first introduction to the BEU. With the BEU's help, the Steelers cornerback started his first business, Keys Auto Detail, later that year. A financial adviser at a bank told him the venture was lucrative, so Keys bought 50 percent of the company. According to Keys, the company "failed miserably," and he lost his $10,000 savings. Yet, he was not deterred.[26]

During the summer of 1966, Keys, along with his mother and a couple of friends, concocted what he called "a superb batter" for chicken. At a family gathering, they served their recipe, and it was well received. After the encouragement, Keys decided to move forward with his plan to begin his own restaurant with fried chicken as the staple product. He encouraged Jim Brown to connect him with Bill Stennis of Golden Bird Fried Chicken and the national vice president of the union. Keys wanted to build a relationship with Stennis, who had established himself in Los Angeles in 1957. Over the next decade, his enterprises became a staple across the city. Keys took notice and wanted to learn from the Philadelphia, Mississippi, native. However, the Golden Bird founder was not initially eager to help Keys because he was under the impression the Steelers cornerback was his competition, but Keys assured him they would not be culinary rivals. Keys recognized, "Once I convinced him that I was not going to compete with him, he began to help me." While working for Stennis pro bono, Keys learned how to manage a business. From that experience, Keys decided to create his own restaurant.[27]

Most Black athletes did well for themselves financially. In 1966, the average family income in the United States was $7,300. Brady Keys earned $45,000 that year with the Steelers. However, he was unable to get the necessary loan to start. Eager to begin his business, the Austin native was dumbfounded by his inability to get vital startup money. He told Robert Lipsyte of the *New York Times*, "Every day I would read in the *Wall Street Journal* and *The New York Times* about all this money available to Negro businessmen." He added, "This is not true. There's money if you want $10,000 for a little drug store if you want to open a fruit stand. As long as you stay a consumer, there's money. But not if you want to be a producer." To secure funding, Keys turned to Steelers owner Art Rooney Sr. He called him, and after a few seconds of presenting the request, all he heard was silence on the line. Keys asked if he was still on the line. Rooney replied, "I am. I'm just trying to figure out how fast to get you the money!" Rooney later wired Keys the $10,000 he needed to get started, and the only repayment he wanted was for him to be "successful." This was a small favor for the All-Pro defensive back that would prove to be fruitful. While the Steelers owner was serious about Brady Keys's business success, head coach Bill Austin was not. He tried to keep Keys from beginning his restaurant. As the Steelers defensive back remembered, coaches did not want their players doing anything "that did not fit the mold."[28]

Most NFL coaches believed football was to be the only focus for players during the season. In their view, players who focused on developing their business plans did not make for a successful year. Brady Keys was a businessman before the NFL allowed its players, Black or White, to be involved in matters off the field. There were no written guidelines on what a player should do during the season because the expectation was that he would focus on his craft as a footballer. In the offseason, athletes were able to do as they wished, since they needed income for their families during the six months they were not covered by their respective teams. From the perspective of Keys, "They wanted to control you. I was one of the last persons to control. They only wanted you to play football." Despite the efforts to block his plans, Keys moved forward as suggested by Rooney and prepared to open his first restaurant.[29]

While a few All-Pro restaurants were opened in 1967, the company had difficulty expanding in 1968. None of the banking institutions that Keys reached out to were willing to lend him financial support. The former Steelers cornerback blamed race: for "a Black man in the sixties trying to raise money, there was nothing but obstacles." He remembered several meetings with potential financial supporters where they were surprised by Keys's presence but not by that of Walter E. Gregg and Tom Reich, the chairman and executive vice president of All-Pro, both of whom were White. Keys believed nobody was willing to support a company where the president and primary stockholder was African American. As Keys recalled, "The banks and the investment house, they gave me canned good excuses. 'Mr. Keys, you don't have enough assets in your company.' Well, if I had enough assets I wouldn't be there asking for money. 'Mr. Keys, you don't have enough management talent in your company.'" He confirmed this was a lie. He noted, "I had a big white lawyer and a bright steel executive on my board, but I made clear that I was the president and the chief officer. So, when they talked about management talent, you know they were talking about me.'"[30]

Keys may have been justified in his claims regarding the racism he experienced during his visits to banks. However, many of the issues financiers brought to his attention had validity. He did not have enough assets as he was just starting his enterprises, which had achieved moderate success at best. Also, many bankers had great reason not to support Keys's ventures: most professional athletes' businesses were not very lucrative despite their celebrity owners. Regardless of the "management talent" supporting him, he was not able to get the financial support he needed. Yet, Keys was not deterred; he was determined to see his business aspirations fulfilled. Fortunately, he would get much-needed financial help from an unlikely source. Buddy Young, one of the early African American players of the NFL with the St. Louis Rams, directed him to financial advisers with First National City Bank of New York. After discussing his business plans with them, All-Pro was given a $150,000 deal, and the bank bought 20 percent of the company. Interestingly, this arrangement did not sit well with his new team despite their initial support.[31]

By 1969, All-Pro had seven franchises worth nearly $2 million. Because of this success, Keys was ready to target the Black community, an area he considered a priority especially regarding his work with the BEU. Therefore, the first restaurant established in a Black community was opened in April 1969 in the Bedford-Stuyvesant area of Brooklyn, New York. Waldo Jeff, an African American man who was a counselor at Queens College and former teammate of Keys at Colorado State University, ran the franchise. Within their first month, the business brought in $4,000 a week. The success of the Brooklyn location demonstrated to potential financiers that All-Pro had the ability to provide a return on their investments, particularly in Black communities.[32]

At the time, White investors avoided supporting Black businesses, especially those in African American neighborhoods, due to the economic ramifications of the riots that engulfed the nation in 1968 in response to Martin Luther King Jr.'s assassination. The damage to businesses that occurred because of the looting scared many banks from supporting African American enterprises. Keys noted, "Now if I had that kind of trouble with contacts and a good job and something of a name, what about other Negroes?" As the All-Pro brand grew and gained recognition, "bankers kept saying, 'Mr. Keys, you're doing something no Negro ever did before.'" The All-Pro president strove to succeed so that his business would be an example that African Americans could accomplish their goals and so that others would not have to endure the hardships he witnessed in the early stages of starting his company.[33]

By May 1970, All-Pro Chicken was recognized as one of the ten largest "minority-owned" businesses in the United States with a total worth of $2.2 million in stock and notes. Several major corporations like Aetna Life, The Travelers Insurance Company, Connecticut Mutual Life Insurance Company, and Berkshire Life Insurance Company bought stock in the enterprise. Their investments served as the impetus for Keys to continue to grow the company by 1972. To do so, a venture was formed with KFC, a food conglomerate that brought in more than $100 million a year with 3,500 franchises worldwide with roughly 3,000 restaurants in operation across the United States, primarily in White communities. KFC sought to expand into Black communities, particularly those in the major urban areas. Dick Beeson, the executive vice president for KFC, contended that African Americans would not buy their fried chicken from a "Kentucky colonel," who, from their viewpoint, was a symbolic bastion of slavery. Fundamentally, KFC officials were aware of the racial dynamics at play. "Black people eat a lot of chicken," Beeson noted. "Why shouldn't we sell it to them?" With the success of All-Pro Fried Chicken in Black communities, KFC leadership recognized that to reach the market of African Americans, they had to change their marketing format. Brady Keys represented the transformation that would allow their brand to extend into Black neighborhoods.[34]

Food First

The BEU also took on a national effort that utilized the work of all the union's offices (with three other chapters opened in Kansas City, Missouri; Washington, DC; and Oakland, California). In February 1970, the BEU began the Food First project to expose the poverty and political inequalities across the United States. This social program was designed to tackle the needs of Black communities nationwide, providing food, clothing, and the necessary tools and information for residents to "broaden their life prospects." The BEU established three goals: provide food and clothing to be dispersed to residents who local leaders identified as needing assistance; seek aid through government programs and donations that provided "food, medicine and the financing of farm and small business development"; and encourage other Black organizations to adopt communities in their respective locales to implement programs of assistance.[35]

Holly Springs, Mississippi, was the focal point for Food First. According to Jim Brown, it was "because Jacob Javits had proclaimed Marshall County the poorest county in the United States . . . and they [also] had political problems as far as elections and so forth." Located in northern Mississippi, thirty minutes south of Memphis, Tennessee, Holly Springs was described as the "seat of

Marshall County . . . submerged in a lake of great trees, and each spring the row of mansions on College and Falconer and neighboring streets, restored years ago to antebellum splendor, are opened to the public for the annual Pilgrimage" where many "gather to relive the fine old minutes of the Old South as Southerners would like them to have been." The county had a population of 26,000, of whom 17,000 (65%) were Black. With an unemployment rate of 60 percent, Holly Springs had a bleak job market. Industrial companies located in the town employed only 160 local African Americans; meanwhile, 1,300 White Americans who lived outside the county worked for companies like Wurlitzer, which manufactured musical instruments. One Holly Springs resident mentioned, "Our unemployment increases yearly. If a white man or woman comes in and applies for a job, then a black man or woman is laid off, so there will be room for him."[36]

As Jim Brown remembered, the objective of Food First was "to motivate the people. . . . We wanted to take that ride to hook up with the people down there, and inspire, and go back and work and raise money and food." More than twenty Black professional athletes convened in Memphis, Tennessee, at the Lorraine Motel. They chose this location as a tribute to Martin Luther King Jr. Ironically, before crossing the state line, the Greyhound bus the group was aboard had some mechanical issues in Tennessee, and one of the passengers joked, "That's the way bussy. If you're going to break down, break down on this side of the border." From there, the group took the one-hour trip to Holly Springs, where they met with local leaders who sought their assistance "against an establishment that so far had thrived on assault by boycott, marches, protests that demonstrated misery." As they assembled at a local restaurant, Jim Brown told them, "Unfortunately, the majority of people in Mississippi who are starving are black and they are because of the political system. . . . The mistake most make is one great thrust with a program, they go back home and the project falls on its face." He wanted those in attendance to understand that they had to keep the program going in their respective cities once they left Mississippi; eradicating poverty was no set it and forget it task.[37]

The history of racial strife in Mississippi created some apprehension among the men in attendance. At the time, sixteen years after the *Brown v. Board* decision, the schools in the city were just being integrated. White residents were not happy about the move to have Black and White children in Holly

Springs attend the same schools. Jim Brown joked with the group, "I've been all over the South, but I used to drive to Alabama, park my car, and fly over Mississippi." While aboard the charter, Brig Owens remembered a group of White men in pickup trucks and brandishing shotguns followed them. He ordered the bus driver to cut the lights off so no one outside could see who was onboard. Many of the players on the trip were on edge. When a photo opportunity came, the flash from a camera went off, and some of the men ducked, thinking shots were fired.[38]

However, there was no racial incident for the travelers. When they arrived in Marshall County, they engaged with the residents, stopping at Rust College, Mississippi Industrial College, and Cadet School. One resident told the group, "We've marched, picketed, boycotted. All have failed, and the major reason they have failed is that we have nobody to turn to. This is a closed society." They added, "There aren't any black-owned stores, no black-owned groceries or industries. You have our support. We don't have anyone else to turn to in Mississippi. We don't have a governor we can go to." Many Black folks in Holly Springs received the contingent of men well, as their status as professional athletes provided them with a certain cachet among the residents. During the players' visit, they saw the dire poverty many people faced. Roy Jefferson, with the Pittsburgh Steelers, said the living conditions of Black people in Marshall County made many of the athletes "cringe." They met a seventy-four-year-old woman, Anna Faulkner, who lived in a two-room home with no bathroom or windows. Her monthly income was $75, of which $55 was from Social Security. By the standards of the 1970s, she lived in poverty, and there was a significant discrepancy between her income and that of the players. William Wright, a forty-eight-year-old man with eight children, had been unemployed for six years because of a heart problem. He received only $18 a month. Sidney Williams remembered that the used clothing and shoes he donated to people were considered "new for them." While many players who made the Food First trip grew up in meager living situations, they had not experienced the type of poverty they saw in Marshall County. The trip to Holly Springs exposed the depth of poverty and illustrated why economic development and social programs were needed. Holly Springs was only a microcosm of a nationwide problem. For these renowned Black men to lend their support was critical to the group's mission of helping on a national level.[39]

When the group left Mississippi, they continued to raise money, food, and clothing for not only Holly Springs but also the Compton area of Los Angeles; East Oakland, California; the Glenville section of Cleveland; Kansas City, Missouri; and the Anacostia neighborhood in Washington, DC. The union conducted several fundraisers, like golf tournaments with the Sixth City Golf Club, basketball tournaments with local organizations and schools, and a tennis tournament with professional tennis player Arthur Ashe. Ashe and Jim Brown competed in matches in New York before thousands of spectators. Other African Americans contributed as well. Black students from Kent State University went on a four-day fast to raise awareness and money for Food First. Yoo-hoo provided two trailers of the "high-protein, milk based" drinks.

The BEU received a check for more than $12,000 from the American Freedom from Hunger Foundation Inc. Political figures also gave public support. Carl Stokes provided support and funds after Jim Brown requested his endorsement of the antipoverty effort. In a letter to Brown, Stokes told him, "Hunger in Holly Springs, Mississippi, Marshall County, as well as in Cleveland and all other cities throughout the United States is, in my opinion, a priority which has to be dealt with." Brown believed the mayor's patronage "better enhance[d] the cooperation of the Cleveland community" with the program. Jesse Jackson, vice president of the Southern Christian Leadership Conference, also gave his support by serving as a keynote speaker for the union's Food First dinner fundraiser.[40]

When members of the BEU returned to Mississippi later that year, they had more than thirty tons of food and clothing to disperse and had raised $25,000. Some of the money was given as loans for Black businessmen in the area to start their own companies, while a portion was given to buy food products for Black residents. Jim Brown believed the loans provided, which "were quietly done," were "the most significant" aspect of the program because there were not many Black businesses in the town. Food First highlighted the poverty throughout the United States and encouraged discussions about the federal government's role in eradicating poverty.[41]

While the union had not intended to get involved in local politics, the election of the first African American to sheriff in Holly Springs was credited to the union's presence. Louis Stokes, a congressman from Cleveland, and Carl Stokes's brother, cited the group's work in the second session of the

Ninety-First Congress. They were praised for "putting action to words." In all, Food First served as a reminder of the power of what collective action coupled with financial support did for the impoverished. The union focused on educational opportunities, unemployment, and poverty through its network of social programs while also giving attention to African American businessmen. Between 1967 and 1972, BEU chapters in Oakland/San Francisco (called the Bay Area chapter), Los Angeles, Kansas City, Cleveland, New York, and Washington, DC, committed themselves to providing financial and technical assistance to Black enterprises within their respective cities.[42]

The BEU and Black Capitalism

To support their plans for national business development, the union aimed to raise $10 million. These funds would allow them to develop offices in major urban areas that could reach branches in the major cities of the United States, provide loans to Black businessmen, give advice and monetary assistance to those ventures that demonstrated a need, and support BEU's social programs. Reaching this goal and acquiring adequate funds was one of the union's biggest obstacles. The group had between five thousand and eight thousand dues-paying members from 1967 to 1972 and different membership levels ($1, $5, $20, and $100 for charter members). The different rates ensured people from different economic backgrounds could join the organization, yet at these rates, the $10 million goal could not be achieved through membership fees alone. For example, the group brought in only around $55,000 in membership fees in 1968.[43]

While Jim Brown originally articulated a vision of the union depending solely on Black folks to raise money, that idea was not sustainable. Many of the Black male professional athletes they depended on for support did not have the financial means to provide assistance. As a result, the BEU sought financial support from nonmembers, both Black and White. Furthermore, the group turned to outside supporters, particularly the federal government and philanthropic organizations, to reach its goals. Some BEU members were apprehensive about this move because they felt Black capitalism "tended to produce Black businessmen who did little for the benefit of the community."[44]

To help them develop their proposals, Jim Brown reached out to Spencer Jourdain, a 1961 graduate of Harvard University. After graduating as one of six African Americans in his class, he visited different parts of Africa to explore the world. He returned the following year and completed his MBA at Harvard Business School. From there, he worked at Corning Glass Works in the marketing and business planning department. However, after a few years there, he heard of an opportunity to connect with the union. Jourdain jumped at the opportunity and helped form the National Business Planning Team (NBPT). This faction oversaw the business proposals presented to the union and determined how to get them funding or whether the BEU would support them from the funds they received. He was a strong proponent of the group's self-sufficiency and Black business development charge. This fact became particularly evident when he told reporters in November 1968 at the official opening of the New York office, "The only people that can help us is ourselves."[45]

To staff the NBPT, Jourdain wanted people with a background in economics or who had experience starting businesses. He turned to those he knew best: Ofia Nwali, John Butler, and Dan Mitchell. Nwali was a PhD student at Harvard who developed a relationship with Jourdain through their "deep" discussions on international economics. Nwali was "super fit" to begin collaborations between African Americans and Africans. Butler was a 1962 graduate of Harvard and later earned an MBA from Harvard Business School. Mitchell graduated from Clark College and had an early history of involvement in the Congress of Racial Equality's sit-ins and voter registration drives, so his knowledge and insight were a welcomed addition to the group to blend civil rights protest and capitalist efforts.[46]

For Jourdain and the NBPT members, working with the BEU "was an era of unlimited optimism and energetic hope." While the office was strategically placed near Wall Street, they did not have easy access to financial support. For instance, the banks they went to for help needed to be convinced of the business ideas the NBPT presented. The financial institutions argued that if Black companies only focused on selling to African Americans, they would not get a return on their investment. As a result, many of the proposals presented by the BEU in New York were never supported.[47]

In 1968, Jourdain continued to seek funding to help support many of the business proposals the organization had received from Black entrepreneurs. In the early part of the year, he applied to the Ford Foundation, a private institution aiming to improve "human welfare" through "the reduction of economic, religious, and racial barriers to equality of educational opportunity at all levels." In March, the union was awarded $520,000 from the philanthropic group. The grant was the largest given by the Ford Foundation, providing twenty-three awards totaling $3.2 million. The BEU was also given $250,000 from the Economic Development Administration to fund the salaries of its staff members. This money helped prepare and retain people who contributed to the organization's efforts in assisting Black businessmen, and provided people in the community with classes on marketing, accounting, advertising, and tax filing.[48]

The BEU's loan process was not very meticulous. "Aspiring" businessmen underwent an interview with the planning team and presented their plans for starting an enterprise or requested support for sustainment or expansion. The planning team analyzed the merits of the proposals and determined what assistance, if any, could be provided. Fortunately, the money the group received from the Ford Foundation allowed it to help several businesses achieve moderate success. That same year, Curtis Robinson, an owner of a small construction company in Cleveland, received a loan from the BEU for $2,000 to purchase equipment for his business. This aid helped him get a contract with the Department of Community Development in Cleveland, where he provided vinyl siding for refurbished homes, making him the first African American in Cleveland to receive this agreement, highlighting the lack of Black Americans in this business realm.[49]

There were other enterprises that benefited from the help of the BEU. New Breed Limited, a clothing group formed in 1967 that specialized in making the dashiki, a shirt described as a "freedom garment" that was "a loosely shaped long-sleeved shirt-jacket, styled with any of 19 large center front pockets," was aided by financial and technical support from the BEU in 1968. New Breed had the people in place who understood the intricacies of the fashion industry. Jason Benning founded the company with Ellis Fleming, Jack Butler, Howard Davis, and Milton Clarke. Benning was a native of Atlanta, Georgia, and graduated from Morris Brown College, earning a bachelor of science in business administration. Fleming and Butler provided the financial support to help get the business started. Milton Clark served as vice president, assisting with the day-to-day activities of New Breed, while Howard Davis oversaw the designs

Davis had experience in the clothing industry from working with Pappagallo, a clothing boutique, for seven years. He was the first African American to win the Designer's Oscar in New York for his fashion motifs. The company had a major impact on the clothing industry during the late 1960s and 1970s. It did this by capitalizing on the sentiments of the Black Power era, a period when African Americans turned away from the misnomer "Negro" and developed a greater understanding of the accomplishments of Black (African) people. The company created the motto, "The New Breed cat is no longer in a future heaven, no longer the product of hazy, fantasy-ridden imaginations."[50]

At its peak, New Breed employed over one hundred people, promoting a pro-Black platform by employing a strictly Black employee base. This was also achieved with the opening of fourteen New Breed stores across the United States in its first two years. Benning noted, "The time may come when we need a particular talent and a white man has it, but we must help our own people first . . . and not through a lot of do-nothing demonstrations . . . and a lot of reports."[51] And by 1970, the operation garnered the financial support to succeed. Initial shares in the company were for one dollar, but after a year, they sold for ten dollars. Writer James Baldwin and actor/comedian Sammy Davis Jr. were two of the company's significant shareholders. As a result, major retail companies like Macy's wanted to get New Breed's clothing mass produced, which meant they needed facilities that would have helped them reach high capacity. This meant more financing, which was beyond their reach. The NBPT in New York developed a relationship with the large chain on behalf of the small Black-owned business.[52]

New Breed tried to develop new ways to connect with Black consumers, especially Black men. Howard Davis noted, "Negroes spend millions on men's and boy's clothing a year, not including shoes . . . and all of it goes to The Man. We just want to keep some of it in the black community, building for us."[53] "The Man" was representative of White corporations that profited the most from Black dollars by having a presence in predominantly Black communities but not reinvesting in the communities they were located, specifically by not providing jobs to African Americans. Davis added in a May 1969 interview, it was evident that New Breed clientele was "the type of guy with the Cadillac and mohair suits. . . . Even the player type, the hustler in the sharkskin suit."[54] While rejecting the "pie-in-the-sky" rhetoric, New Breed also was against what they deemed "White dress" because Black folks looked "ridiculous in something designed for a blue-eyed European."[55] Interestingly, New Breed had a decent following with White consumers, as White men in particular made up 20 percent of the company's total sales. The company's clothing was also utilized in two motion pictures, *Up Tight* and *Putney Swope*. In Houston, Texas, a group of Black doctors requested an order of clothes from New Breed instead of the typical scrubs worn in the hospital. Overall, the company was able to tap into different markets.[56]

Despite the financial obstacles, New Breed kept its fashion goals in mind. Kathy Aldrich, a fashion editor with the *Amsterdam News*, believed wearing dashikis was simply a fad. She argued, "It will start to disappear in a year or two, but it won't go away lightly. There has to be a drastic change in social patterns between the races." While many wore New Breed and similar styles, the dashiki was linked to recognizing and embracing one's African heritage. That was a significant contribution to the company. As history has shown, many Black people across the United States wore the dashiki as part of the more significant cultural movement connected to the Black freedom struggle. This period signified a change in Black attitudes toward self-image.[57]

This cultural shift in Black awareness inspired new economic and entrepreneurial pursuit. In the fall of 1968, John Wooten, Jim Shorter, and Sidney Williams decided to move forward with supporting a venture in cosmetology. They helped create Magnificent Natural Products Company, an enterprise initiated in Los Angeles by Dennis L. Taylor and his business partner Wilbert Jackson. The men targeted African Americans who wore their hair without any chemical relaxers. At this time, the Afro hairstyle was popular, and with the hair care industry grossing $1 billion per year, Magnificent had a profitable market to explore. Its motto, "Products designed with you in mind," was adorned on all promotional materials with a Black female and male wearing Afros. Its primary products were the Magnificent Protein Enriched Holding Spray and the Hair and Scalp Care Shampoo. The company also sold creams, a setting lotion, and a conditioner. These items were the biggest sellers and made the company profitable. The two-man operation expanded to a business with "hundreds of employees" by the early 1970s. This was mainly due to the work of the NBPT, which helped establish connections with distribution centers across the nation. It also negotiated the loans Magnificent received to get started and helped the company establish a national manufacturing plant. Magnificent Natural Products lasted over a decade before the company was sold to Asian investors, as companies like Magnificent Natural Products needed larger financial contributions for wider success and reach.[58]

The Highs and Lows of Black Capitalism

Several other Black businesses could sustain themselves and grow with the help of the BEU and federal contracts. One example was Namax Builders Inc., created in 1967 by Nathan Beavers, a thirty-nine-year-old graduate of Howard University. In 1968, he received a $2,000 loan from the BEU to assist with his construction company, which, prior to the financial assistance, only employed three workers and was "on the verge of collapse." The money the union provided Beavers allowed him to accept a contract from the US Gypsum Company to restore 54 apartment units in the Hough area that had been destroyed in the riots two years earlier. Based on Beavers's work, the Better Homes for Cleveland Foundation presented him with a contract to renovate another 150 apartments in the Hough community. Carl T. Rowan noted, "Namax Builders could not have met its payroll until the time came when it could draw money against the two contracts if [John] Wooten and Union had not provided the $2,000 loan." In less than ten months, the company grew to over seventy employees and, with the number of subcontracts it obtained, had "$2.3 million worth of work on the books and [were] negotiating for $17 million more in contracts."[59]

With Namax's success, other Black construction groups were able to get contracts. McKinney Plumbing Co., another Cleveland-based group, was a three-man operation that got few work opportunities in its early beginnings and, like Beavers's group, was on the verge of failure. However, the BEU provided a subcontract for the group worth $200,000. This allowed the company to grow to sixteen workers. American Steel and Fabricating Company, led by Nolan Williams, received a contract for $26,000 and hired four others to help with the construction work. Like Beavers, Williams owed his early success to a loan and negotiating assistance from the NBPT. By the end of 1968, American Steel grossed $400,000.[60]

Because construction had historically been difficult for African Americans to enter, the Society of Registered Contractors was formed, with Nathan

Beavers named president. Through his leadership, Beavers helped other African Americans get deals. For example, Richardson Electric Company rose from three workers to twelve with $80,000 in contracts because of Beavers's help. As he put it, "Men who were just crap-shooters on the city streets are now proud members of the community." Helping Black men and women from the area was his main motivation. He added, "We took one man from the ghetto and made a first-rate carpenter out of him in six weeks. And what is so impressive is that the workmanship and loyalty of these people is a bit better than that of the employees who come through more normal channels." Many companies were reluctant to hire African Americans. The thought process was that they needed more training for jobs, and White business leaders were not keen on teaching "basic" responsibilities to new employees. It was a simple excuse to rationalize the exclusion of Black people from their companies. These types of actions were prevalent not just in Cleveland but also across the country. As a result, the federal government made efforts to fix this problem.[61]

Several Black construction contractors in DC with whom Brig Owens worked had problems securing support. He noted, "We went through the whole process of going through all the hurdles minority businesses had to jump to survive. Jim's philosophy is that you have to give them the tools to survive to make changes. You can't give handouts." Initially, he and Mitchell directed business owners to the Small Business Administration (SBA) for support. The SBA instituted a "6x6" program for businessmen who could not obtain funding through traditional means, like banks, by providing $6,000 over six years. However, after seeing how restricted companies became after seeking help from the SBA, they realized a relationship with the SBA was not beneficial to Black businessmen because the federal agency "tie[d] your hands and shoes so tight that once you went through them you could not do anything else. They wanted your first-born." Businesses that received aid from the administration could not get money from banks or other financial lending institutions. If the agency declined individual support, it made their attempts to get help elsewhere much harder. After establishing bank relationships, the union acquired conventional financing for DC businessmen. They were criticized, but as Brig Owens explained, "People were better off for it."[62]

By the summer of 1970, the BEU's Washington, DC, branch dedicated much of its attention to technical assistance for people who wanted to improve their businesses. Like Cleveland, they had different initiatives, such as loan programs and weekly advertising clinics attended by over seventy businesses in clothing, liquor sales, food, and other markets. These seminars discussed how to create newspaper advertisements, what print materials to promote their products, how to buy radio time, and examined the best insurance policies. By 1971, the DC branch assisted forty-four businesses with technical and, in some cases, financial support. Moreover, they were able to help companies build relationships with banks that could educate them on the best ways to grow their business. However, the technical assistance sometimes did not equate to long-term success.[63]

Out of the trunk of his car in Washington, DC, Nathaniel Williams started his custodial business, Clean Rite Maintenance Company. A graduate of Dunbar High School, the DC native got his start working two jobs: daytime with the US Patent Office and nighttime with a janitorial firm. In 1968, Williams was elevated to manager at his second job and quit his federal position. This promotion ignited his interest in starting his own business. Fortunately, in 1969, he received a $2,500 loan from the BEU's DC office to start. In 1972, the SBA contacted Williams for work opportunities, primarily cleaning federal buildings, specifically the White House and Blair House, the official guest residence of the president. He was provided $300,000 a year for these locations. A few months later, he was awarded three more contracts, which totaled $3 million, to cover Andrews Air Force Base, Fort Belvoir, and Goddard Space Flight Center. While Williams brought in large contracts, the time commitment to run his business prevented him from pursuing other outside appointments. This prevented him from acquiring any extra money for the cleaning company and essentially left him at the whim of the SBA for work prospects. In addition, the significant properties required a more extensive employee base, which forced Williams to hire more workers. However, his "rags-to-riches" story was coming to an end. By 1976, he owed over $100,000 due to bad negotiations and miscalculations on federal taxes. As Vernon Thompson for the *Washington Post* reported, federal allocations were "so haphazard" for Clean-Rite that Williams "eventually had to apply for credit to pay his employees on time," which damaged his ability to secure future contracts.[64]

His quarter-of-a-million dollars home was foreclosed, and so were his offices. He also had to surrender his two Mercedes-Benz sedans to a collection agency.

Along with those losses, he owed creditors more than $500,000, which forced the Internal Revenue Service to freeze his assets. With such a large debt unsettled, there were financial ramifications that affected Williams's family. His son dropped out of college to earn extra income for the family since Williams's salary as Keene Elementary School's principal was insufficient. It took years before they were able to pay off their debt. Nathaniel Williams believed that if he had not gotten involved with the SBA, his business would not have suffered such a fate where his livelihood was wiped away. Considering Williams's fiscal decisions during his tenure over his enterprise, the SBA was the only significant factor in his financial demise. The lack of technical support, manpower, and federal limitations played a role. Clean-Rite Maintenance is an example of the difficulties Black businessmen experienced, particularly with government funding.[65]

Namax Builders, New Breed, and Clean-Rite were a few models of how African Americans were producers in the US economy. While these enterprises had relative success and did not endure as long as their owners had hoped, they were a stark reminder of the realities of Black capitalism. If given the proper resources and support, Black businesses could have substantial success. However, the opportunities they were given did not always equate to long-term growth. That was simply the reality of an economic system that was based on unpredictable markets and parameters. While the BEU assisted African Americans with creating enterprises, many of the group's members also established their own ventures. Some developed restaurants, film companies, and agencies representing athletes in professional sports. The BEU wanted to create businesses to provide financially for themselves, especially when their playing careers were over. They were cognizant of what to expect from a society largely structured around race and socioeconomic status. With that understanding, they were not looking to assimilate into White society per se, nor were they striving to keep "larger society at arm's length." The BEU was looking for, as William Van Deburg attests, "equal opportunities, privileges, and respect." No BEU chapter exemplified this goal more than the one in Kansas City. Spearheaded by Curtis McClinton, the BEU's most successful chapter experienced all the highs and lows Black capitalism had to offer.[66]

5

Two Different Worlds

Kansas City and the BEU

On Sunday, January 15, 1967, Super Bowl I was held at the Los Angeles Memorial Coliseum. It was a sunny and hazy afternoon with a game-time temperature of seventy-two degrees and slight wind blowing to the east. The game featured the Green Bay Packers, representing the NFL, playing against the Kansas City Chiefs of the AFL. With more than sixty thousand attendees, the spectacle created around the game solidified professional football's dominance in the United States. Unfortunately, for the Chiefs and those who wanted the AFL to illustrate its ability to be competitive, they lost to the Packers by a score of 35–10. The lone bright spot for the Chiefs was Curtis McClinton's seven-yard touchdown catch from Len Dawson in the second quarter. After the game, Packers head coach Vince Lombardi told reporters, "I think the Kansas City team is a real tough football team but doesn't compare with the National Football League teams." Although the Chiefs' loss solidified arguments for the NFL's superiority, the Chiefs stamped themselves and the AFL as formidable foes. It also provided the Kansas City (KC) sporting community with a team it could support.[1]

Professional football had been an important part of KC's identity. The NFL had its earliest presence in the city in 1924 with the Kansas City Blues. They went as the Kansas City Cowboys the following two seasons before folding in 1926 after the team merged with the Cleveland Bulldogs. It would take more than thirty-seven years for pro football to return to town. In 1963, the Dallas Texans of the AFL, under the ownership of Lamar Hunt, moved to Missouri. Hunt, who came from a wealthy oil family, was previously denied entry into the ranks of NFL owners in 1960. That bloc denied his application fearing expansion was not advantageous to the financial strength of the league. To address the NFL's monopoly, he and other businessmen created the AFL, placing teams in the cities of rival NFL teams, like Dallas, New York, and Los Angeles. They also put franchises in places with exclusive market control, such as Buffalo, Oakland, and Denver. Hunt's Texans played in Dallas for three years before moving to KC and were rebranded as the Chiefs.[2]

Coming to Missouri was a new beginning for the Hunt family, and a homecoming for McClinton. While the Chiefs warmed to the idea of having the most racially integrated team in professional football, the city itself was cold to the idea of racial harmony projected by the AFL champions. The popularity of professional football allowed both the Hunts and McClinton to have early success in the city, and McClinton, in particular, was able to contribute to Black business development in KC. Professional sports, and the athletes who played them, influenced the social, economic, and political realities of cities across the nation. However, for Black members of the Chiefs, football gave them a livelihood that allowed them to improve their own financial prospects.

While the playing field provided privilege, they were still limited by the conventions of racial segregation. This chapter focuses on the obstacles Black athletes faced when they inserted themselves into the civil rights and Black Power movements in KC. By examining the life of Curtis McClinton and his formation of the KC chapter of the Black Economic Union (BEU), we see how Black business development brought individual victories but largely failed as a means of Black collective uplift. Examining his experiences illustrates how economic freedom could not have been achieved in the 1960s and 1970s; the financial commitments at the local and national levels were largely insufficient. The problems that plagued Black communities in Cleveland, Los Angeles, and DC were no different in KC, and they could not be remedied by the adoption of Black capitalism. There were structural issues that money alone could not solve. It raises the question whether Black athletes and their promotion of Black capitalism were ever a reliable tool in the fight for freedom, justice, and equality.

New Beginnings

Curtis Realious McClinton was born on June 25, 1939, to Mary Ella McGee and Curtis Realious McClinton Sr. in Muscogee, Oklahoma, and raised in Wichita, Kansas. His father operated a grocery store before becoming a statehouse representative from 1956 to 1963. In 1959, he and James P. Davis (the only two Black members of the state legislature) passed a law that all hotels, motels, restaurants, and businesses providing public accommodation could no longer discriminate based on race. McClinton Sr. was also elected as the state's first Black state senator, serving one term and continuing to push for the end of segregation in public spaces. His father's political experiences helped McClinton comprehend the roles Black men could play in society. He remembered, "My capacity of what I could do was defined for me at an early age. My father played baseball for recreation but was a scholar, a political science major, and a teacher. He exposed me to the institution and the abilities of Black men." When the elder McClinton was in politics, he did not receive a salary for his efforts. He was primarily into it to help his community. As such, he left the family grocery store under the management of his wife, while he was away for four months of the year. The notion of sacrifice one had to make for their community, coupled with the cultural investment in the lives of other Black people, made an impression on the younger McClinton.[3]

Early childhood experiences prepared McClinton for the opportunity to attend the University of Kansas (KU) in 1957, where he was a member of the varsity football team. McClinton likened his time there to "a bent, crooked-growing tree. It was slow and backward." Lawrence was much different from Wichita, as few Blacks in Lawrence had "jobs of any importance." He likened it to attending a school in the Deep South, where at least one knew "where a white man stood then [*sic*] to be in an environment where a white man would grin in my face and shake my hand to make me think that he is not big-oted . . . but he is." Adjusting to the collegiate ecosystem of KU was not easy.[4]

With the support of his family and coaches, he was able to make it home. He majored in business and education, two areas that would serve his interests once he left KU. On the athletic field, McClinton led the football team in rushing in 1959 and garnered some attention from NFL scouts, as the Los Angeles Rams selected him as the 110th pick in the tenth round. Playing in California would have forced him to be far away from his family and without a college degree, so McClinton decided to return to Kansas. McClinton built a community with Black students on campus by becoming a member of Kappa Alpha Psi fraternity. In the spring of 1960, he won the sixty-yard-high hurdles at the Big Eight Conference meet, and in the fall of that year, he received Big Eight Conference honors for football. The next season, McClinton played well enough to garner second-team All-American honors. He was drafted by the Dallas Texans on December 5, 1961 and signed with the team after the Bluebonnet Bowl. McClinton graduated from Kansas with a degree in business education and many athletic accolades. Leaving Lawrence forced him to begin his transition to Dallas.[5]

For McClinton, playing for the Texans was a welcomed new beginning. "To say I'm not going to Los Angeles, but rather Dallas was based on the value of the owner," he remembered. The Texans owner's ability to engage players reflected what McClinton called "phenomenal interpersonal skills." McClinton "made a business decision" to go to the South; he knew the region's culture and that people like Lamar Hunt "was good people." To be on a sports team at this level also required a commitment to winning. While college football was centered on community and pageantry, professional football focused on profit margins and victories.[6]

The Hunt family owned the Texans, but the team was in the making and image of coach Henry "Hank" Stram. Born Henry Wilczek to Polish immi-grant parents in Chicago in 1923, the sartorially aware football coach was keen on order. On game day, all team members were required to wear a suit or sport coat with dress pants. The game uniforms were to be identical for all players from head to toe, with matching socks and shoes. When the national anthem played, they were to line up in numerical order with their right hand over their heart and helmet cupped with their left arm. Stram believed the will of the collective was more important than that of the individual, and he pressed that belief on his players. Such beliefs were designed to keep team quarrels to a minimum.[7]

While balancing their lives away from the field, players (especially rookies) were keen on ensuring they never had a knock on their door during training camp. This greeting was followed by, "Coach Stram wants to see you over in his office and bring your playbook." This meant one's time on the team was coming to an end. Curtis McClinton had no intention of being cut, so he relied on some of his teammates to help him understand and fulfill the expectations of the pro game. One of the most important persons in his development was his backfield mate Abner Haynes. One of the first Black football players at North Texas State University, Haynes was drafted by the Texans in 1959 and won the league MVP the following year in 1960. He and McClinton served as an impressive duo for the Texans. During the 1962 season, Haynes led the league in rushing touchdowns for the third consecutive year, while McClinton earned AFL's Rookie of the Year. His recognition as one of the best new talents led the *Philadelphia Tribune* to call him "the AFL's answer to the Cleveland Browns Jim Brown." The Texans earned a record of 11–3 and won the AFL championship, defeating the Houston Oilers 20–17 in double overtime.[8]

In 1962, the Hunt family chose to move the team to Kansas City, Missouri. The Texans had finally achieved a successful season, but the team could not overcome the presence of their NFL rival. The AFL's headquarters were in Dallas, but the Texans could not surpass the NFL's brand power in the city competing with the Cowboys. Thus, the AFL brass had to adjust. They worked on a deal with Mayor H. Roe "The Chief" Bartle about moving the team to KC. Hunt promoted the narrative that the Chiefs were "mid-America's team," staking claims to Missouri and Kansas along with the surrounding states of Oklahoma, Nebraska, Iowa, and Arkansas, which were included in the team's new logo. Since there were no remotely close AFL or NFL teams, this strategy allowed the Chiefs to grow their fan base exponentially.[9]

The Hunts looked to expand their reach in 1963, but the transition to KC was difficult. Getting buy-in from a new fan base was the biggest issue, so Lamar Hunt was motivated to put the best team on the field. While he did not present himself as a champion for civil rights in KC, others placed the label on him. This was mainly due to the makeup of his teams. Like the

Cleveland Browns of the 1940s–1960s, the Chiefs were a favorite of African Americans across the country. When many professional football teams were overwhelmingly White, the Chiefs were different. Hunt noted, "We weren't looking to make any grand social statements. We just wanted to find the best players." In 1963, the number of Black players on the training camp squad was in double digits, with notable draft selections of Bobby Bell from the University of Minnesota and Buck Buchanan and Stone Johnson from Grambling State University, two of sixteen from the HBCU in Louisiana to be taken by NFL and AFL teams that year. Bell and Buchanan were considered "the biggest names in college gridiron warfare." Johnson was a 1960 US Olympic team member and held the world record in the 200 meters, so Stram wanted to utilize his speed at the flanker position. So, a player's abilities often superseded their race on the team, making the Chiefs one of the most racially diverse teams in the league. Of the fifty roster spots, twelve were Black players. This starkly contrasted the 1962 Dallas Texans, who only had three Black players: Haynes, McClinton, and Dave Grayson.[10]

On August 30, the Chiefs played a preseason game against the Houston Oilers before eleven thousand fans during a preseason game in Wichita. While making a block, Johnson fractured his fifth cervical vertebrae in his neck. The injury caused paralysis of his legs and arms, and doctors performed surgery on him that night. He later died on September 8 because of his injuries. Abner Haynes was deeply affected and took the blame for Johnson's death. He later recalled, "I was the cause of him being here. I felt responsible for him being there and getting killed." Johnson's untimely death sent shockwaves throughout the team and the league. It took a while for members of the Chiefs to focus on winning again. That season, they went 5–7–2, the team's worst record in their short history. Over the 1964 and 1965 seasons, the Chiefs earned 7–7 and 7–5–2 records, failing to reach the playoffs both years, but the team was competitive.[11]

Black Chiefs

As KC was getting adjusted to professional football, Black players were trying to get accustomed to living in a city that was still governed by racial segregation. They were not allowed to enter many of the same places or find housing in areas that their White teammates could. Shortly after McClinton arrived in KC, the city council proposed a resolution for integrating public facilities. It passed with the final count of 50.9 percent in favor. The margins for equal access were slim. If it were not for five thousand new voters who registered for the election, of which 80 percent were Black, the ordinance would not have passed. For Curtis McClinton, "This ignited a very ticklish fiber in my body and motivated me to get involved in the community where I was going to make a living." As Ivan Carter and Blair Kerkhoff noted, considering the realities of Black members of the Chiefs, "winning games was only part of the battle. Earning respect and retaining dignity in the face of racial intolerance took just as much courage."[12]

Playing for the Chiefs did not provide Black players an exception to the racial covenants that existed throughout the city. The integrated culture of KC was largely influenced by various jazz communities and barbecue restaurants. For example, Gale Sayers, who played at KU, was presented with two options heading into the 1965 season. In November 1964, the Chiefs chose him with the fifth overall pick of the AFL Draft, while the Chicago Bears selected him with the fourth pick of the NFL Draft. However, the racial climate around housing in KC influenced Sayers's choice to go to the Windy City. The Chiefs selected Bobby Bell in the 1963 draft, and the Minnesota Vikings selected him in the NFL Draft. He chose to sign with KC, and when he arrived, he felt like he was "going back into the South." Attending the University of Minnesota, he had grown accustomed to some of the trappings given to star college athletes. Bell said, "In Minneapolis, you could live where you wanted to live, eat where you wanted to eat. Down here, there were places you could live and places you could not, places you could eat and places you could not—it was a different world." He viewed more than two hundred homes throughout the city and suburbs only to have banks refuse to sign the paperwork for the necessary loan. Even Coach Stram tried to intervene on his behalf, but his vouching was useless.[13]

Bobby Bell noted, "You could call a restaurant on the phone and make a dinner reservation, then when you showed up with your wife, they wouldn't have a table for you." Black athletes were not shielded from racial discrimination in KC. Police harassment was also a major issue. He remembered, "You would get pulled over all the time when you drove through a white neighborhood. Things like that were common, you know." Such matters did not deter Bell or other Black members of the Chiefs, but they did take a toll on them and their families. Abner Haynes indicated, "Nobody understood what the top athletes were going through. It was difficult to keep marriages. Your wife wasn't prepared. Your kids weren't prepared." Haynes added, "If you fought for your rights and dignity, you made white people mad. If you didn't do it, you made black people mad." The dilemma of being a professional athlete was difficult for him and so many others. Black athletes in White-dominated spaces experienced what sociologist W. E. B. DuBois described as "double consciousness." Their actions were calculated through multiple prisms. Haynes had built a reputation for not accepting the status quo. He and other Black players decided to boycott the 1965 AFL All-Star Game held in New Orleans, Louisiana, after they experienced segregated living spaces with their hotel arrangements and were refused service by restaurants and taxis in the city. They wondered why they played a game in a city where they were not welcomed. Haynes, a former league MVP, refused to bow to racist practices. Before the start of the next season, the Chiefs traded him to the Denver Broncos. The problems he left in KC were awaiting his replacement.[14]

In the 1966 NFL Draft, the Chiefs and the Los Angeles Rams chose Heisman Trophy Winner Mike Garrett from the University of Southern California. He chose KC once the Hunt family offered him a contract worth $500,000. When he arrived in the city, he found only three complexes willing to rent to him, but none of them were suitable. He looked to get a place to live in the Country Club District, an upscale area of the city, but his applications were declined. This part of the city was created in 1906 by Jesse Clyde "J. C." Nichols as "a wonderland of posh homes, tree-lined vistas and cul-de-sacs." By the 1950s, the area consisted of more than five thousand acres. Despite the *Shelley v. Kraemer* (1948) ruling, which made it illegal to enforce housing covenants based on race, African Americans were still denied access to real estate they desired. Nichols instituted these measures by creating homeowners' associations and deeds on the properties. While Nichols was not the originator of such practices, he spread their use throughout the United States through the real estate groups of which he was a member. Garrett had the financial means to pay for a home, but his race restricted those possibilities. He knew of various White teammates who had no problems. He ended up rooming with Black teammate Aaron Brown.[15]

To address racial segregation in KC housing, Curtis McClinton and Bobby Bell developed a proposal with Freedom Inc., a grassroots organization of Black activists. They planned a complex of integrated apartments called McClinton Courts, with air-conditioning and a football-shaped pool on the west side of Swope Park. The plan never materialized because the city council refused to make the zoning changes for a complex in the area. McClinton and Bell played on their identities as members of the Chiefs to provide better housing opportunities for KC's Black citizens with no luck. In response, Bruce R. Watkins, the first Black member of the city council and cofounder of Freedom Inc., sponsored a Fair Housing Ordinance to change those restrictions.[16]

A year later, evidence of the measure proved fruitful for some. In July 1967, six months after the Chiefs loss in Super Bowl I, their work led the city council to pass a measure that banned racial discrimination in housing. Mike Garrett was able to get an apartment in the Country Club District. Bobby Bell found a home in the suburbs of Prairie Village, Kansas, but through unconventional means. A White friend bought the house and rented it to the Chiefs All-Pro until he could find a bank to provide his loan. By this point, Bell was heading into his fifth season with the Chiefs, but some of the banks he visited had questions about his ability to pay the mortgage. They argued that since his employment with the Chiefs was not guaranteed, they wanted to avoid taking a chance on him defaulting. While the lack of job security associated with playing professional football was used as a demerit against Bell, many of his White teammates on the Chiefs did not experience those same issues when securing their loans.[17]

The freedom to exist was limited for Black people throughout KC and in communities on the fringes. Some establishments held unwritten "Whites only" policies. For example, in 1967, a Black Conception Seminary College student, Clarence Thomas, was studying to become a Catholic priest. He would have been the first African American in that position in his hometown of Pin Point, Georgia. One night, Thomas and a White friend from the seminary, Tom O'Brien, scheduled a double date. The plans for the meeting fell through, and both men decided to go to Shakey's Pizza Parlor in Overland Park, Kansas, an affluent suburb ten miles from KC. They intended to hang out and have some beers. They put their order in with the waitress, and twenty minutes passed before the manager approached their table with security. He said, "We've had complaints about you guys. You've been too loud." O'Brien told them they had the wrong people. The manager replied, "No! This is the right table. A bunch of complaints, you've been too loud. You all need to leave." O'Brien, who had been to Shakey's numerous times, tried to plead his case. Thomas grabbed his arm to leave, telling him, "Man, it ain't the volume." O'Brien failed to realize there had never been Black patrons at the establishment. Many African Americans knew how to read situations and spaces that were keen on upholding racial segregation. Unfortunately, well-meaning White friends were oblivious to the persistence of these practices. White businesses in KC and across the United States had no problem limiting their clientele. That was not the case for Black athletes, who had to come up with different ways to make a living especially with few networks and financial resources. Thus, the creation of a chapter of the BEU in KC made sense.[18]

The Makings of the Kansas City BEU

As much as the BEU was based on the personality of Jim Brown, the Greater Kansas City chapter, as it was officially called, took on the identity of the Chiefs running back. Brown was happy McClinton was willing to start an office in KC but let him know all the office responsibilities would be on him and his organizing skills. Building off their connection since the Ali Draft Summit, McClinton remembered Brown told him, "If you can go to Kansas City with no money and without help from the national office, then go to it." The reality was the other offices around the country struggled to secure their own funding. Thus, providing the KC chapter with money from the grants and donations they already secured would have hurt operations. Brown "was very straightforward in regard to the fact that it would be an initiative that I would have to lead and fund. There would be no resources except for leadership from the board." Accepting those parameters, McClinton's goal was to use the BEU to help Black entrepreneurs already in existence and new ventures begun by some of the Black members of the Chiefs.[19]

The BEU in KC officially opened on Saturday, June 8, 1968, at 3402 East Thirty-First Street. However, many Black residents were not initially welcoming. They saw the economic-focused mission of the organization and deemed them "Uncle Toms for promoting capitalism" and "relying on White people" for financial support as "handouts." This was different from the community reception of the Cleveland office. McClinton recognized the validity of such sentiments, saying, "Sometimes it's hard for them to relate that I can feel the common need. There's a constant challenge of being accepted by those with whom I'm working on a day to day [*sic*] basis." He was not given access simply because he was Black or an athlete. There was a level of trust he knew he had to develop. Just because he was a member of the Kansas City Chiefs did not give him an automatic pass to become the racial representative of Black people in the city. Unlike members of the Cleveland chapter who lived among many of the Black folks they were helping, McClinton's living situation was not the same. Despite that reality, community members wanted to know that he had their best interests in mind; it was about the good of the whole, not the individual. While many African Americans wanted their funding to come from within, taking funding from White businesses and the government was considered a handout that took away agency and power from them. So, they had to be very strategic about how they disseminated their efforts.[20]

In KC, the Black newspaper, *The Call*, was a significant help in promoting the BEU. Black newspapers like the *Chicago Defender*, *Pittsburgh Courier*, and *Atlanta Daily World* served as sources of information on the happenings in Black communities across the US. *The Call* served a critical role for the Black community in KC. As historian Manning Marable noted, "the Black press became the chief vehicle to control and to exploit the Black consumer market, as well as to promote the ideology of Black Capitalism to the masses." The BEU benefited immensely from the coverage provided by the Black-owned *Call*, and two White papers: the *Kansas City Star* and the *Kansas City Times*. Using these media was one of the foundational tools of the organization's efforts. The newspapers highlighted upcoming workshops, which helped businesses understand the best ways to navigate funding obstacles. The BEU hosted ten- and sixteen-week courses on business administration. In its first year, the BEU in KC garnered $460,000 in contracts and loans. One of the primary foci of the organization was construction. This was an untapped business area for African Americans nationally, but especially in KC. McClinton and his board members saw this as a space to provide numerous African Americans in the city with job opportunities.[21]

In a 1968 *Kansas City Star* article, sportswriter Dick Wade wrote, "Trust between men is as rare in the ghetto, where it is needed so badly, as a balanced diet. Wherever there are poor, there are those who exploit the poor. Where there is exploitation, trust dies." The BEU served as a metaphorical bridge between the middle class and the poor, or "student" and "teacher," as Wade defined them. He also provided some statistics: African Americans made up 11 percent of the national population, with 20 percent living in urban areas; however, they controlled only 3 percent of the invested capital in the United States. McClinton knew that every Black person in KC would not embrace his approach to Black capitalism, but he was committed to showing that it could be useful. Getting access to capital was the most important step.[22]

While getting the day-to-day essentials came with its own hassles, it was customary for many professional sports teams to help their players get jobs in the offseason. The salaries of professional football players in the 1960s did not provide the luxury of just tending to their profession on the gridiron. Most players needed another job to hold them over financially. Chiefs management aimed to secure jobs for its players when they arrived at training camp in late summer, so by the time the season ended the following January, they did not have to worry about their next paycheck. Curtis McClinton was able to find an opportunity in banking. Since February 1965, McClinton had been a full-time employee of Douglass State Bank in KC, Kansas, during the offseason and part-time during the season. Founded in 1947, Douglass was the first Black-owned bank west of the Mississippi River. McClinton's time there helped him better understand the financial parameters of loans and mortgages. From his view, these were the two most essential funding sources to help Black people who were looking to create businesses and secure housing. In his time at Douglass, McClinton became keen on the obstacles Black businesses faced. Through his observations, he attributed some of the problems of Black businessmen in Kansas City to "poor lighting, poor parking, poor streets, and . . . crime. But the biggest problem is the inability of the black businessman to attract consumers and the dollar outside of the inner-city area." Segregation forced many Black enterprises to rely on the Black dollar. However, by the mid-1960s, the national push for integration created more competition as Black clientele patronized White businesses. Although many companies McClinton observed lacked management skills and the financial means to be effective, he knew the most significant factor was customers. He told the *Kansas City Town Squire*, "Even when a man has these things and is interested in doing business, he must have the customers to open."[23]

Relying on Black consumers was important for most Black entrepreneurs since they were in Black communities. This belief fitted the self-help ethos that characterized the historical experiences of Black capitalists and was most viable in restaurants and beauty (i.e., barber and cosmetology services). This was a positive by-product of segregation. However, other segments of the populace believed relying solely on the Black dollar was impractical. In the 1960s and the decade that followed, there was an evolution of commerce that saw Black goods and services gain access to different markets. By the late 1960s, African American families made 63 percent of the median income of White families, with nearly $30 billion in purchasing power. The issue for many businesses was accessing those dollars while reaching clientele outside of the Black community. White establishments had the luxury of being racially exclusive because of sheer population size; that was not the case for Black businesses. A solution needed to be developed for this lack of support.[24]

On Monday, July 1, 1968, McClinton officially opened Swope Parkway National Bank (SPNB), the first Black-owned bank in Missouri. He received the charter for the bank in 1966 and began an eighteen-month process to secure investors. The bank had $750,000 in capital and fifteen staff members. McClinton also put up some of his funding to open the bank, and teammate Willie Lanier also invested $5,000. Assisting with the organization of SPNB was LaVannes C. Squires, who served as executive vice president. He and McClinton connected through their work at Douglass and were both KU alums. Squires, like McClinton, grew up in Wichita and in 1950 was the university's first Black student to play on the men's basketball team, earning the Freshman Basketball Award in 1951. The following year, he helped the team win the 1952 national championship. Squires's ties to KU and willingness to help build the Black business community in KC were major factors in their relationship.[25]

McClinton's development of Swope Parkway was in the same spirit of Jackie Robinson who served as chair of the board of directors for Freedom National Bank, founded in Harlem in 1964. Robinson had created the bank in concert with Dunbar McLaurin, a Black businessman in the borough. Robinson noted, "I became fascinated with the way big business was conducted, with the operation of the stock market and the power which exists in the hoard rooms of banks and corporations." He added, "Black people were coming to the point where they would be crying out in behalf of Black Power, but it was pathetic to realize how little we knew of money." The legendary baseball player admitted that if African Americans had organized around the vote and economics, there would be "a much easier fight on our hands." Most African Americans had lower income than White Americans and were considered financial risks because of bad credit. They also had to battle the stereotype of being untrustworthy. As Robinson experienced, despite all the discrimination in the form of denials for mortgages and loans, Black people "faithfully and religiously deposited their savings in white banks."[26]

SPNB faced many obstacles in its first year of operations. Because the Federal Reserve Bank refused to provide any financial support, in November 1968, SPNB purchased $5,000 worth of State of Israel bonds. Squires explained, "Ours is a new bank, and Israel is one of the world's youngest democracies. The economic growth of the inner-city area of Kansas City is our objective, just as the economic growth and development of the state of Israel is the purpose of Israel bonds." He concluded, "Both purposes are parallel in their goals." This move provided the bank with a 5.5 percent return. These types of investments, along with a growing number of patrons, helped the bank by 1970. By that time, the bank had doubled its employees and held more than $7 million in capital. Swope Parkway was the first bank from 1940 to 1970 to earn a net profit in its first year of operation. Across the United States, Black businesses had difficulty getting adequate funding and lines of credit from White banks, and insurance companies imposed higher interest rates for Black business owners. SPNB helped alleviate some of those problems for Black companies, especially those in need of financial support. However, SPNB also had to address the conflicts its financial leanings created. To be invested in the State of Israel while looking to develop Black businesses put the bank at odds with Black Power advocates, who supported Palestine. As Squire posited, the bank's success was interconnected with the fate of Israel. His position did not resonate with all the customers SPNB served, but the bank's leadership saw it as a way of doing business.[27]

The lack of management skills and financial capital were some of the early problems the BEU identified with Black businesses. McClinton noticed, "Even when a man has these things and is interested in doing business, he must have the customers." He encouraged those who came to him for help to get out to the predominantly White suburbs in Raytown and Johnson County, two prime locations for businesses to attract clientele. With the high overhead to operate in suburban locales, African American business owners were limited in their reach. There were also restrictive codes in the suburbs that limited the opportunities for Black folks to live in these areas. Thus, opening a store in communities where African Americans were denied the right to live was a hard sell for many Black businessmen. In 1970, a Black real estate company encountered racial hostility when it opened its doors to attract Black people to the Johnson County community. It was not long before White residents disapproved of the company's presence and broke the office's windows. While Black-owned businesses in KC faced many problems, their issues were a microcosm of a national matter. According to the Ford Foundation, in 1969, there were 163,000 Black corporations in the United States with revenue of $4.5 billion. However, the total receipts for all businesses combined in the United States were over $1 trillion that year. Black companies accounted for only a tiny fraction of the capital. Ford concluded that Black spending power was estimated at $30 billion, but more than 80 percent of expenditures from African Americans went to businesses owned by people who were not Black.[28]

Despite financial restraints, community organizations joined in support of SPNB and BEU. In March 1969, the South KC branch of the National Association for the Advancement of Colored People (NAACP) protested the school board's refusal to deposit funds into SPNB. After a 4–2 vote, they sent funds from the Teacher Corps program to Baltimore Bank and Trust. Dr. Vernon E. Rice, president of the chapter, said, "The black community in this city is quite disturbed by the board's action. So disturbed that if you keep adding fuel to the bomb, it's going to go off." He told the board that 47 percent of the school's population was Black, so funding should also go to Black-owned businesses. He added, "We often hear the trite statement . . . that black people should determine their own future. When we assert ourselves and show self-determination, then you take away the boot strap." Henry P. Poindexter, vice president of the school board, noted the money went to the banks in districts that paid the most taxes. Rice replied, "We're not asking for favoritism . . . we're just saying the Negro community contributes large amounts of tax money to the district and we don't get any of it back in our institutions." Many African Americans were ready and willing to support McClinton and his bank. Rice told McClinton, "Now is the time for all Black men to come together hand in hand if we are to ever achieve these goals."[29]

To expand the BEU's reach, Curtis McClinton made sure to connect with sectors outside of the Black community in KC. His goal was to get assistance and input where possible. He utilized all the connections he had built throughout the city as a member of the Chiefs. For instance, he developed a partnership with the Tri-Presbytery Committees of Northwest Missouri and Northeast Kansas. They aimed to work "together to achieve greater impact on metropolitan problems." Religious entities played a critical role in community efforts. Merrill Proudfoot, a professor at Park College and chair of the Topeka-Highland Presbytery, noted, "A survey has shown that churches have a considerable amount of undesignated liquid wealth, which is indicative of much greater underlying economic power." Groups across the city were looking for partnerships that would allow them to capitalize on the economic efforts that were being promoted locally and nationally. The BEU had moderate success getting funding to support its efforts. The Office of Economic Opportunity provided them with a federal grant worth $100,310 to be used as operating funds to support businesses, youth development programs, and staffing. The union used these funds to create a daycare center, florist shop, printing plant, variety store, commercial bakery, men's apparel shop, carpet cleaning business, service station, boarding home, and beauty shop. In total, these enterprises employed sixty-five people with a payroll of $175,000 and revenue of $1.4 million.[30]

One of the first businesses the BEU helped was Leon's United Super Market, KC's first Black-owned grocery store, started by Leon Sullivan. Despite its historical significance, it was subject to both good and bad times. On August 23, 1968, four Black men robbed the grocery store and some of the patrons at gunpoint after having customers lie on the ground while they checked their pockets and purses. As the four fled Leon's, they got into a shootout with police, and one of the men died from a gunshot wound he suffered. Brenda Conrad, a nine-year-old girl who was on a swing set at the adjacent Seven Oaks Park, was also wounded during the shootout. While Leon's was a staple in the community, it was not immune to the social ills in low-income communities plagued by poverty, hunger, and unemployment.[31]

The BEU also helped Black businesses get into the automotive industry. In March 1969, it helped fund Butler Auto Parts, founded by Phil Butler. He was directed to two initiatives: the Operation Mainstream program under the Small Business Administration (SBA) and Chrysler's Mopar division, which served as a direct connection for automobile parts. The business was the first Black auto parts shop to be sponsored by the SBA and Chrysler. Butler Auto was a family affair: Phil had the help of his brother, David, and father, Ernest, and his wife, Beverly, managed the company's books. In the 1970s, Butler Auto and other new businesses like it faced the reality that nationally, many companies did not survive their first eighteen months of existence, and 57 percent stopped operating within five years. The business lasted well into the 1980s. This partnership served as the impetus for more considerable dealings; a few years later, the BEU partnered with Chevrolet to get more Black owners of dealerships. Of the 6,100 Chevrolet dealers across the United States, only 32 were owned by "minorities." The biggest issue was that 50 percent of those that went into business were closed after eighteen months.[32]

In July 1969, the BEU celebrated its first four hundred days of operation. It held a weeklong citywide celebration from July 6 to 13 to commemorate its work but also was working on ways to expand its efforts. The culminating event was held on Sunday, July 13, a banquet held at the U-Smile Stadium Inn. Jim Brown served as the keynote speaker and told the 350 people in attendance, "We are not the Uncle Toms and we are not radicals. We do not believe in separatism, but neither do we believe in bowing down. We are for self-help and black pride. We also believe in whites and blacks working together." He added, "Black citizens in the United States must be given total freedom or placed in concentration camps." Brown also called on the federal government to prevent armed struggle. He asked, "But what if a group of young men decided guerilla warfare is the only way to achieve freedom in this country? What if they decided to destroy whiteness and burned homes and churches with people inside?" He played on the fears of the White business community. A year before, the country had a reckoning when Martin Luther King was killed in Memphis. The nation did not want to deal with that type of destruction again. Brown stuck to his script; he wanted the Black community to know that for those who were not with the "Uncle Toms" or the "radicals," the BEU was their alternative. He also reminded attendees they had nothing to fear as the United States had "the greatest system in the world." Brown was not going to advocate for revolution, only Black capitalism. His presence at the celebration helped bring new supporters to the KC chapter. Four hundred days was a milestone worth celebrating, but it was a small feat in the grand scheme of the BEU trying to achieve national prominence where it could wield social, economic, and political power.[33]

The BEU embraced interracial coalitions that contributed to its efforts to aid Black businesses. This was illustrated with its collaboration with John H. Wandless in 1969. A native of Pittsburgh, Pennsylvania, Wandless made his way to KC after serving four years in the US Navy and enrolled at Rockhurst College. Upon graduation, he worked as an Urban Affairs Specialist with the Office of Economic Opportunity in KC. In this role, he wrote *Minority Economic Development: Opportunities and Approaches*. This report had two goals: first, help the BEU in KC develop a business plan for economic development, and second, create an evaluation process to determine how to accept business proposals that are presented to them.[34]

While Black Power had many meanings to many people, so did Black capitalism. This was illustrated through Nixon's revamping of the phrase, and even Jim Brown's use of green power. There was no clear distinction between the two. However, Wandless provided his own assessment of Black capitalism. He stated the objectives of this economic philosophy were not to "create more jobs for ghetto residents; generate profits to investors; experiment with neighborhood capitalism; adequately supply the consumer needs of the ghetto residents; cool the ghetto." His take addressed some of the perspectives that saw Black capitalism as a cure-all for the problems in Black communities. Wandless argued the "real objectives" were "taking the lid off the aspirations of minorities so that America is really a land of opportunity; developing, pride, solidarity and achievement; developing minority capacity to influence and participate in community-wide decision making; developing wealth in minority communities—the acquisition of capital and the availability of credit; and ultimately banish the ghetto as a center of defeat and exploitation."[35]

Wandless also urged the White business community to be invested in the "basic justice of public and private support" of Black business development. It was his argument that the White community had "failed in several instances to compensate the [Black] man for his 200 years of labor in building this nation without pay." His sentiments echoed a call for reparations, which garnered him support from BEU leadership. In his proposals for the organization, he recommended it concentrate its efforts, specifically in the areas of manufacturing and housing, within a three-hundred-mile radius of KC. This covered a five-state area, including the highly populated cities in Kansas, Oklahoma, Missouri, Iowa, and Nebraska, and largely aligned with the Chiefs' fan base. As a result, McClinton brought Wandless on as director of operations to help lead the BEU's efforts.[36]

Going Out on Top

As the BEU's efforts ramped up in the fall of 1969, the Kansas City Chiefs were on the precipice of the ultimate team goal: winning a Super Bowl. That year, the Chiefs were heralded for being the first pro sports team with a majority Black squad. Based on the forty-man roster limits of NFL teams, twenty-two were African American with eight starters on the defensive side of the ball. Stram lauded the group as "the best defensive club we've had in Chiefs' history." The coach added, "We don't particular care what color he is, what nationality, what anything, the only concern we have is bringing him in with the idea of competing for our squad and if they earn the right to be a member of our 40 man squad then they are going to be here." Willie Lanier, who had never been on an integrated sports team until he joined the Chiefs in 1967, was pleased by the meritocratic approach of the coach. He said, "If there were any quotas here, it was not obvious to me. Hank took the position that whoever performed the best would start. It appeared to me that there were quotas elsewhere, but I really didn't see any restrictions on this team."[37]

The Black presence on the Chiefs must be attributed to Lloyd Wells, a former college athlete on the football team at Texas Southern University and Korean War veteran. Wells was a newspaper photographer with the *Houston Forward Times* and *Houston Informer*. His insights helped build one of the AFL's best teams in the 1960s and 1970s. The belief was his eye for talent developed from his time as a videographer for Muhammad Ali. The boxing champion stayed with him several times when he visited Houston, especially during his trial over enlisting in the US military during the Vietnam War. Wells gained notoriety within the professional football ranks after he was able to lure Otis Taylor away from the Dallas Cowboys. He also developed a pipeline with historically Black colleges and universities (HBCUs), helping the Chiefs sign talent that was either less desirable or overlooked by many teams because of their race or where they attended school. Institutions like Prairie View A&M, Morgan State, and Grambling State were a few of the schools Wells introduced to KC. Such qualities led the team to hire him as the first full-time Black scout in the AFL in 1963. As much credit has been attributed to Stram for the team's winning culture, Wells was just as influential.[38]

The Chiefs earned an 11–3 record during the 1969 season. When it came to Black players on the Chiefs, the adage "winning cures all" had a bit of truth. Some of the off-field discrimination changed after January 11, 1970. That day, they played the Minnesota Vikings in Super Bowl IV. This game was the last time the AFL and NFL would play as two separate leagues before both merged under the NFL banner the following season. It was also the first Super Bowl in New Orleans, as both leagues agreed to play the annual season finale below the Mason-Dixon Line. By the end of the first half, KC led 16–0. Those points were enough, considering they arguably had the league's best defense, led by Bobby Bell, Buck Buchanan, Willie Lanier, and Emmitt Thomas. The Chiefs were dominant, winning 23–7. The triumph in New Orleans was the first championship for KC since the Kansas City Monarchs won the Negro League World Series in 1942. Chiefs fans from all over America came out to celebrate the momentous occasion. Winning even brought Black players congratulatory messages, public adulation, and perks around town like free meals and drinks, but they still had much to overcome in the grand scheme.[39]

Shortly after Super Bowl IV, President Richard Nixon wrote a letter to McClinton on January 22, expressing his admiration for the efforts of the KC BEU office. He said, "The outstanding efforts of the Kansas City chapter of the Black Economic Union to provide new employment and business opportunities and the black communities have come to my attention and I want to commend you and your associates for your important contribution." The president had been made aware of the work of McClinton across the city and wanted to make sure he extended his gratitude for demonstrating how beneficial Black capitalism could be for African American communities. Nixon added, "I understand that you have set ambitious goals and have made remarkable progress in achieving them. It is a pleasure to congratulate you for your excellent work and to wish you continued success in the days ahead." Nixon's letter signaled how the president looked to connect with proponents of Black capitalism, especially Black athletes. The Chiefs winning the Super Bowl was also a benefit to McClinton getting access to networks that had yet to manifest.[40]

In Super Bowl I, Curtis McClinton had been a major contributor to the Chiefs. By 1970, he played a less significant role with the team, which had been relying more heavily on other running backs like Mike Garrett, Wendell Hayes, and Warren McVea. Although he had not planned it, Super Bowl IV would be McClinton's final professional football game. He knew the power of sport and realized athletics had given him a certain fame and recognition. It also allowed him "the ability to speak and be heard by individuals who have something to say that can't be heard." It was his goal to use his platform to be a voice for those who did not have access to the same spaces. Reflecting on his impending retirement, he said, "I always said I would play for five years. . . . Then, I began to seriously address the future that lay before me. I knew it was not in football." McClinton had played eight years of professional football, and coaching or having a managerial position with the Chiefs or elsewhere was not viable. There were no Black head coaches in the league in 1970 and only a few assistant coaches. The Pittsburgh Steelers hired Lowell Perry as their receivers coach in 1957. Since his hiring in the "Steel City," few Black men were allowed to coach at that level. McClinton did not want to involve himself "in anything that [had] fixed opportunities." After the game, McClinton began to shift more of his focus on the work of SPNB and the BEU.[41]

The experiences of Black athletes, when it came to their motivations for preparing for life after football, were not always the same. Just because one was popular in the sporting arena did not always translate to financial prosperity away from it. Whether one had success or failure was dependent on the details. Some could go into movies, like Jim Brown. Others sought to become sports agents, like John Wooten and Brig Owens. Curtis McClinton wanted to develop business ventures that would have a generational impact. Prior to the start of the 1970 season, McClinton retired. It had become apparent to many that he was done playing professional football—not because his body had begun to fail him, but because he had grown a beard, breaking from the clean-shaven rules of Coach Stram. He had a longer career in the NFL than most and left with his reputation intact. He was considered "the type of player who made a contribution merely by being in uniform." Now thirty-two years old and out of football, he had time to focus on his business interests and that significant goal: creating fifty thousand new jobs through business development worth $500 million. An assessment of the BEU in 1968 would show that McClinton's intentions were good, but nothing about the organization gave the impression that it could yield those results; the office needed more personnel to handle the proposals presented to it from Black business folks who came for help. The BEU also needed more office space, supplies, classrooms, a meeting space, and funds to support its community awareness programs. Most of all, there was no "seed money" to help Black businesses ready to expand. However, by 1970, the BEU had gotten the resources it needed through federal government agencies and external contributors.[42]

Produce, Achieve, and Prosper in KC

While SPNB was developing into a reliable financial resource, the bank was not the BEU's slush fund. Due to the various statutes and regulations associated with operating a financial institution, running afoul of those measures would be costly. So, McClinton's goal upon retiring was securing funding to support the day-to-day operations of the BEU. He pushed a narrative of economic self-sufficiency and believed this could be done through membership fees and increasing the organization's membership to at least 300,000 people. With the lowest option for dues at $5, the minimum the KC office would bring in was $1.5 million. By 1970, KC had a population of 500,284 people, of which African Americans comprised 22.1 percent. Even if every Black person in KC paid the membership dues, McClinton would have had to depend on outside funding sources from non-Black individuals and government agencies. Federal grants and outside contributions would be significant factors for the BEU.[43]

While financial resources were a great need, so was human capital. For the daily operations of the BEU during football season, McClinton had relied on the resourcefulness of Fran Wyatt and Alexander Harris. Wyatt, a native of Kansas City, Kansas, was chief administrator of planning and programming. A review of her job description includes eighteen tasks, including organizing community relations, developing evaluation reports, researching, and completing applications for funding from different foundations and government agencies. She coordinated many of the grant proposals the KC office submitted to various national and local agencies. Harris, a native of Kansas City Missouri, was the chief housing administrator. Discharged from the US Army as a master sergeant, he later worked with the Land Clearance and Redevelopment Authority of Kansas City. This work and the connections he made through his father, Ray Harris Sr. (one of three Black contractors in the city), made him an asset to the BEU, connecting Black companies to the housing and rehab opportunities in the city. Retirement liberated McClinton from the time demands of football. It had given him the appropriate time to dedicate himself to different projects and funding opportunities, and he had the Nixon administration to thank.[44]

Over the 1960s and 1970s, the federal government created various initiatives to vitalize cities. One effort was Model Cities, which was created under the Johnson administration. This project supported antipoverty programs and improved social services in urban communities, where residents also helped implement programs. KC was also one of several major cities to get funds through the Urban Renewal Project (URP), which included many rehab opportunities for construction companies. Over eleven thousand buildings were identified through URP for renovations, but only a few Black contractors had successful bids. The most significant issues were the "inability to submit accurate and competitive bids," lack of insurance coverage, no access to bonding, insufficient operation funds, and inadequate resources for economic assistance. The BEU made the goal of helping Black contractors get proposals submitted on spaces with substandard housing and poverty. They also helped develop budgets that reflected how much it costs to rehab and renovate office buildings, homes, and residential communities. To help contractors, McClinton established a partnership with the Extension Division of the University of Kansas. He believed there were many valuable contracts in rehab and helping Black contractors get access was a worthy cause. Knowing how to structure their bids was the first step; qualifying for private and government loans was the next.[45]

The BEU created Mo-Kan Contractors to help Black businesses secure grants and contracts. Construction of housing for low-income families became a primary focus for the BEU through several of its initiatives: the United

Trade Association (UTA), the Minority Contractors Association (MCA), the Business Institute Training Center (BITC), and the Economic Rehabilitation Program (ERP). Spearheaded by Alex Harris, Mo-Kan assisted in construction and remodeling, providing a wealth of opportunities that Black contractors historically had been shut out of for decades in KC. For example, in December 1969, Mo-Kan negotiated on behalf of the Sam J. Persley Construction Company, helping them get a $550,000 contract to remodel the St. Regis Hotel as part of the Mid-City Towers Project and Rent Supplement Program under the Federal Housing Administration. Persley was a longtime resident of KC since 1936, and at the time, it was the largest building contract for a Black-owned company. His goal was to turn the building into low-income housing by constructing eighty-five units where residents would not pay more than 25 percent of their monthly income for rent. On the rehab front, Persley was responsible for remodeling common space for residents, kitchens, and bathrooms, installing new carpeting, elevators, new roofs, new plumbing and wiring, and updates to the interior and exterior of the building. Previously, Mo-Kan helped Persley get a $100,000 contract to build the Good Samaritan Baptist Church in southeastern KC. The BEU was helping numerous Black businesses prosper.[46]

While certain Black businessmen were able to benefit from federal and local contracts, African Americans on the whole were not benefiting from the individual successes. At the heart of the matter, much of the bulk of Black earnings were spent on housing and food. For example, KC resident Carl Vann and his wife and four kids moved from the Chouteau Courts housing project to a four-bedroom, three-story house. Through UTA, MCA, and ERP, the home underwent a full rehab: a new roof, refinished floors, new plumbing and electric wiring, painted and papered walls, carpet and new cabinets installed, garage repaired, and a newly cultivated yard. While providing housing for low-income persons, they also tapped into the community to participate in building projects. While this effort improved housing prospects for community members, it also provided jobs for Black youth, many of whom had dropped out of school or were deemed "unemployable" because of their extensive police records. This allowed them to learn a trade that would allow them to make an honest living.[47]

Despite a national shortage of homes, the reality in KC was much different. There were thousands of vacant homes across the city, but most were in high-crime areas. This was a significant impetus for the urban renewal projects across KC and the United States. In March 1970, Housing Secretary George Romney pushed for Operation Breakthrough, a program created to develop new techniques in housing. The program assessed how European countries handled housing to determine if any approaches could help improve conditions in the United States. While it was tasked with looking for new strategies to build housing unit developments, the BEU's delegation went looking to negotiate contracts with companies in Amsterdam to see if they could operate plants in the United States; unfortunately, nothing materialized from the visit.[48]

In 1970, 61 percent of Black people in KC lived in low-income areas, with 32 percent of that population living below the poverty level, which for a family of four was $3,968. Poverty was a grave reality in KC, especially for African Americans. Nationally, the poverty level had increased by 1.2 million people, or 5.1 percent, with the poverty rate of Black Americans three times that of White Americans. Interestingly, African Americans who lived above the poverty level were more likely to live in low-income areas than White Americans of the same economic status. While the BEU and other organizations had the goal of eradicating poverty, creating solutions was not easy. The US Census Bureau reported that to raise above the poverty line the income of all low-income families and individuals nationwide, $11.4 billion would be needed.[49]

By the spring of 1971, the efforts of the BEU and McClinton had garnered significant attention. They had obtained millions of dollars in federal contracts and loans for Black businesses across the city. SPNB was operating with $12 million in capital, and McClinton was making a seamless adjustment to life after professional football. Mayor Charles B. Wheeler Jr. recognized him on Tuesday, May 11, 1971, with "Curtis McClinton Day." However, examining the financial realities of the war on poverty reveals that all was not well. While the BEU received aid, the amount it was provided did not solve significant issues of poverty in KC. For example, in 1971, the SBA gave $66 million in contracts to minority businesses, the largest allocation at that time. However, it represented only 0.1 percent of the federal government's $76 billion contract allocation. This alone illustrated that Nixon's war on poverty was not focused on eradicating poverty's causes. Community organizations like the BEU had to get creative with funding to help develop Black businesses. They were not adequately resourced.[50]

Despite the financial limitations, the BEU continued its efforts in business development. It was supported by the Department of Commerce's Office of Minority Business Enterprise, the Economic Development Administration, and the SBA. It also developed an MBA program with the University of Missouri–Kansas City, where attendees took courses in accounting, bookkeeping, marketing, sales, customer service, advertising, taxes, budgeting, and business plan development. The BEU continued to have weekly programs, this time adding workshops that explored the history of the African American experience, "junior achievement" sessions that focused on the personal development of teenagers and youth, and education courses for those who had dropped out of high school. By the fall of 1971, the UTA and BITC, equipped with research teams of attorneys, certified public accountants, architects, bankers and financiers, market research analysts, and engineers, were operating as go-to educational resources for businesses.[51]

While the BEU continued to help numerous businesses across KC "produce, achieve, prosper," the organization also faced several issues with community partners. In September 1971, the Jackson County Bar Association and the Kansas City Bar Association of Kansas initiated a boycott against the BEU for being left out of the BEU's annual business directory. The two associations were critical of the BEU since they did not recall McClinton or anyone from the BEU ever asking Black attorneys to be part of its efforts. For them, how could an organization claiming to be for the advancement of the Black community not use Black lawyers? Benjamin E. Franklin, president of the Kansas City Bar Association, mentioned, "I know of no black attorney that they have ever sought out [for] volunteer services." Franklin's sentiments speak to the disconnect between the three organizations. Since law firms provided pro bono services, there was some confusion among many Black lawyers in KC why they had not been contacted by the BEU. John Wandless, the director of operations for the BEU, told the associations that the oversight was an honest mistake and that they would be included in the next year's promotional. Much of the BEU's legal assistance and guidance was volunteer based as McClinton had received some pushback for using a "Jewish attorney." Wandless said, "We certainly intended to use black attorneys in the future, and some have already been engaged." The BEU and bar associations tried to have meetings in September and October, but the BEU canceled each time. They finally met in late November, and both bar associations addressed their grievances with McClinton. Since the BEU presented itself as a unifying force for Black Kansas City, leaving out the associations and neglecting to engage any of its members for legal issues, intentionally done or not, created an unnecessary rift. Fortunately, all parties were able to put their egos aside and left the meeting with an understanding of how they would work together.[52]

Life Changes

From a United States context, the civil rights and Black Power movements were significant components in the narrative of the 1960s. During the same time, there were also liberatory movements across Africa, and more than half of the countries on the continent gained independence from colonial rule. By the early 1970s, many African leaders wanted to find new ways for economic development. One such gesture to grow their economies was the first All-African Trade Fair sponsored by the Organization of African Unity, held February 23 to March 5, 1972, in Nairobi, Kenya, the country deemed to be "setting the pace" for economic development.[53]

Led by President Jomo Kenyatta, Kenya was looking to move from an agriculture-based economy to an industry-based economy. McClinton was also looking to grow his enterprises by developing a connection with his "African brothers and sisters." From his perspective, the two men could discuss the possibilities of business developments around oil. The grand idea of sitting with Kenyatta never materialized. However, one of the Kenyan businessmen he met mentioned an interest in connecting with the BEU-sponsored company Aquarius, which made and installed fiberglass bathtubs and shower stalls. However, no plans, contracts, or agreements were made during the visit. McClinton took part in the conference and explored the country, specifically the coastal city of Mombasa, for nearly a month, looking for ways to link with the "mother continent" to develop new business partnerships. McClinton made it known that the "BEU [was] considering an approach based on joint ventures with the Kenya government and private African Kenyan businessmen." He wanted to ensure he did not embrace elements of paternalism or suggest that the BEU was coming to save Africans.[54]

With representatives from thirty-seven African countries, there were vast possibilities. McClinton met with various government officials, banks, and businesses in an effort to build connections in the country. He was also invited to sing at several embassies. A bass-baritone singer, McClinton was inspired by Paul Robeson's life, and singing was one of his immense passions. Although many of the attendees often got football confused with soccer when he referred to his former professional sports exploits, he could engage in fruitful conversations about potential opportunities and the work of the union. Upon returning from Kenya, McClinton enrolled at the Kennedy School of Government at Harvard University. After five years of being associated with the BEU and SPNB, he sought new opportunities for many reasons. In 1973, he married Marguerite DeVonne French, a Muscogee, Oklahoma, native like himself, who practiced pediatrics in Tulsa, Oklahoma. They had been dating since 1972 and had known each other since being introduced by McClinton's mom at a Christmas party in the mid-1950s. By this time he realized that his ability to make the necessary impact was starting to wane and that the organization needed new leadership. But most importantly, McClinton had faced a major setback: the collapse of SPNB.[55]

On January 4, 1975, SPNB became the Deposit Insurance National Bank of Kansas City. The Federal Deposit Insurance Corporation (FDIC) had taken over the bank and deemed it insolvent because of citations for "imprudent loans." The financial institution that served as a staple in the Black community and symbolized the fortunes of green power for many Black business folk in KC had been taken over by the federal government. Those customers with $40,000 or less in the bank could recover their savings. However, the shareholders in the bank were the biggest losers. Of all the accounts with SPNB, only ten had more than the protected sum, most of which were government agencies at the federal and city levels.[56]

When the bank was formed in 1968, the board was racially diverse, but by 1975, all the White members had resigned. In the spring of 1973, the bank's funds were misappropriated as money was stolen, and several imprudent loans were never paid back. While this news was not made public to bank patrons, the board tried to facilitate business as usual. However, the bank's accrued losses were difficult to overcome, and the lack of oversight led to its downfall. A serious question to ask about McClinton and SPNB's leadership was whether they were giving enough scrutiny to loan applications. This lack of attention increased the high number of bad loans. Because it offered financial literacy assistance and loans to first-time borrowers, SPNB had to be less strict with its lending policies and how it handled requests than traditional (White) banks. Bank officials wanted to assist Black businesses, but unfortunately for them, they had given loans to businesses that eventually defaulted on their payments. This led to the bank's demise. While McClinton had to deal with the public fallout from the bank closing, he also had to manage the anguish of losing $500,000 of his own money that he had invested in the bank. Because of the insolvency, there was hope that another Black-owned bank would be created to replace SPNB, but that goal never materialized. The bank officially closed in May 1976.[57]

According to the BEU's records, in 1976, they provided roughly $9.5 million in grants and loans, which accounted for 422 jobs in construction and 329 jobs with other small businesses. It was not close to the 50,000 jobs nor the $500 million valuation McClinton wanted to achieve in 1968. Nevertheless, their efforts with various community partners, foundations, and governmental agencies over the years continuously met obstacles that "green power" could not solve. The economic freedom so many wanted through Black capitalism was limited. While the median income for Black families increased, the number of African Americans below the poverty level did as well. Reflecting on the realities of Black capitalism forty years after he initiated the BEU in KC, McClinton remarked, "Our dollars went to other places with a major loss of Black capital, and jobs have never been regained. There are economic models within the system that cater to the Black market that are specialized." He added, "Like Black tailors, grocery stores, liquor stores, [the] assimilation of that, where you have goods and services that are incorporated by the major community. Our market goes elsewhere 10 to 1." Even when Black businesses were present, that did not guarantee the profits they needed to survive.[58]

More Money, Same Problems

In the fall of 1977, McClinton was named director of the Office of Special Projects for President Jimmy Carter's administration under the US Department of Commerce. He lived a commuter lifestyle, mimicking his father's congressional life by working in DC while his wife and daughter lived in KC.

Even when he was no longer leading the BEU, Curtis McClinton stayed true to creating pathways of green power for Black people in the KC community. Upon a visit home, he ran into Anne Lambert Johnson at the grocery store. After exchanging pleasantries and getting the family updates, Lambert Johnson told him about her desire to open her dental office. A native of Richmond, Virginia, she and her husband, Nelson Johnson, had moved to KC in 1974, where she had been practicing with Frank Haugh at his office at Thirty-Ninth Street and Indiana Avenue. She informed McClinton that she had encountered discrimination to get a loan to purchase a location at Gregory Boulevard and Cleveland Avenue. When she went to a local bank, "the guy looked at me like I was crazy. He had never heard of such a thing as a black female, woman, dentist." She had a degree in biology from Virginia Union University, a master's degree in molecular biology, and a doctorate in dental surgery from Howard University. Even when she showed the loan officer her qualifications to prove she was a dentist, he refused to help her.[59]

McClinton was baffled but not surprised, telling her, "That's a shame what happened to you, but we'll see that you get a loan, and we'll see that you get the money you need for your building," she recalled. The BEU's recommendation through Bank of America approved the loan she needed. In 1978, she officially opened her general practice at 3715 East Gregory Boulevard, making her the first Black dentist in KC specializing in preventive dentistry and full-mouth rehabilitation. Across the nation, there were only forty-five Black female dentists at that time. As of 2023, Lambert Johnson has served the KC community for more than forty-five years with the tongue-in-cheek motto "I know the tooth, the whole tooth, and nothing but the tooth." Through McClinton's assistance, Lambert Johnson began a pipeline of Black female dentists in KC.[60]

Curtis McClinton continued to be engaged in economic development after he left the BEU. He took postgraduate courses at Central Michigan University, Harvard University, and the University of Pennsylvania. Following graduate school, he served as director of real estate marketing with Amtrak in the early 1980s, where he managed $3 billion in property (e.g., train stations, buildings and facilities, leases, and bond finance). US president Jimmy Carter appointed him the director of special projects with the Department of Commerce's Economic Development Administration in 1980. The administration wanted him to replicate much of the success he directed in KC through his work with the BEU identifying where financial assistance could be given to Black businesses. The result of his work garnered him the Parren J. Mitchell Special Achievement Award for his "untiring support and assistance" to finance "minority business." In 1983, he was chosen by Mayor Marion Barry to be deputy mayor for economic development in Washington, DC. In this role, he helped businesses in the district secure funding from financial institutions, even building partnerships for the nation's capital during visits to China.[61]

While the expectation was that McClinton would return to KC to lead the BEU after his time in DC, he decided to end the commuting grind and expand his construction projects in KC. His time with the organization had come to an end. Yet the issues the BEU experienced while he was leader continued. His selection of Chang D. Hwang, a business associate, was a major issue. McClinton considered him a reputable man who could help grow the BEU. Yet, there was a problem among the BEU's base: Hwang was not Black. Many African Americans around KC had a difficult time entrusting a non-Black person to lead an organization that consisted of Black people. There was also "the lack of capital and the lack of opportunity" that Hwang identified in September 1978. At that time, Mayor Wheeler and Mayor Jack Reardon of Kansas City, Kansas, were developing programs to help support "minority businesses" around the metro area. Many of the same grievances the BEU experienced in 1968 were still prevalent. With no significant restructuring of society, the existence of racism and sexism, minuscule financial investments, and shortsighted planning, the financial crises African Americans had experienced for decades continued. Black capitalism had limitations.[62]

Organizations and movements are impacted by the cult of personality, where a central figure or figures dictate the modus operandi, and their followers are only engaged because of those individuals. In his operations, Curtis McClinton was against such positioning, often deferring the head positions of the BEU and SPNB to avoid such conflicts and relying on group dynamics. He argued, "The true meaning and capacity of any institution is to divest itself of personalities. It has constant objectives but no commitment to personalities. Because the BEU is an institution, it will divest itself of me. I'm merely an individual contributor." As a result, when he left the organization, it continued to operate focusing on housing development and opportunities for Black Kansas City.[63]

Pathways to economic security were never definite for African Americans. Black business development throughout the 1960s and 1970s was predicated on funds from their personal savings or bank loans. The former was nonexistent for many aspiring business folks, and the latter was difficult to obtain because of the various stipulations. Thus, creating generational wealth through enterprise was no guarantee. No matter the number of Black banks that Curtis McClinton created or Willie Lanier supported, African Americans lacked the financial means to advance. As scholar Jared Ball noted, "Black people do not have enough to deposit, wealth to offer as collateral, nor the ability to circumvent persistent White supremacist devaluations of Black housing, land, or business to generate the kinds of banking (economic) strength required to serve the needs of a Black community."[64]

Despite those realities, the BEU believed that Black capitalism could be a formidable instrument in changing the plight of Black communities. The shortsightedness (and shortcoming) of Black capitalism was that it was not going to liberate African Americans. The civil rights and Black Power movements of the 1960s and 1970s demanded an end to racial discrimination, job creation, better educational opportunities, and improved housing. By the 1980s, none of those goals had been achieved. The wealth gap between White and Black Americans had not closed but was instead exacerbated. Affirmative action programs helped curtail some of the employment and schooling prospects, but they only helped a small segment of the Black population. Capitalism was an economic system that many people benefited from materially. However, the living conditions of Black people were not improved by their engagement in it, whether they owned the businesses or not. Thus, putting race to a profit motive and calling it "Black capitalism" did not change the realities of large segments of African Americans. Black athletes like Jim Brown and Curtis McClinton had a significant impact on the greater public, and although much of this effect was linked to their athletic identity, after their playing careers, they made concerted efforts to insert themselves in the movement for freedom, justice, and equality by taking up the mantle of Black capitalism.

More Than an Athlete

Of the many chapters of the Black Economic Union (BEU) that were founded, only two—Cleveland and Kansas City—have continued their work in the twenty-first century. Long gone from the BEU are the men who initiated these offices. Most of the original members left the group by 1975 as they began to develop different visions and expectations for their lives. There were also financial reasons. While Jim Brown wanted African Americans, and particularly Black athletes, to fund the organization, the reality of opening different chapters across the country proved to be difficult, as can be seen in the example of Curtis McClinton and the Kansas City chapter. Securing funding was critical to whether the BEU could keep its doors open on local and national levels. The reliance on governmental funding and support from large corporations and foundations was a tedious process that kept the organization reliant on outside entities for its existence. Although the salaries of many BEU members were considerably higher than that of the average American, they were not financially well off after their playing careers were over. As A. Deane Buchanan noted, "Most of the athletes were dealing with survival issues." While the players could give financially, many of the programs the BEU created depended primarily on grants and money raised, not capital gained from sales. This greatly affected their utility since there were regulations and stipulations on allocating the money.[1]

Assisting African American enterprises was a major priority for the organization, and often, quantity took precedence over quality. Jim Brown contended that the Union helped four hundred Black businesses over the organization's tenure from 1966 to 1974. However, many enterprises did not have longevity due to a lack of profit making, poor marketing, and loan defaults. It was helpful when entities like the Ford Foundation granted the BEU financial support, but the funding had time restrictions, usually two to four years. This created problems for businesses supported by the BEU, which could not be overcome, as many failed after three years. In the 1970s and 1980s, White businesses were able to profit in the range of billions from Black dollars, all under the guise of integration and equality. Thus, Black enterprises were hurt as Black consumers had more options for services and goods. Unbeknownst to many civil rights advocates, integration harmed Black institutions. The financial development the BEU sought where the Black community was its economic base was unachievable. While the organization failed to take on the full-scale national presence Brown envisioned, BEU members stayed committed to being involved in the economic improvement of the Black communities where they lived.

When the headquarters of the BEU moved to Los Angeles in April 1971, John Wooten began exploring other interests. Carl Stokes had appointed him to the Cleveland City Planning Commission, and the following year, he helped form Pro Sports Advisors Inc. In this sports management agency, he served as president and represented over one hundred professional football, basketball, and baseball players. He served in this role for several years before becoming a scout with the Dallas Cowboys in the late 1970s. For over a decade, Wooten held numerous high-level positions in the NFL. In 1989, he was promoted to director of pro personnel for the Cowboys. Two years later, he was appointed director of NFL player programs. In 1994, he was named vice president and director of player personnel operations with the Philadelphia Eagles, making him one of the highest-ranking African Americans in the league. Wooten's tenure in the NFL exposed him to racial inequalities among players and even coaches. This eventually led to his involvement with the

Fritz Pollard Alliance—an organization dedicated to the eradication of the "good-ole-boy system" and the promotion of "minority" head coaches in the NFL. He served as the group's chair, raising awareness about the league's shortage of Black coaches, general managers, and owners.[2]

By 1974, Brig Owens was no longer working with the BEU, and after thirteen years in the NFL, he retired in 1977. From 1979 to 1984, he utilized his juris doctorate from the Potomac School of Law as assistant executive director and associate counsel to the National Football League Players Association (NFLPA). After leaving the players' association, he started Super Leaders, a nonprofit organization that aspired to help schoolchildren from Washington, DC, graduate from high school. The organization assisted fifty to one hundred students each year from seven schools in the DC area. In 1990, the National Collegiate Athletic Association gave Owens the NCAA Silver Anniversary Award for his community service in the nation's capital. By 1994, Super Leaders had aided more than two thousand students in completing their educational requirements through a support system composed of volunteers from the organization. In addition to his work in the nonprofit sector, Owens was hired as a sports agent representing many notable players, such as Washington Redskins players Doug Williams and Art Monk, 1994 top overall pick Dan Wilkinson, and New York Knicks basketball player Charles Smith. He served as a partner with Bennett & Owens, a law agency that catered to sports management and real estate, until his death on June 21, 2022.[3]

After his playing days, John Mackey served as a representative for players with the William Morris Agency, Incorporated. He also worked as the history management coordinator for the Indiana Black Expo, which was "known for its extensive programming for youth and families, health initiatives and business workshops." In 1992, twenty years after he retired, John Mackey was enshrined in the NFL Hall of Fame, a long overdue selection since his peers recognized him as the greatest tight end to play the game. He attributes his long-awaited induction to his involvement with the NFLPA. In a 2000 interview, Mackey stated that his push for better pay and health care benefits for retired players displeased Hall of Fame selection committee members. More than fourteen years after his induction, the NFLPA and the NFL agreed to a much-improved player retirement package. A section entitled the "88 Plan," dedicated to Mackey for his hard work and commitment, guaranteed retirees

"$88,000 a year for nursing or daycare for any former players with dementia or Alzheimer's disease, or $50,000 a year for home care." A few years later, Mackey was diagnosed with dementia. He died on July 6, 2011, in an assisted living facility in Baltimore. His fate was directly related to the numerous concussions he suffered in his career. Posthumously, it was confirmed that his brain had signs of chronic traumatic encephalopathy. This finding brought attention to NFL players' physical and mental well-being after their playing careers.[4]

Long known as the Jackie Robinson of professional football in Washington, following his retirement after the 1968 season, Bobby Mitchell served in the front office with the team as director of pro scouting, executive assistant to the president, and assistant general manager. The latter position he held for nineteen years. While he had minor aspirations to become a coach, his primary goal was to be the team's general manager, but after forty-four years with the team, the opportunity was never presented to him. It was an ordeal that Mitchell greatly resented. In 2003, Mitchell was awarded the inaugural Paul "Tank" Younger Award by the Fritz Pollard Alliance. While holding back tears, he told those in attendance, "I spent over 40 years with the Washington Redskins, and the best I could do was an internship. I interned for 40 years. Maybe this alliance won't let that happen again." Aside from his work in the NFL, Mitchell also worked closely with the Leukemia/Lymphoma Society in Washington, DC, helping it raise millions of dollars in donations for research. Mitchell died on April 5, 2020.[5]

More than forty years after he played his first professional football game, Walter Beach was still concerned with how Black athletes presented themselves within the NFL. In 2003, he wrote an op-ed for the *New York Times* addressing on-field antics. He wrote, "When watching games now, it saddens me to observe some players' behavior. Often, they are dancing and making faces (sometimes signing a football or talking on a cellphone) after a successful play, even if their team is losing." He added, "Scoring touchdowns, making tackles and interception passes are what professional players are supposed to do. That is their job. The dancing and jiggling that goes on after these plays often seems like show-business behavior and cheapens athletic excellence." Beach concluded, "You don't get extra points for how well you dance in the end zone." Touchdown celebrations, in Beach's view, are disrespectful to the game. His sentiments illustrate how conscious Black athletes from the 1960s and 1970s were about Black identity. Beach also stayed connected to community work. In the 1990s and early 2000s, he served as chief of recreation for Brooklyn parks with New York City's Department of Parks and Recreation. He also directed the East Coast operations in New York of Jim Brown's Amer-I-Can.[6]

Jim Brown was elected to the NFL Hall of Fame the first year he was eligible in 1971. He continued his acting career over the next forty years, starring in over thirty films. His most notable movies were *100 Rifles*, *Three the Hard Way*, and *I'm Gonna Git You Sucka*. Brown also lent his time and money to a film company, Nathaniel Productions, and partnered with famed comedian and actor Richard Pryor to form Indigo Productions, where he served as president. In 1988, Brown founded the Vital Issues Project, which grew into Amer-I-Can, a life skills development program that reaches out to gang members, prisoners, and students in US schools. Twenty-four years since its inception, the program continues to teach a fifteen-step course that provides its participants with the "foundation and tools for achieving a prosperous life." Over Brown's life, the program had been sponsored in fourteen states.[7]

Despite his business interests, over the years, Brown held steadfast to the belief that professional athletes, especially Black players, can change American society through political and social activism. For him, "If they came together, they could raise millions of dollars from the government, millions of dollars from the public." He added, "They can have a tremendous impact on the violence, a tremendous impact on the schools. But they have to do it collectively. Everyone does it individually now. Individual charity work is like giving someone a fish. Collective change is what's needed. That's like teaching people how to fish."[8]

For much of the latter part of the twentieth century, Black athletes have supported their own charitable foundations. This period lacked a collective effort that addressed social, political, and economic issues outside of the playing field. In 2006, Brown proclaimed that the 1960s and 1970s "was an era of political consciousness" when many Black athletes chose to advance the cause of freedom, justice, and equality. In the present, he felt there was a great disconnect with contemporary athletes as they were consumed by a period "of money and buffoonery and fooling around. . . . These guys are just interested in a new contract." Brown was speaking to a moment where many Black athletes ignored what Howard Bryant calls "the heritage," a recognition of their responsibility to be voices for the Black community. There was a lull in the activism of Black athletes in the first decade of the twentieth century. A series of new realities had changed much in the country: the attacks on September 11, 2001; large endorsement deals and contracts; and the advent of a so-called postracial society with the election of Barack Obama as US president in 2008. Black athletes moved differently. It was not until the death of Muhammad Ali on June 3, 2016, that a global reminder of the legacy of athletes being a voice for social, economic, and political issues was celebrated.[9]

Months after the global admiration of Ali, Colin Kaepernick's protest of the national anthem in August 2016 initiated a new discourse on the role of athletes. On Monday, August 29, 2016, Brown was on an NFL Network panel discussion speaking in support of Kaepernick's protest, stating, "He's within his rights, and he's telling the truth as he sees it. . . . I am with him 100 percent." While he acknowledged he would not protest similarly, he was supportive. He was inspired by Kaepernick's actions and the backing other athletes had given him. In his view, there was a new wave of athlete activism. The following month, Brown addressed the lack of activism and the inability of most athletes to address social issues. He told *Time*, "The agents tell these young people that you can get endorsements, you can get a lot of money, don't rock the boat." He added, "Money becomes the objective, and individuals protect their image, make sure they have the right image to represent corporations. And now what is happening is there seems to be a reversal."[10]

In August 2017, Brown urged the former quarterback to decide whether he would be an activist or play in the NFL. He said, "If I sign for money then these people I sign with, they have rules and regulations. . . . I'm going to give you the real deal. I'm an American. I don't desecrate my flag and my national anthem. I'm not going to do anything against the flag and the national anthem." This sentiment starkly contrasted his ordeal with Art Modell and whether he was to attend training camp in 1966. The checks the Browns owner signed throughout his career were never a deciding factor in the various positions Brown took during his playing career. Thus, he contended that athletes needed to oblige the whims of the NFL brass. Kaepernick was no longer in the NFL at this time, but numerous players, like Michael and Martellus Bennett, Marshawn Lynch, Eric Reid, and Kenny Stills, continued to protest during the anthem. By Thursday, October 11, 2018, Brown was articulating a different position regarding Kaepernick's protest. With his wife Monique and music artist Kanye West, Brown met at the White House with President Donald Trump to discuss federal support for Amer-I-Can. The rationale for his different feelings had become evident. There was speculation that if he wanted Trump's support, he would have to distance himself from Kaepernick.[11]

The media coverage of the gathering brought Brown into a national conversation about his allegiances, as confusion among many of his supporters and fans had been building around the rationale for the meeting. Brown had been unaware of the contempt many of his Black supporters held against him for taking on this meeting. Historically, he had been given an audience with every president since Nixon, although President Obama never met with him to discuss the work of the nonprofit. Brown had withdrawn his support of taking a knee. Brown's decision to meet with Trump raises the question whether Black liberation is achievable in a society based on racial segregation and economic inequalities.[12]

In the 1960s, Jim Brown and many BEU members believed they could assess the conditions of Black communities and transform them through a philosophy and praxis of business growth and development. The problem with this belief is that capitalism, whether Black or not, cannot free African Americans. Although examples of thriving Black communities, like Harlem, Tulsa, DC, and Atlanta, exist, they prove to be exceptional cases in a society structured on labor exploitation with the haves and have-nots. Jobs, housing, formidable education, and access to health care were critical basic needs that millions of African Americans advocated and fought for during this period.

Today, some of the same questions are raised about the contributions of African American athletes to the larger Black freedom struggle. There has been a more significant presence of Black men in the professional sports ranks. By 2023, the NFL and NBA had revenues of $11.9 billion and $10.5 billion, respectively. Such profit making illustrates that the earning potential of Black athletes supersedes their predecessors. Despite these fortunes, they continue to express their displeasure about the power dynamics within the professional ranks. In October 2022, Nielsen, an information company that helps businesses understand the buying attitudes of consumers, published a report called *Amplifying Black Voices in Media: Creating Informed, Thoughtful, and Authentic Experiences*. They predicted that by 2025, Black Americans would have a spending power of $1.98 trillion. While rated as one of the largest consumer groups per capita, African American support of Black-owned enterprises has not matched the support of the White citizens and their patronization of White-owned businesses. Thus, promoting green power has elevated Black enterprises, produced numerous employment opportunities, and created economic independence for African Americans. With Nielsen's findings, the landscape of the economic realities in the United States has changed, as have the various technological shifts and advances since the BEU's founding.[13]

Throughout their journeys in locales like Kansas City, Cleveland, Los Angeles, DC, New York, and the Bay Area, African Americans realized capitalism (and its Black manifestation) had limitations in the larger freedom struggle. Assisting people with the development of their businesses was commendable and necessary; however, the social, political, and economic inequities that existed were often too significant to overcome. The structure of society was predicated on labor exploitation with the haves and have-nots. Jobs, housing, formidable education, and access to health care were critical basic needs that millions of African Americans advocated for and fought to receive. There were individual success stories, but a society where all African Americans existed outside of poverty was utopic, considering the realities of capitalism. For Black liberation to come to fruition, the United States needed—then and, in many ways, now—a complete overhaul. While a restructuring of society along political, social, and economic lines has not materialized, Black athletes will continue to play a critical role.

Throughout the twentieth and twenty-first centuries, Black athletes have been celebrated for their physical abilities. However, outside the sporting arena, that admiration often diminishes particularly when they take leadership roles on social and political matters. There have been numerous examples of Black athletes joining forces to address issues around citizenship. Historian Louis Moore notes that in the summer of 2020, the More Than a Vote initiative, spearheaded by LeBron James, was "the largest Black athlete social justice network" since the BEU. In the summer of 2020, NBA and WNBA players brought voter suppression to the forefront during the global COVID-19 pandemic. This collective greatly influenced the outcome of the presidential election of 2020, as well as other political campaigns like Raphael Warnock's US senatorial campaign in 2021. There are also the efforts of Colin Kaepernick's

Know Your Rights Campaign and the Players Coalition. These two entities have made strides to build connections with communities across the United States, focusing on educational opportunities for youth, economic development, and criminal justice reform. As such, present and future professional athletes can see themselves in the same fashion and play meaningful roles in their communities—as more than athletes.[14]

Acknowledgments

This book stems from my parents' introduction of sports and "race men" to me at a very young age. Jim Brown, Muhammad Ali, and Bill Russell were a trio whose athletic abilities along with their stances on political and social matters were a major influence. My own research as a teenager led me to the likes of Tommie Smith and John Carlos. I obviously never saw any of them compete live, but their approach to the world consumed much of my early athletic identity. I have been enamored of athletes who have shown they were more than what they did on the playing field. Mahmoud Abdul-Rauf, Colin Kaepernick, Maya Moore, Joshua Perry, and Michael and Martellus Bennett have provided contemporary inspiration. To my mother and father, Marjorie and Robert A. Bennett Jr., you have been a great support system for me since day one. If it were not for your many sacrifices, I would not have the many opportunities afforded to me. Your encouragement kept me focused on finishing. This project also would not have been possible if not for the early lessons of what it means to be a human. This has been an arduous task, and the many sacrifices you have made over my life have served as a true example of love.

A chance phone call to the Fritz Pollard Alliance in 2010 set this book in motion. John Wooten's willingness to talk to me about my project led to one of the most eventful times in my life as a young scholar. It also led to a conversation with Jim Brown, which resulted in numerous conversations over two years with him and other members of the Black Economic Union (BEU) who provided insight about their lives. A lot of those experiences have been shared in this book. Other things will have to be taken to the grave, as the old saying goes. In all, I am grateful for the many connections and transformative relationships that have developed with many of them, including Walter Beach III, Jim Brown, A. Deane Buchanan, Mike Garrett, Spencer Jourdain, Brady Keys, Willie Lanier, Curtis McClinton, Bobby Mitchell, Brigman Owens, Sidney Williams, and John Wooten. To the families of Beach, McClinton, and Wooten, I owe a deep appreciation for allowing me to be part of your lives outside of this project.

Trying to piece together numerous individuals' memories of sixty-year-old happenings is a difficult process. To the former members of the BEU, I am truly grateful for your patience and willingness to assist in this scholarly effort. I hope that I have done justice to capturing aspects of your lives and contributions. Thank you, all, for the countless telephone and in-person conversations. Special thanks must be given to Jim Brown, John Wooten, Walter Beach III, and Curtis McClinton, with whom I was able to develop strong relationships beyond the dissertation phase. Many thanks must also be given to Gail Boyd, Kim Brown, Monique Brown, Davonne McClinton, Margo McClinton Stoglin, Terri Mitchell, and Juanita Wooten for their assistance with this project. Special gratitude must also be given to Sababa Akili: thank you for your perspective on the union's early years and insight on the complexities of Black life in Cleveland. To Jim Coleman, I appreciate you for connecting me to the BEU community in Kansas City and providing a bridge to an untapped history.

Several people provided invaluable insight in helping me initiate this project. As a graduate student at The Ohio State University, I was researching the commodification of enslaved Black women in the antebellum United States. A chance meeting with Leonard N. Moore changed that focus immediately. He challenged me to consider what my motivations were as a scholar. Sports have been a love of mine my whole life, and focusing on their sociocultural aspects has been life-changing. Thanks for that unsolicited feedback. Leslie Alexander helped guide me through that journey. Going from eighteenth and nineteenth-century foci to a twentieth-century concentration was difficult, but her support throughout the process has helped me lead a life of joy. Much respect for her willingness to help in my early journey. Samuel Hodge helped solidify my focus on athletics. I am appreciative of his mentorship and friendship over the years, from the basketball court to the classroom; he has been a critical part of my growth as a human. Hasan Jeffries has served as a friend and mentor for more than half of my life. Thank you for the challenge to raise my standards as a historian. Jelani Favors demonstrated what the writing grind entailed. When transforming a dissertation into a book, there are no shortcuts. Thank you for the conversations on believing in self and how to keep going. To Derrick White, the second-greatest Alpha I know, I must express my deepest gratitude to you. Your support and encouragement have been invaluable throughout this process. You helped me see the true value of my work, even when I doubted myself. Your support was unwavering. During the editing phase, I questioned whether I could see this project get finished. Your patience and understanding during a challenging period in my life provided me with the strength to keep going. Without your guidance and reassurance, this book would not have been completed. Thus, I am truly grateful for your kindness and wisdom. This book reflects your countless efforts of support. Louis Moore, your guidance was vital. You provided much-needed direction that helped shape and refine many ideas in this book. Your keen insights and thoughtful feedback not only strengthened my arguments but also brought to light critical aspects of the BEU that had previously remained hidden. Your expertise and willingness to engage in many conversations helped me uncover new meanings for this work that I would have otherwise missed. For your intellectual generosity and ability to challenge my thought process, I am truly appreciative. Thank you for being a critical part of this book.

There are many other writers and scholars who have contributed to my growth: Marcellus Barksdale, Albert Bimper Jr., Howard Bryant, Adrian Burgos, Akilah Carter-Francique, Kenyatta Cavil, Langston Clark, Nyron Crawford, G. Christopher Cutkelvin, Harry Edwards, Cherese Fine, Marcis Fennell, Tomika Ferguson, Theodore Foster, Gerald Gems, William Godfrey, C. Keith Harrison, Louis Harrison, Asa Hilliard, Alton Hornsby, John Howe, Marcus Johnson, A. J. Keaton, Darren Kelly, Valerie Lee, Sam Livingston, Luis Macias, Jacquelyn Meshelemiah, James Moore III, Ashley Patterson, Walter Rucker, Martin Smith, Daniel Thomas, Christopher Towler, Akinyele Umoja, Devin Walker, Anne Watts, Vincent Willis, Javier Wallace, Matthew Wynter, James Young, Kurt Young, and David Wiggins.

I am also thankful to the Denison University community, which offered support throughout my writing process. This includes Lauren Araiza, Raj Bellani, Kim Coplin, Jstn Clmn, John Davis, Paige Feeney, Fareeda Griffith,

Toni King, Ayana Hinton, Tess Lanzarotta, Veerendra Lele, Yen Loh, Melanie and Greg Lott, Lew Ludwig, May Mei, Emily Nemeth, Heather Pool, Trey Proctor, Megan Threlkeld, Adam Weinberg, Eric Winters, and Hoda Yousef.

The professionals at numerous archival locations were helpful in the process of writing this book. They include the staff at the Case Western Reserve Historical Society, the Cleveland Public Library, and the Kansas City Public Library; Phyllis Andrews at the Rare Books and Special Collections at the University of Rochester Libraries; Branson Wright with the *Cleveland Plain Dealer*; Kevin Carroll with ProQuest; Kathy Lafferty with the Kenneth Spencer Research Library at the University of Kansas; Kailee Faber from the Schomburg Center for Research in Black Culture; James Watts, Carmaletta Williams, and Larry Lester with the Black Archives of Mid-America in Kansas City, along with Vewiser Dixon, Ollie Gates, and Colin Shipley-Gates; Ryan Pettigrew, Carla Braswell, and Elizabeth Macias with the Richard Nixon Presidential Library and Museum; and Jan Grenci with the Prints and Photographs Division of the Library of Congress. Most importantly, getting to these archives would not have been possible without the help of my brother Brian Murphy. Most of all, I am thankful to the University Press of Kentucky staff, especially Ashley Runyon and Alice Fugate Brown.

There are an abundance of people who provided encouragement and love over the years as I went through the writing process: Shakeer Abdullah, Temi and Ayo Adesanya, Aisha and Joseph Amos, Niles Alburg, Alex Allen, Nnaemeka Anene, Tracy and Osei Appiah, Neal and Nelson Austria, Vada Azeem, Grace Azenabor, Shawn Bailey, Steven and Leondra Baker, Lisa Barclay, Chassidy and Quinn Barham, Kellen Beckwith, Ennise and Carlton Bell, Ghanasyam Bey, Brandon Bianco, Kenneth Blacks, David Bolisomi, Rick Boyages, Vincent Briley, Chris Branton, Jasmine Brown, Kurby Brown III, Derrick Bryan, Christian Bryant, Beth and Bob Buehler, Tamara Butler, Quinn Capers IV, Carter Cassell, Benjamin Caswell, Ashley Evans and Maurice Clarett (Jayden, Titan, and Ashton), Whitney and Kwame Christian (Kai and Dominic), Tai Cornute, Shirnelle and Morris Council III (Dallas and Zayd), Ojea Cruz Banks, Daron Davis, Nan Carney-DeBord, Mike Deegan, Maykel Desir, Mariame Diabate, Leslie Dillon, Jasmine and Mike Doss, Steve Doty, Ty Douglas, Simone Drake, Chigo Ekeke, Stanley Ellison, Zarius Eusebe, Michelle and Erik Farley, Jennifer Faison-Kelly, Britney and Phil

Farmer (PJ and Payton), Chase Farris, Paige Feeney, Marcis Fennell, Russell Field, Bri Fields, Theodore Foster, Sayvon Foster, Kyven Gadson, Marquis Gaines, Javaune and Dimitri Gaston, Melanie and Alfonzo Gilette, Donte Goosby, Ashli Evans and Alisha Gordon (Venice), the Gordon family (Gail, Robyne, Ralph, Jenny, and Jenese), David Graham, Scottie Graham, Curtis Grant, Doran Grant, Claiborne Green, Lauren Grogan, Kenneth Guiton, Jonathan Hall, Marlisa Halm, J. R. Hammond, Nii Hammond, Marlon Hayles, Paul Harris, Tricia Harris, Shantelle and Andre Hill, Erik Hines, Daniel Herron, Demetrius Kweku Hobson, Keisha Hunley-Jenkins, John Jackson, Rashida Jeffries (and Asha, Aliyana, A'laila), Alexander Jones, Ashleigh Jones, Cardale Jones, Keandre Jones, Ross Jordan, Abby and Najib Kamagate (Norin), Susan Kennedy, Valerie Kinloch, Theresa Kline, Matthew Klugman, Linda Krumholz, Charles Lawrence Jr., Megan Lawther, Caroline Little, Tina Ligon, Cindy Londot, Kimberly Lowe, Diana Mafe, Sam Maier, Scott and Tuere Marshall, Marques and Meliha Martin (Mama K, Mira and Maia), Christian Martinez, Dimitrio Martinez, Renae Mayes, Leon McDougle, Jeremy McDowell, Jae and Justin McGee, Hayley and Travian Mitchell, Prince Moody, Daniel Newhart, Jack Nimesheim, Tiffany Ozbun, Luther Palmer, Kelsey Paras, Greg Parini, Melissa and Kenny Parker (Kyndal, Kaden, and Kellen), Ron Parker, Omari Patterson, Kelly-Ann and Ernest Perry, Jailen Pierre, Christa and Franklin Porter, Devon Price, Ethan Quinn, Martha Rachedi and the Barton family, Chay Rankin, Jamal Ratchford, Sid Reeves, Ronald Richards, Willie "Mukasa" Ricks, Heather Rhodes, Eliza Roach, Ryne Romick, Anthony Rooney, David Schilling, Beau Scott, Abby Scully, Karen Powell Sears, Lauren Secaras, Tyiesha Radford and Marshall Shorts Jr., Armond Sinclair, Robert Solomon, P. J. Soteriades, Tina Spiert, Takeo Spikes, Travis Spurley, Ryan Stamper, the Stavridis family, Bruce and Justin Stewart, Tina and Mac Arthur Stewart, Tera James Stewart, Chris Sullivan, Ben Tate, Melanie Taylor, Chila and Dan Thomas, Damion Thomas, Devin Thomas, Tamara Afia Thompson, Eric Trenz, Kaitlyn Tyler, Desiree Vega, Shafa and Alex Vigo, Troy Vincent, Edie Waugh, Eric White, Joel Williams, Marlon Williams, Lawrence Williamson, Corey Willoby, Justin Wooden, Kelly Wise and the Institute for the Recruitment of Teachers at Phillips Academy, the Denison Black Student Athlete Association, the Gahanna Basketball Association, and the Morehouse Football Alumni Association.

Many thanks must also be given to my family: Carl Bailey Jr.; Shirley Banks; Alonza Bennett; Asha Bennett; Leroy Bennett; Jabari Bennett; Wayne Bennett; George L. Marion; Sharon Marion; Allison, Courtney, Gloria, and Clyde Bennett; Allison and Courtney Bennett; Antron Birch; Jasmine and Barry Bradley (Ava and Peyton); Ayo, Shimika, and Abayomi Brame; Curtis Brame; Kimani, Kamau, Tracey, and Kenyatta Brame; Pearl Brame; Billy and Tamika Brame; Brenda and Walter Brame; Vikki and Rhondo Cooper; Audrey Davis; Al, Pat, and Mone Doucet; Shameka Edmonds; Nikki Graves and Edward Henderson III; Ana and Douglas Jeter; Lucky and Horace McKennie; Libra and Walter McKennie; Anita McKoy; Joyce, Preston, and Lee Moreaux; Coreyan, Ahanu, and Awan Roberts; Gail Sims; Dorothy and Harry Weaver II; Dawn, Somi, Cuatro, and Harry Weaver III; Veronica Watford; Lorrine West; Nicole and Rodney West (Xavier, Tyler, and Sydney); Britney and Pernelope Whitby; and the many other extended family members from the Bennett and Brame communities.

Gratitude must also be given to my best friend, Gisell Jeter-Bennett. Through this process, I have come to understand, on a profound level, the notion of marrying someone who is a true partner in every sense. Thank you for helping me see this book to the finish. You served as my most ardent supporter, keeping me encouraged throughout this process. Beyond this book, I am also thankful for the journey we have shared—from navigating the challenges of grad school (and marriage) to embracing the joys and responsibilities of parenthood. Raising our sons, Amari and Karim, has been a beautiful struggle. Thank you for taking your shades off.

To my sons, the writing of this book has been a process we have done together. You do not realize the ways in which you have influenced and inspired me, but know that every moment of this process was influenced by my love for you both. It is my hope that, through the lives explored in this book, you will find lessons that help you understand the complexities of life. May they guide, challenge, and encourage you to move through the world with prudence, resilience, and compassion. Love you.

Notes

Introduction

1. Branson Wright, "Black Sports Stars United behind Ali after '67 Summit in Cleveland," *Cleveland Plain Dealer*, June 3, 2012, A10.

2. Michael Ezra, "Main Bout, Inc., Black Economic Power, and Professional Boxing: The Cancelled Muhammad Ali/Ernie Terrell Fight," *Journal of Sport History* 29, no. 3 (2002): 417; "Won't Accept Army Induction: Athletes Fail to Sway Clay," *Washington Post*, June 5, 1967, D1; "Jim Brown Leads the Effort: Negro Stars Fail to Talk Ali into Joining the Army," *Chicago Daily Defender*, June 5, 1967, 1, 3; "Jim Brown to Urge Clay to Enter Army," *Cleveland Press*, June 3, 1967.

3. Robert L. Allen, *Black Awakening in Capitalist America: An Analytic History* (Garden City, NY: Doubleday, 1969), 163–64, 228–29; William L. Van Deburg, *New Day in Babylon: The Black Power Movement and American Culture, 1965–1975* (Chicago: University of Chicago Press, 1992), 117; For more on Black capitalism see Robert E. Weems Jr., *Desegregating the Dollar: African American Consumerism in the Twentieth Century* (New York: NYU Press, 1998); Laura W. Hill and Julia Rabig, eds., *The Business of Black Power: Community Development, Capitalism, and Corporate Responsibility in Postwar America* (Rochester, NY: University of Rochester Press, 2012); Brandon K. Winford, *John Hervey Wheeler, Black Banking, and the Economic Struggle for Civil Rights* (Lexington: University Press of Kentucky, 2020); Marcia Chatelain, *Franchise: The Golden Arches in Black America* (New York: Liveright, 2021).

4. Additional historical accounts of Black athlete activism include Sheldon Anderson, *The Politics and Culture of Modern Sports* (Lanham: Lexington Books, 2015); Cheryl Cooky and Michael Messner, *No Slam Dunk: Gender, Sport, and the Unevenness of Social Change* (New Brunswick: Rutgers University Press, 2018); Lane Demas, *Integrating the Gridiron: Black Civil Rights and American College Football* (New Brunswick: Rutgers University Press, 2010); N. Jeremi Duru, *Advancing the Ball: Race, Reformation, and the Quest for Equal Coaching Opportunity in the NFL* (New York: Oxford University Press, 2011); Mike Freeman, *Football's Fearless Activists: How Colin Kaepernick, Eric Reid, Kenny Stills, and Fellow Athletes Stood Up to the NFL and President Trump* (New York: Sports Publishing, 2020); Gerald Gems, *Before Jackie Robinson: The Transcendent Role of Black Sporting Pioneers* (Lincoln: University of Nebraska Press, 2017); Pamela Grundy, *Learning to Win: Sports, Education, and Social Change in Twentieth-Century North Carolina* (Chapel Hill: University of North Carolina Press, 2001); Aram Goudsouzian, *King of the Court: Bill Russell and the Basketball Revolution* (Berkeley: University of California Press, 2010); Simon Henderson, *Sidelined: How American Sports Challenged the Black Freedom Struggle* (Lexington: University Press of Kentucky, 2013); Gregory J. Kaliss, *Beyond the Black Power Salute: Athlete Activism in an Era of Change* (Urbana: University of Illinois Press, 2023); Michael Long, *First Class Citizenship: The Civil Rights Letters of Jackie Robinson* (New York: Times Books, 2007); Charles Martin, *Benching Jim Crow: The Rise and Fall of the Color Line in Southern College Sports, 1890–1980* (Urbana: University of Illinois Press, 2010); Fritz G. Polite and Billy Hawkins, *Sport, Race, Activism and Social Change: The Impact of Dr. Harry Edwards' Scholarship and Service* (San Diego: Cognella, 2012); David Wiggins, *Glory Bound: Black Athletes in White America* (Syracuse, NY: Syracuse University Press, 1997); David Wiggins, *Out of the Shadows: A Biographical History of African American Athletes* (Fayetteville: University of Arkansas Press, 2006); Dave Zirin, *What's My Name, Fool? Sports and Resistance in the United States* (Chicago: Haymarket, 2005).

1. Standing on Their Image

1. Marc E. Lackritz, *The Hough Riots of 1966* (Cleveland, OH: Regional Church Planning Office, 1968), 7–9; Leonard N. Moore, *Carl B. Stokes and the Rise of Black Political Power* (Urbana: University of Illinois Press, 2002),

48. The bar was in the heart of the Hough area on East Seventy-Ninth Street and Hough Avenue.

2. Lackritz, *Hough Riots of 1966*, 7–9; United Press International, "White-Hater Sees More Riots Ahead," *Washington Post*, July 29, 1966, A4; Alvin War, "A Look at Hough July 1967," *Cleveland Call and Post*, July 22, 1967, 9B; Moore, *Carl B. Stokes and the Rise of Black Political Power*, 48.

3. War, "A Look at Hough July 1967."

4. United Press International, "Testimony in Cleveland," *New York Times*, August 3, 1966, 19; Van Deburg, *New Day in Babylon*, 12–13; For more information on the Lowndes County Freedom Organization, see Hasan K. Jeffries, *Bloody Lowndes: Civil Rights and Black Power in Alabama's Black Belt* (New York: NYU Press, 2010); Clayborne Carson, *In Struggle: SNCC and the Black Awakening of the 1960s* (Cambridge, MA: Harvard University Press, 1981). The Black Panther Party in Alabama had no affiliation with the Black Panther Party for Self-Defense in Oakland, California, although the former inspired the latter.

5. Sababa Akili, telephone interview with the author, digital recording, June 20, 2012, Atlanta, Georgia. Recording in possession of author; Daisy Cragett, "City Limits: What Price Glory?," *Cleveland Call and Post*, July 16, 1966, 3A.

6. Hal Lebovitz, "3 Browns in the Know Reflect on Situation in Hough," *Cleveland Plain Dealer*, July 24, 1966, 1C.

7. Ibid.

8. US Census Bureau, *Sixteenth Census of the United States: 1940—Population*, vol. 1, Number of Inhabitants (Washington, DC: US Census Bureau, 1942), 837; "Cleveland: The Friendly City to Negroes," *Jet*, November 25, 1954, 10–13.

9. Jim Brown, telephone interview with the author, digital recording, October 26, 2011, Los Angeles, California, recording in possession of author; "Cleveland Pioneered in Opening Doors to Negroes in Pro Sports," *Cleveland Call and Post*, June 24, 1961, 3E.

10. "Cleveland Nine to Be Named Buckeyes by Local Owners," *Cleveland Call and Post*, December 6, 1941, 11A; "Grays, Buckeyes, Meet Tonight; Series to Begin Sunday," *Cleveland Call and Post*, September 14, 1944, 10; "Bucks Fear Gibson's Bat in Negro Series," *Washington Post*, September 14, 1945, 17; Moore, *Carl B. Stokes and the Rise of Black Political Power*, 2–5.

11. Moore, *Carl B. Stokes and the Rise of Black Political Power*, 2–5.

12. Ibid., 31–36.

13. Ibid.; "Constantly Yours," *Cleveland Call and Post*, March 12, 1966, 1B; Walter Burrell, "The Soul Side," *Cleveland Call and Post*, November 4, 1967, 3B; Lin Hilburn, "Black History Is a Continuing Process," *Los Angeles Sentinel*, February 10, 1972, A7; Jevaillier Jefferson, "Maverick's Flat Is Historical Landmark," *Los Angeles Sentinel*, July 5, 2000, A1; Yussuf J. Simmonds, "John Daniels/Maverick Flats," *Los Angeles Sentinel*, October 14, 2010, A14.

14. Theresa Moore, *Third and Long: The History of African-Americans in Pro Football 1946–1989*, produced and directed by Theresa Moore, 180 min, T-Time Productions, 2011, documentary; John Wooten, telephone interview with the author, digital recording, July 27, 2010, Arlington, Texas, recording in possession of author.

15. James Melvin Washington, ed., *A Testament of Hope: The Essential Writings and Speeches of Martin Luther King, Jr.* (New York: HarperSanFrancisco, 1991), 629–30; James Farmer, *Lay Bare the Heart: An Autobiography of the Civil Rights Movement* (Fort Worth: Texas Christian University Press, 1998), 210.

16. Tex Maule, "The Curtain Falls on a Long Run," *Sports Illustrated*, July 25, 1966, 20.

17. Bob Schlesinger, "Build Up, Don't Burn Down—That's John Wooten's Message," *Cleveland Press*, June 28, 1968, C1, C10.

18. Ibid.; Jim Brown, telephone interview with the author, digital recording, November 10, 2010, Los Angeles, California, recording in possession of author; Jefferson, "Maverick's Flat Is Historical Landmark," A1; Simmonds, "John Daniels/Maverick Flats," A14; "Mantan Moreland Is Star of Coast Film," *Chicago Defender*, September 2, 1939, 20; "Maggie Hathaway Gets Break with Warner Brothers," *Chicago Defender*, May 27, 1944, 8; Jim Brown with Steve Delsohn, *Out of Bounds* (New York: Kensington Publishing, 1989), 46; A. S. Doc Young, "The Unforgettable Maggie Hathaway," *Los Angeles Sentinel*, November 18, 1993, 7; John Wooten, "History of Negro Industrial and Economic Union," appendix 2, 3; "NAACP Charters Hollywood Unit," *Cleveland Call and Post*, April 21, 1962, 1C; Clayton Moore, "Another Golf Hassle: Western Ave. Rejects Hathaway Again!," *Los Angeles Sentinel*, April 9, 1964, B4; William Jackson, "Negro Golfers Need Money Sponsors," *Cleveland Call and Post*, July 4, 1964, 6A.

19. Display ad 103, *Chicago Tribune*, November 22, 1964, M11; display ad 387, *New York Times*, November 22, 1964, BR52; Associated Press, "Bomb Threat Made against Jim Brown," *Washington Post*, September 23, 1964, C4; Sid Ziff, "Jim Brown Reveals Cribbing Scandal," *Los Angeles Times*, November 3, 1964, B1.

20. Jim Brown with Myron Cope, *Off My Chest* (Garden City, NY: Doubleday, 1964), 167.

21. Stan Isaacs, *Jim Brown: The Golden Year 1964* (Englewood Cliffs, NJ: Prentice Hall, 1970), 58; Associated Press, "Bomb Threat Made against Jim Brown," *Washington Post*, September 23, 1964, C4.

22. Isaacs, *Jim Brown*, 50; Brown with Delsohn, *Out of Bounds*, 55–56; J. Brown, telephone interview, October 26, 2011.

23. Delsohn, *Out of Bounds*, 55–56; Brown, telephone interview, October 26, 2011.

24. Wooten, telephone interview, July 27, 2010. The "talented tenth" is a concept developed by sociologist W. E. B. DuBois discussed in his article "The Negro Problem," published in 1903.

25. Charles Heaton, "'My Biggest Thrill,' Says Brown," *Cleveland Plain Dealer*, December 28, 1964; United Press International, "Browns Blank Colts: Collins Scores 3 TDs," *Chicago Daily Defender*, December 28, 1964, 25; United Press International, "Browns Brown Wins S. Rae Hickok Award," *Chicago Daily Defender*, January 25, 1965, 21; Moore, *Third and Long*.

26. Jim Brown, interview by Alex Haley, *Playboy*, February 1968, 60; Brown with Delsohn, *Out of Bounds*, 66.

27. Brown with Delsohn, *Out of Bounds*, 47, 67.

28. Stephanie Capparell, *The Real Pepsi Challenge: The Inspirational Story of Breaking the Color Barrier in American Business* (New York: Wall Street Journal Books, 2007), 268–69.

29. Wooten, "History of Negro Industrial and Economic Union," appendix 2, 2; Brown with Delsohn, *Out of Bounds*, 58–59; J. Brown, telephone interview, October 26, 2011.

30. Brown with Delsohn, *Out of Bounds*, 58–59; Brown, telephone interview, October 26, 2011.

31. J. Brown, telephone interview, October 26, 2011. For more on Booker T. Washington, see his autobiography *Up From Slavery* and Louis R. Harlan's

two volumes, *Booker T. Washington: The Making of a Black Leader, 1856–1901* and *Booker T. Washington: The Wizard of Tuskegee, 1901–1915*. Please see *Selected Writings and Speeches of Marcus Garvey* and Ula Yvette Taylor's work *The Veiled Garvey: The Life and Times of Amy Jacques Garvey* for details concerning the Universal Negro Improvement Association and the life of Marcus Garvey. Booker T. Washington, *Up from Slavery: An Autobiography* (New York: Doubleday, Page, 1901); Louis R. Harlan, *Booker T. Washington; the Making of a Black Leader, 1856–1901* (New York: Oxford University Press, 1972); Louis R. Harlan, *Booker T. Washington: The Wizard of Tuskegee, 1901–1915* (New York: Oxford University Press, 1983); Marcus Garvey and Robert Blaisdell, *Selected Writings and Speeches of Marcus Garvey* (Mineola, NY: Dover, 2004); Ula Y. Taylor, *The Veiled Garvey: The Life & Times of Amy Jacques Garvey* (Chapel Hill: University of North Carolina Press, 2002).

32. Kwame Ture and Charles V. Hamilton, *Black Power: The Politics of Liberation in America* (New York: Vintage), 44.

33. Van Deburg, *New Day in Babylon*, 25.

34. Ibid.; John Wooten, telephone interview with the author, digital recording, August 3, 2010, Arlington, Texas, recording in possession of author.

35. "Touchdown Scored for Business," *Cleveland Call and Post*, March 12, 1966, 3C.

36. "Overflowing Crowds Pack NIEU at Official Opening," *Cleveland Call and Post*, March 12, 1966, 1A; "Jim Brown and Pro Mates: Back Negro Industrial and Economic Union," *Cleveland Call and Post*, February 5, 1966, 1A; Lumpkin Photo, "NIEU Leaders," *Cleveland Call and Post*, February 19, 1966, 3A.

37. "John Mapp, Heads Lee-Harvard Group," *Cleveland Call and Post*, May 25, 1963, 6A; Bob Williams, "At NIEU Breakfast: Bradley Gets Praise," *Cleveland Call and Post*, April 9, 1966; "Lawyer Seeks U.S. House Seat as 1st Ohio Negro," *Jet*, May 5, 1966, 47. The LHCA met at the Lee Road Baptist Church at 3970 Lee Road.

38. Wooten, telephone interview, July 27, 2010.

39. Ibid.; Wooten, "History of Negro Industrial and Economic Union," appendix 2, 4; Articles of Incorporation of The National Negro Industrial and Economic Union, roll B459, frame 283; Dave Brady, "Jim Brown Maps Plan for Economic Revolution," *Washington Post*, March 6, 1966, C4.

40. J. Brown, telephone interview, October 26, 2011; Articles of Incorporation of The National Negro Industrial and Economic Union; "Cooper

Resignation Due Tuesday: Hewitt Is School Board Hopeful," *Cleveland Plain Dealer*, March 26, 1967, 18A; "James Young Joins Insurance Company," *Cleveland Call and Post*, September 5, 1959, 2A; "Arnold Pinkney Named Campaign Director for Judge Charles White," *Cleveland Call and Post*, September 17, 1966, 4A; Julian Krawcheck, "After the Ball Is Over: Pals Disagree on Jim Brown," *Cleveland Press*, April 24, 1966; Arnold Pinkney was a member of the United Community Development Program, a group of African American lawyers and businessmen in Cleveland who developed a housing project and shopping center in Cleveland. Carl Stokes also served on the board of trustees for the union.

41. Associated Press, "Wide Business Interests May Lead Brown to Quit," *Washington Post*, January 14, 1966, C3; Brown with Delsohn, *Out of Bounds*, 109.

42. Brown with Delsohn, *Out of Bounds*, 109.

43. Ibid.

44. William N. Wallace, "Jim Brown Uncertain about Pro Football Career," *New York Times*, May 29, 1966, S1; "'Happy to Be Home': It's Movies and NIEU for Retired Jim Brown," *Cleveland Call and Post*, October 1, 1966, 2A; Hal Lebowitz of the *Cleveland Plain Dealer* was able to get the firsthand account from Brown about why he was retiring.

45. Brown with Delsohn, *Out of Bounds*, 109–12.

46. Akili, telephone interview, June 20, 2012; Associated Press, "Brown Will Star in World War II Movie in Spring," *Washington Post*, January 28, 1966, D2; Wallace, "Jim Brown Uncertain about Pro Football Career," S1. Akili was born in Clarksdale, Mississippi, on November 30, 1947. His family moved to Cleveland, Ohio, in 1956. Several NIEU members who also played for the Browns and Washington Redskins participated in the summer recreation programs: Paul Warfield, Jim Shorter, Walt Roberts, and Walter Johnson.

47. Akili, telephone interview, June 20, 2012.

48. Akili, telephone interview, June 20, 2012; conversation with John Wooten, December 7, 2023, Arlington, Texas.

49. Akili, telephone interview, June 20, 2012; "Afro Art Shop Hints Sabotage," *Cleveland Call and Post*, June 22, 1968, 3A; Alvin Ward, "Akil Claims He's Political Prisoner," *Cleveland Call and Post*, May 24, 1969, 16A.

50. "Afro Art Shop Hints Sabotage," *Cleveland Call and Post*.

51. Hal Lebovitz, "3 Browns in the Know Reflect on Situation in Hough," *Cleveland Plain Dealer*, July 24, 1966, 1C.

52. Ibid.; Francis Ward, "Jim Brown Tackles Film and 'Black Power,'" *Jet*, August 11, 1966, 22; Brad Pye Jr., "Bass Is a Big Fish for Rams," *Los Angeles Sentinel*, September 1, 1966, B2; Wooten, telephone interview, July 27, 2010.

53. Bill Lane, "The Inside Story: Business Help," *Los Angeles Sentinel*, December 29, 1966, A3. While the event was scheduled to commemorate Brown's football career for October 16, scheduling conflicts forced the event to be held on January 29, 1967.

54. Jim Brown and Jeff Baxter, *Jim Brown Tells It Like Is* (Cleveland, OH: Main Line, 1968).

55. J. Brown, telephone interview, October 26, 2011.

56. Brian Glick, *The War at Home: Covert Action against U.S. Activists and What We Can Do About It* (Boston: South End Press, 1989); Thomas Vail, "Excerpt of Jim Brown's Farewell Night Speech," *Cleveland Plain Dealer*, February 5, 1967, C8. The NOI, SNCC, SCLC, and the Revolutionary Action Movement were the four groups identified for surveillance, but COINTEL-PRO called for other organizations to be watched as well.

57. Vail, "Excerpt of Jim Brown's Farewell Night Speech"; Brown and Baxter, *Jim Brown Tells It Like Is*.

58. J. Brown, telephone interview, October 26, 2011; "Jim Brown's Album Explodes with Truth," *Cleveland Call and Post*, February 11, 1967, 9A. *Jim Brown Tells It Like It Is* was produced and written by Jeff Baxter. The two-sided album comprised four tracks on each side. On side one was "Jim Brown Farewell Day Speech," "Press Interview: How the Negro Industrial and Economic Union (N.I.E.U.) Works," "Comments on Black Nationalism," and "Comments on Racial Violence." Side 2 contained "Jim Brown Interviewing New N.I.E.U. Member," "Negro Pride and Heritage," "Comments on Black Muslims," "Comments on Cassius Clay (Mohammed Ali)." Jim Brown's proceeds from the sale of the album went to the NIEU.

59. J. Brown, telephone interview, October 26, 2011; Walter Beach III, interview with the author, digital recording, April 12, 2011, Macungie, Pennsylvania, recording in possession of author.

2. The Ali Draft Summit

1. United Press International, "Sayers Will Join Rally to 'Enlist' Clay," *Chicago Tribune*, June 3, 1967, B1; United Press International, "Brown, Taylor in Group: Negro Athletes Will Try to Make Ali See Light," *Washington Post*, June 3, 1967, D3.

2. United Press International, "Brown, Taylor in Group"; United Press International, "Sayers Will Join Rally to 'Enlist' Clay."

3. Robert L. Teague, "Via Stolen Bike: The Road to Rome," *New York Times*, August 14, 1960, S3; Shirley Povich, "This Morning . . ." *Washington Post*, August 23, 1960, A15; Gentry Estes, "Spalding University Honors Muhammad Ali by Renaming the Building Where He Learned to Box," *Courier Journal*, January 17, 2018, https://www.courier-journal.com/story/sports/boxing/muhammad-ali/2018/01/17/muhammad-ali-columbia-gym-spalding-university/1040315001/. William Reynolds, an affluent metal manufacturer of Reynolds Aluminum Company served as Clay's sponsor before the Summer Olympics.

4. A. A. "Doc" Young, "The Biggest Mouth in Boxing: Clay Big in Handlers, Too," *Chicago Daily Defender*, November 28, 1962, 24.

5. Ibid.; Howard Zinn, *A People's History of the United States*, (New York: Harper, 2005). 469–501; Thomas Hauser, *Muhammad Ali: His Life and Times*, (New York: Simon & Schuster, 1991), 91; Michael Ezra, "Main Bout, Inc., Black Economic Power, and Professional Boxing: The Cancelled Muhammad Ali/Ernie Terrell Fight," *Journal of Sport History* 29, no. 3 (Fall 2002): 417; United Press International, "Clay to Turn Pro," *New York Times*, September 7, 1960, 50; United Press International, "'Brainwashing': Father Says Clay Joined Muslims at 18," *Washington Post*, February 7, 1964, B1. While a high school student, Clay wanted to write a paper for his English class that focused on the NOI, but his teacher disapproved of the topic. Clay would later sign with trainer Angelo Dundee, who contributed to his success as a professional boxer.

6. The surname X was given to converts to replace their last names. According to NOI doctrine, the letter took the place of what they called "the name of the slave master." Hauser, *Muhammad Ali*, 63–67; Manning Marable, *A Life of Reinvention* (New York: Viking, 2011), 280–81. Elijah Muhammad instructed all NOI ministers to refrain from commenting on the death of the president. This was a decision based on strategy. Elijah Muhammad had been outspoken about the president's "New Frontier" plans, and any slight of Kennedy's death would bring unwanted attention to the organization. However, on December 1, Malcolm X failed to refrain from commenting on the president's death. Speaking before a crowd of about seven hundred at a NOI rally at the Manhattan Center in New York City, he proclaimed that he "never foresaw that the chickens would come home to roost so soon. . . . Being an old farm boy myself, chickens coming home to roost never did make me sad; they've always made me glad." Attendees

laughed and applauded these sentiments. Malcolm X added that the killings of Congo prime minister Patrice Lumumba and Mississippi NAACP field secretary Medgar Evers, and the bombing of Sixteenth Street Baptist Church in Birmingham, Alabama, where four young African American girls were killed, were enough evidence for the "roost."

7. Randy Roberts and Johnny Smith, *Blood Brothers: The Fatal Friendship between Muhammad Ali and Malcolm X* (New York: Basic Books, 2016), 162; Robert Lipsyte, "'I Don't Have to Be What You Want Me to Be,' Says Muhammad Ali . . . 'I'm Free to Be Who I Want,'" *New York Times*, March 7, 1971, 1967, 24–25, 54, 59, 62, 67; Hauser, *Muhammad Ali*, 66–67.

8. Brown, telephone interview, November 10, 2010; Jim Brown, telephone interview with the author, digital recording, February 25, 2011, Los Angeles, California, recording in possession of author.

9. Brown, telephone interview, February 25, 2011.

10. Dave Brady, "Joe Louis Claims Clay May Last 9 or 10 Rounds," *Washington Post*, January 15, 1964, C2; Claude Andrew Clegg, *An Original Man: The Life and Times of Elijah Muhammad* (New York: St. Martin's Griffin, 1998), 210; Michael Ezra, *Muhammad Ali: The Making of an Icon* (Philadelphia: Temple University Press, 2009), 88–89.

11. Clegg, *An Original Man*, 187–88; Marable, *Malcolm X*, 287; Hauser, *Muhammad Ali*, 105–107.

12. Clegg, *Original Man*, 212–13; Lloyd Garrison, "Clay Makes Malcolm Ex-Friend," *New York Times*, May 18, 1964, 40.

13. "We Shall Overcome . . . Someday!," *Cleveland Call and Post*, May 18, 1963, 16A; Louis Lomax, "Louis Lomax–Malcolm X Speeches at CORE Rally Shake Up the City," *Cleveland Call and Post*, April 11, 1964, 1A; William Walker, "Down the Big Road: Ballots and Bullets; Intelligence and Courage," *Cleveland Call and Post*, April 11, 1964, 2B.

14. Brown with Delsohn, *Out of Bounds*, 190; Robert Lipsyte, "The Last Preliminary: Clay's Main Bout, Inc., Seen Final Step in a Project to Bolster Negro Business," *New York Times*, January 9, 1966, 4S; Clegg, *Original Man*, 247.

15. Associated Press, "Wide Business Interests May lead Brown to Quit," *Washington Post*, January 14, 1966, C3; Robert Lipsyte, "Clay's Main Bout, Inc. Seen Final Step in a Project to Bolster Negro Business," *New York Times*, January 9, 1966, 4.

16. Lipsyte, "Clay's Main Bout, Inc. Seen Final Step in a Project to Bolster Negro Business."

17. "Ain't Nobody Gonna Take This," *Jet*, November 19, 1964, 36; Jack Olsen, "A Case of Conscience," *Sports Illustrated*, April 11, 1966, 95; Steve Rushin, *The Caddie Was a Reindeer and Other Tales of Extreme Recreation* (New York: Atlantic Monthly Press, 2004), 188.

18. David Remnick, *King of the World: Muhammad Ali and the Rise of an American Hero* (New York: Random House, 1998), 289–90.

19. Brown with Delsohn, *Out of Bounds*, 186; "Athletes Face Call in Draft Step-Up: U.S. Sports Stars Facing the Draft," *New York Times*, February 20, 1966, S1.

20. Brown with Delsohn, *Out of Bounds*, 186.

21. Ibid.; Arthur Daley, "Sports of the Times: Visit with Jimmy Brown," *New York Times*, June 13, 1967, 78.

22. Brad Pye Jr. "Jim Brown Says Bigots Delay Clay-Terrell Bout," *Los Angeles Sentinel*, March 10, 1966, B1, B4; Associated Press, "Clay-Terrell License Ruled Illegal: Champion Refuses to Apologize," *Washington Post*, February 26, 1966, D1.

23. A. S. "Doc" Young, "Fight Telecast Here," *New York Amsterdam News*, March 26, 1966, 33; Francis Ward, "Jim Brown Tackles Film and 'Black Power,'" *Jet*, August 11, 1966, 20–25.

24. Young, "Fight Telecast Here."

25. Dave Brady, "Jim Brown Claims Racial Bias Haunts Fight," *Washington Post*, March 11, 1966, D1. John Wooten, John Brown, Sidney Williams, Ernie Green, Walt Johnson, Bobby Mitchell, Lonnie Sanders, and Executive Director John Daniels were the union brass heavily involved in Main Bout.

26. Brady, "Jim Brown Claims Racial Bias Haunts Fight," D4. Fullmer became a prominent boxer after defeating "Sugar" Ray Robinson for the middleweight championship in 1957.

27. "100 Theatres to Show Clay Bout on Giant Screen," *Chicago Daily Defender*, October 18, 1966, 26; Brad Pye Jr., "In Astrodome: Angelenos Back Clay," *Los Angeles Sentinel*, November 17, 1966, B2.

28. "Will Ali-Terrell Settle It All?," *Los Angeles Sentinel*, December 15, 1966, C4; "Cassius to Defend Title in Honolulu," *Chicago Daily Defender*, December 19, 1966, 26.

29. Willie Hamilton, "After 17-Day Tour: Bass Reports from Vietnam," *Los Angeles Sentinel*, March 30, 1967, B2; Hauser, *Muhammad Ali*, 103.

30. "Clay Stops Folley in Seventh Round," *New York Times*, March 23, 1967, 1; "Ali (Clay) Wins Induction Delay," *Chicago Daily Defender*, March 28, 1967, 26; Elliott J. Gorn, ed., *Muhammad Ali: The People's Champ* (Urbana: University of Illinois Press, 1995), 136; "Pvt. Joe Louis Says," poster, University of North Texas Libraries Government Documents Department, World War Poster Collection, World War Two Collection, 1942.

31. Ed Meagher, "Cassius Refuses to Enter Army; Faces Prison Term, Fine," *Los Angeles Times*, April 29, 1967, 1, 8; "Victory in Sight?," *Chicago Tribune*, February 23, 1966, 16; A. Robert Smith, "Senator Morse's Advice and Dissent," *New York Times*, April 17, 1966, 249; Associated Press, "District Court Denies Clay's Final Appeal," *Los Angeles Times*, April 28, 1967, C1; Lipsyte, "'I Don't Have to Be What You Want Me to Be'"; Associated Press, "No Army, No Title for Clay, Say Ring Officials," *Los Angeles Times*, April 22, 1967, A1; "Clay's Lawyers Begin New Court Maneuvers," *Los Angeles Times*, April 30, 1967, I1; William Jackson, "Heavyweight Ill-Advised," *Cleveland Call and Post*, May 6, 1967, 9B.

32. "Clay's Abdication," *Cleveland Press*, April 29, 1967, 1.

33. "Dr. King Accuses Johnson on War: Asserts Westmoreland Was Returned to Quiet Dissent—Praises Clay on Draft," *New York Times*, May 1, 1967, 1, 10.

34. Bayard Rustin, "Reverberations: In Defense of Muhammad Ali," *New York Amsterdam News*, June 3, 1967, 14.

35. Jonathan Eig, *Ali: A Life* (Boston: Houghton Mifflin Harcourt, 2017), 247; Branson Wright, "Black Sports Stars United behind Ali after '67 Summit in Cleveland," *Cleveland Plain Dealer*, June 3, 2012, A1; Brown with Delsohn, *Out of Bounds*, 190–91.

36. Delsohn, *Out of Bounds*, 190–91.

37. Wooten, telephone interview, August 3, 2010; Wright, "Black Sports Stars United behind Ali after '67 Summit in Cleveland," A1, A10; Joe Falls, "If I Fail, It Won't Be Because of My Race," *Detroit Free Press*, September 18, 1966, 6C; Michael Covan, "The Emergence of the Black Athlete in America," *Black Scholar* 3, no. 3 (November 1971): 24; Aram Goudsouzian, "Bill

Russell and the Basketball Revolution," *American Studies* 47, no. 3/4 (Fall/Winter 2006): 61–85.

38. "Alcindor May Go Right into NBA," *Washington Post*, February 13, 1965, D9; Robert Lipsyte, "Alcindor Accepts U.C.L.A Basketball Scholarship from 60 College Offers," *New York Times*, May 5, 1965, 56; David Condon, "In the Wake of the News . . . ," *Cleveland Plain Dealer*, January 26, 1967, K1; Associated Press, "UCLA Captures Title, 79–64: Alcindor, Warren Pace Triumph over Dayton," *Chicago Tribune*, March 26, 1967, B1; Jeff Prugh, "Opponent, Writers Find Alcindor Stuffy," *Washington Post*, February 5, 1967, C4. The *Chicago Tribune* attributed Alcindor's talent as the reason for the "reviving interest" in college basketball.

39. Prugh, "Opponent, Writers Find Alcindor Stuffy," C4; conversation with John Wooten, December 7, 2023, Arlington, Texas.

40. Bill Russell with Tex Maule, "I Am Not Worried about Ali," *Sports Illustrated*, June 19, 1967, 18–21; Bill Russell and William McSweeny, *Go Up for Glory* (New York: Coward-McCann, 1966), 166; Brown with Delsohn, *Out of Bounds*, 191; Wooten, telephone interview, August 3, 2010; Demas, *Integrating the Gridiron*, 28–48.

41. Brown with Delsohn, *Out of Bounds*, 191.

42. Wooten, telephone interview, August 3, 2010.

43. Wooten, telephone interview, August 3, 2010; "Clay to Attend 'Mystery Meeting,'" *Plain Dealer*, June 4, 1967, 7C; Milton Gross, "Clay 'Absorbed in Beliefs,'" *St. Petersburg Independent*, June 8, 1967, 15A.

44. Brown with Delsohn, *Out of Bounds*, 54; Wooten, telephone interview, August 3, 2010; Associated Press, "Mitchell Gets Army O.K. to Play Sunday," *Chicago Daily Tribune*, November 4, 1961, B2; Dave Brady, "Only Three Redskin Players 1-A in Draft, Survey Reveals," *Washington Post*, April 23, 1967, D4; "U.S. Olympic Hopes," *Atlanta Daily World*, April 8, 1956, 8; Walter Beach III, telephone interview with the author, digital recording, August 3, 2010, Macungie, Pennsylvania, recording in possession of author. In *Out of Bounds*, Brown discusses some of the racial discrimination he faced while fulfilling his military obligations in Alabama.

45. Associated Press, "Huff, Other NFL Stars Make Hit with American Troops in Vietnam," *Washington Post*, January 30, 1966, C3; Eig, *Ali*, 247;

Curtis McClinton, telephone discussion with the author, June 15, 2010, Kansas City, Missouri; Curtis McClinton, telephone interview with the author, digital recording, October 5, 2010, Kansas City, Missouri, recording in possession of author; personal résumé of Sidney Williams, submitted with project proposal for Job Interest and Motivation to Mayor's Council on Youth Opportunity on behalf of the National Negro Industrial and Economic Union, February 29, 1968. Major Barney Gill, the group's escort, told the press what the players did was valued since many of the places they went to were "not the most secure places on the campus."

46. "Jim Brown to Urge Clay to Enter Army," *Cleveland Press*, June 3, 1967; Chuck Heaton, "NIEU Huddle Result: Cassius Still Won't Go," *Cleveland Plain Dealer*, June 5, 1967, 59, 61; William (Sheep) Jackson, "Muhammad Ali Stands Firm on His Rights, Religious Beliefs," *Cleveland Call and Post*, June 10, 1967, 1A, 15A.

47. Heaton, "NIEU Huddle Result," 59; Jackson, "Muhammad Ali Stands Firm on His Rights, Religious Beliefs," 15A; conversation with John Wooten, December 7, 2023, Arlington, Texas.

48. Jackson, "Muhammad Ali Stands Firm on His Rights, Religious Beliefs"; Brigman Owens, telephone interview with the author, digital recording, March 3, 2011, Washington, DC, recording in possession of author.

49. "Won't Accept Army Induction: Athletes Fail to Sway Clay," *Washington Post*, June 5, 1967, D1; "Jim Brown Leads the Effort: Negro Stars Fail to Talk Ali Into Joining the Army," *Chicago Daily Defender*, June 5, 1967, 1, 3; Wright, "Black Sports Stars United behind Ali after '67 Summit in Cleveland," A12; John Wooten, telephone interview with the author, digital recording, July 27, 2010, Arlington, Texas, recording in possession of author.

50. Wright, "Black Sports Stars United behind Ali after '67 Summit in Cleveland," A12; Eig, *Ali*, 247; "Jim Brown to Urge Clay to Enter Army," *Cleveland Press*, June 3, 1967; Heaton, "NIEU Huddle Result: Cassius Still Won't Go," 59, 61.

51. Russell with Maule, "I Am Not Worried about Ali," 18–21; "Color Question," *New York Amsterdam News*, June 10, 1967, 15.

52. Sidney Williams, telephone interview with the author, digital recording, March 24, 2011, Los Angeles, California, recording in possession of author; McClinton, telephone interview, October 5, 2010.

53. Moore, *Third and Long*.

54. Moore, *Third and Long*; Wright, "Black Sports Stars United behind Ali after '67 Summit in Cleveland," A10.

55. "Convict Clay; 5-Yr. Term: Jury Takes 20 Minutes for Decision," *Chicago Tribune*, June 21, 1967, 1; Remnick, *King of the World*, 291; Mike Marqusee, *Redemption Song: Muhammad Ali and the Spirit of the Sixties*, 2nd ed. (London: Verso, 2005), 227.

56. Marquesse, Redemption Song, 32–39; Eig, *Ali*, 246; Robert Lipsyte, "Sports of the Times: Foodstuffs," *New York Times*, November 21, 1968, 57; Hans J. Massaquoi, "The Unconquerable Muhammad Ali," *Ebony*, April 1969; Leonard Sloane, "Name Franchising: It Takes More Than a Star to Sell Goods," *New York Times*, October 25, 1970, F2.

3. Challenging the National Football League

1. "Gridders Rebel Nationwide," *Los Angeles Sentinel*, July 27, 1967, B1.

2. Ibid.

3. Ibid.

4. William Wallace, "Pros' Popularity Keeps Soaring," *New York Times*, August 27, 1967, S1, S7, S9; United Press International, "Negroes Publicize Plight: Sports Becomes Vehicle of Protest," *Washington Post*, December 22, 1968, E2; Associated Press, "Browns Coach Is Slated at Federal Hearing Today," *New York Times*, November 16, 1970, 64; "I Was Blacklisted— Parrish," *Chicago Tribune*, November 20, 1970, C5; "Beach Is Linked to League Probe," *Cleveland Call and Post*, December 5, 1970, 13B; Associated Press, "Beach Sues NFL, Browns for Job Loss," *Washington Post*, June 11, 1971, D3.

5. "Beach Is Linked to League Probe," *Cleveland Call and Post*; Moore, *Third and Long*; Bernie Parrish, *They Call It a Game* (New York: Dial Press, 1971), 172. In a telephone conversation on September 11, 2012, Walter Beach mentioned that while Art Modell questioned his choice in literature, he did so to make sure that some of his White southern teammates did not get word of the defensive back's reading material.

6. Hal Lebovitz, "3 Browns in the Know Reflect on Situation in Hough," *Cleveland Plain Dealer*, July 24, 1966, 1C; Parrish, *They Call It a Game*, 172; Philip C. Suchma, "From the Best of Time to the Worst of Times: Professional

Sport and Urban Decline in a Tale of Two Clevelands, 1945–1978" (PhD diss., Ohio State University, 2005).

7. Parrish, *They Call It a Game*, 172.

8. Parrish, *They Call It a Game*, 172–74; Sidney Williams, telephone interview with the author, digital recording, March 29, 2011, Los Angeles, California, recording in possession of author; "Schafrath Browns' Captain," *Cleveland Plain Dealer*, July 23, 1966, 56; Moore, *Third and Long*; Walter Beach III, in-person interview with the author, digital recording, December 28, 2011, Macungie, Pennsylvania, recording in possession of author; United Press International, "Ex-Cleveland Back Hedges about Role in NFL Probe," *Los Angeles Times*, November 12, 1970, H3; "Beach Sues NFL, Browns for Job Loss," *Washington Post*, June 11, 1971, D3.

9. "Strike of 5 Browns Irks Boss Modell," *Chicago Tribune*, July 23, 1967, B7; "Gridders Rebel Nationwide," *Los Angeles Sentinel*, July 27, 1967, B1; Parrish, *They Call It a Game*, 113.

10. United Press International, "Atty. Raps Browns Owner: Says Race Not an Issue in Holdout by 5 Players," *Chicago Daily Defender*, July 25, 1967, 24; United Press International, "Five Browns Still Out, Money Not Only Issue," *Chicago Daily Defender*, July 26, 1967, 28; "Strike of 5 Browns Irks Boss Modell," *Chicago Tribune*, July 23, 1967, B7. Brown's lawyer James Berick scheduled the meeting.

11. "Players Go into 4th Day of Mass Holdout," *Las Vegas Daily Optic*, July 25, 1967, 4.

12. Associated Press, "Browns Set Up Talks on Holdouts," *Chicago Tribune*, July 25, 1967, B3; United Press International, "Jim Brown Lauds Striking Browns," *Washington Post*, July 28, 1967, D2; "Strike in Pro Football," *New York Times*, July 30, 1967, 145.

13. "Browns Set Up Talks on Holdouts," *Chicago Tribune*; Bill Scholl, "Pact Believed Near $50,000," *Cleveland Press*, June 17, 1960

14. "Strike in Pro Football," *New York Times*; United Press International, "Jim Brown Lauds Striking Browns," *Washington Post*, July 28, 1967, D2.

15. United Press International, "Jim Brown Lauds Striking Browns," *Washington Post*, July 28, 1967, D2.

16. United Press International, "Giants Cut Linebacker Williams Lions, Steelers Trade Linemen," *Washington Post*, August 24, 1967, B4; "Shinnick Out;

Colts Activate Williams," *Chicago Tribune*, September 29, 1968, B4; United Press International, "Brown's Holdout Ended; Kelly Plays Out Option," *Chicago Daily Defender*, August 8, 1967, 25; United Press International, "Compromise Ends Holdout by Browns, but Nobody's Happy," *Los Angeles Times*, August 8, 1967, C1, C4; NEA, "Negro Athletes and Society: Boycotts on the Ballfields?," *Kingsport News*, August 12, 1967; William N. Wallace, "Sports of the Times: The Group," *New York Times*, August 1, 1967, 36.

17. Wallace, "Sports of the Times."

18. "Brown's Holdout Ended; Kelly Plays Out Option," *Chicago Daily Defender*; "Compromise Ends Holdout by Browns, but Nobody's Happy," *Los Angeles Times*.

19. "Players Gain in 'Holdout,'" *Cleveland Call and Post*, August 12, 1967, 1A; Edward R. Garvey, "From Chattel to Employee: The Athlete's Quest for Freedom and Dignity," *Annals of the American Academy of Political and Social Science* 445 (September 1979): 99; "Stars Host Stokes Party," *Los Angeles Sentinel*, September 21, 1967, A1, 2D; Moore, *Carl B. Stokes and the Rise of Black Political Power*, 5.

20. Wooten, telephone interview, August 3, 2010; Associated Press, "Browns Get No Offers for 2 Players Cut," *Chicago Tribune*, July 21, 1968, B8. While the situation with Fichtner was strenuous in 1968, Wooten admitted in a telephone interview they have "shaken hands and hug, and it's all behind us."

21. "Fichtner, Wooten Have Their Say to Sports Ed.," *Cleveland Call and Post*, July 13, 1968, 8B.

22. "Browns Involved in Racial Incident-Fichtner, Wooten Placed on Waivers," *Washington Post*, July 20, 1968, D3.

23. United Press International, "Browns Enroll 3 Backs," *New York Times*, June 13, 1964, 17; Wooten, telephone interview, August 3, 2010.

24. Wooten, telephone interview, August 3, 2010; conversation with John Wooten, in-person with the author, digital recording, December 7, 2023, Arlington, Texas; William N. Wallace, "Unwanted Wooten Weighs New Move after His Release," *New York Times*, July 25, 1968, 45.

25. Wooten, telephone interview, August 3, 2010.

26. Wooten, telephone interview, August 3, 2010.

27. Ibid.; Williams, telephone interview, March 29, 2011.

28. Williams, telephone interview, March 29, 2011.

29. "New Demands Hit Browns," *Chicago Defender*, August 31, 1968, 15. Pinkney and Wooten were married to twin sisters. While Pinkney represented John Wooten in the racial dispute with Fichtner, he kept open communication with Modell despite Wooten's release.

30. "New Demands Hit Browns," 15.

31. United Press International, "N.F.L. Leads Race for Collegians: But A.F.L. Is Making Best Showing since Inception," *New York Times*, June 16, 1963, 16; Bob McCullough, *My Greatest Day in Football: The Legends of Football Recount their Greatest Moments* (New York: Thomas Dunes, 2001), 156–58. Ironically, Jim Brown, initially a walk-on at the school, had his way paid by forty-four people from the neighborhood where he grew up in New York.

32. Roy Damer, "All-Star John Mackey Seen as New Pro Ditka," *Chicago Tribune*, June 8, 1963, C2; United Press International, "Colts Sign Mackey," *Washington Post*, May 28, 1963, C5; Associated Press, "Colts Sign Four Veterans, Give Walkout Warning," *Washington Post*, July 30, 1966, D3.

33. United Press International, "NFL Player Boss, John Mackey Quits," *Chicago Defender*, September 13, 1973, 32.

34. Owens, telephone interview, March 3, 2011.

35. Rich Roberts, "Brig Owens Switches Fields, but Continues His Will to Fight," *Los Angeles Times*, February 11, 1982, B14.

36. Ibid.

37. Ibid.; Owens, telephone interview, March 3, 2011. Owens was born on February 16, 1943, in Linden, Texas. When he was young, his family moved to Orange County, California, for better job opportunities. In an interview about his transition from California to Ohio, he remembered, "There was curiosity. People asked, 'How did you guys get this guy all the way from California?' I was considered a Blue Chipper. Others queried, 'How did you get this young man all the way from California who could turn our program around?' I had a very good spring game, and very welcomed by the Black community, and the overall community of Cincinnati. It was a great experience. A family [of Dr. Martinell Walton] adopted me, a home away from home. I became his adopted son."

38. Owens, telephone interview, March 3, 2011; Brigman Owens, telephone interview with the author, digital recording, March 14, 2011, Washington, DC, recording in possession of author; Edward R. Garvey, "From Chattel to

Employee: The Athlete's Quest for Freedom and Dignity," *Annals of the American Academy of Political and Social Science* 445 (September 1979): 92; Lawrence M. Kahn, "The Effects of Race on Professional Football Player's Compensation," *Industrial and Labor Relations Review* 45, no. 2 (1992): 295–310; Robert G. Mogull, "Football Salaries and Race: Some Empirical Evidence," *Industrial Relations* 12, no. 1 (1973): 109–12.

39. Owens, telephone interview, digital recording, March 14, 2011, Washington, DC.

40. Garvey, "From Chattel to Employee," 92; Kahn, "Effects of Race on Professional Football Player's Compensation," 295–310; Mogull, "Football Salaries and Race," 109–12.

41. Bob Oates, "NFL Players to Demand Reduction of Rozelle's Authority," *Los Angeles Times*, July 2, 1970, D1, D9.

42. William N. Wallace, "Football Players to Seek New Contract," *New York Times*, March 28, 1970, 39.

43. "NFLPA Negotiations to Start Soon," *Oakland Post*, April 2, 1970, 18; Associated Press, "NFL Players Association Seeks Bargaining Power," *Washington Post*, June 9, 1970, D2; Associated Press, "N.F.L. Players Claim Unfair Labor Practice," *Chicago Tribune*, June 19, 1970, C4; Associated Press, "NFL Players OK Strike if Demands Not Filled," *Los Angeles Times*, July 4, 1970, C5; Associated Press, "Don't Go to Camp, NFL Players Told," *Washington Post*, July 10, 1970, D1; Associated Press, "NFL Bars Veterans from Training Camps: Rookies Ordered to Report on Time," *Washington Post*, July 14, 1970, D1.

44. Kenneth Denlinger, "Redskin Veterans Work Up a Sweat: Heat's on at Georgetown," *Washington Post*, July 18, 1970, E1; United Press International, "Meeting Set for Tomorrow: NFL Players Seek Federal Mediation," *Chicago Daily Defender*, July 21, 1970, 26.

45. Bob Oates, "It's Official: NFL Players on Strike: Mackey Claims 1,300 Veterans Support Action," *Los Angeles Times*, July 31, 1970, C2, C6; Kenneth Denlinger, "Chiefs Decline Invitation: Players Assert Solid Support for Present Position," *Washington Post*, July 24, 1970, D1, D3; "NFL Owners Make Offer: $18 Million in Benefits," *Los Angeles Times*, July 24, 1970, F1, F10.

46. "NFL Owners Make Offer: $18 Million in Benefits," F10; "Hall of Famers Shut Out," *Los Angeles Times*, March 16, 1972; Kenneth Denlinger,

"Position Paper Picks Holes: Players Challenge Owners' Assertions," *Washington Post*, July 26, 1970, E1, E3.

47. Oates, "It's Official," C2, C6; "All-Time NFL Selections," *Washington Post*, September 7, 1969, 45; Associated Press, "Colts' End Mackey Put on Waivers," *Los Angeles Times*, September 14, 1972, D6; United Press International, "Month-Long Session Expected: Probe of NFL Opens Monday," *Washington Post*, November 15, 1970, C5; United Press International, "Grand Jury Probe: Parrish Predicts NFL Indictments," *Washington Post*, November 20, 1970, D3; "I Was Blacklisted—Parrish," *Chicago Tribune*, November 20, 1970, C5; Parrish, *They Call It a Game*, vii. Parrish stated the BEU provided "financial and moral support at crucial times" in the publication of the book. The two men Parrish mentioned who were caught in Modell's ire were Ross Fichtner and Larry Ben.

48. Associated Press, "Sample Tells Probers He Was 'Blackballed,'" *Chicago Tribune*, December 15, 1970, C1, C6; United Press International, "Baltimore Colts Sign John Sample," *Chicago Defender*, June 27, 1969, 24; George Strickler, "Colts Retain Title; Beat Giants, 31–16," *Chicago Daily Tribune*, December 28, 1959, C1; Associated Press, "Sample Blames Rozelle in NFL Blacklist Case," *Los Angeles Times*, December 15, 1970, F7; Johnny Sample with Fred J. Hamilton and Sonny Schwartz, *Confessions of a Dirty Ballplayer* (New York: Dial Press, 1970). Weeb Ewbank, head coach of the team, remarked Sample's "speed and size certainly qualify him for the job." Unfortunately, Sample did not win the lawsuit. In July 1971, Sample was arrested for cashing stolen checks totaling more than $5,000.

49. Associated Press, "Beach Sues NFL, Browns for Job Loss," *Washington Post*, June 11, 1971, D3; William Wallace, "2 Dozen Suits Plague N.F.L.," *New York Times*, May 28, 1972, S12; William N. Wallace, "They Sue and Sue . . . but the N.F.L. Show Goes On," *Chicago Tribune*, September 17, 1972, F25. Walter Beach's suit was filed with the Equal Employment Opportunities commission.

50. Owens, telephone interview, March 3, 2011; Brigman Owens, telephone interview, March 14, 2011.

51. Associated Press, "Colts' End Mackey Put on Waivers," *Los Angeles Times*, September 14, 1972, D6; Associated Press, "Mackey Goes to San Diego," *Washington Post*, September 18, 1972, D4; Associated Press, "Mackey Is Charger

Now," *Chicago Tribune*, September 19, 1972, C5; Deane McGowen, "People in Sports: Healthy Mackey Retires," *New York Times*, July 26, 1973, 48; United Press International, "NFL Player Boss, John Mackey Quits," *Chicago Defender*, September 13, 1973, 32; "Mackey to Be Player Agent," *New York Times*, September 13, 1973; George Solomon, "Mackey Accepts Post with Talent Agency," *Washington Post*, September 13, 1973, D3.

52. McCullough, *My Greatest Day in Football*, 156–57; John C. Weistart, "Judicial Review of Labor Agreements: Lessons from the Sports Industry," *Law and Contemporary Problems* 44, no. 4 (Autumn 1981): 109–46; John C. Weistart, "League Control of Market Opportunities: A Perspective on Competition and Cooperation in the Sports Industry," *Duke Law Journal* 1984, no. 6 (December 1984): 1013–70; "Releasing Superstars from Peonage: Union Consent and the Nonstatutory Labor Exemption," *Harvard Law Review* 104, no. 4, (February 1991): 874–95; Richard E. Bartok, "NFL Free Agency Restrictions under Antitrust Attack," *Duke Law Journal* 1991, no. 2 (April 1991): 503–59; Kahn, "Effects of Race on Professional Football Players' Compensation," 295–310.

4. In the Community

1. John Wooten, "The Human Environment: Poverty," *Nation's Business* 56 (June 1968): 60–61.

2. Wooten, "History of Negro Industrial and Economic Union," appendix 2, 3, The Western Reserve Historical Society, Carl B. Stokes Papers, Manuscript Collect No. 4370; "We made the first step . . . Now It's Up to YOU!!," NIEU pamphlet, Manuscript, Archives, and Rare Book Library, Emory University, Joseph Vaudrey Baker papers, 1935–74, Manuscript Collection No. 982, Box 2, Folder 20; Hill and Rabig, *Business of Black Power*, 1.

3. "NIEU Gets Grant from the Greater Cleve. Foundation," *Cleveland Call and Post*, March 11, 1967, 1A, 16A.

4. Ibid.

5. J. Brown, telephone interview, February 25, 2011; Alvin Ward, "A Look at Hough July 1967," *Cleveland Call and Post*, July 22, 1967, 9B, 10B; "Project JIM Provides Needed Community Program," *Cleveland Call and Post*, September 2, 1967, 10B.

6. Wooten, "History of Negro Industrial and Economic Union," appendix 2.

7. David J. Garrow, *Bearing the Cross: Martin Luther King, Jr., and the Southern Christian Leadership Conference* (New York: Perennial Classics, 1999), 223; United Press International, "King Warns of Racial Violence in Cleveland," *Los Angeles Times*, April 27, 1967, 7; United Press International, "Dr. King Says Police Invite Riots In Ohio," *New York Times*, June 10, 1967, 19; "Money: The President Battles with Congress," *Los Angeles Times*, October 8, 1967, M4; United Press International, "Mayor Stokes Calls for War on Two Fronts," *Chicago Daily Defender*, March 12, 1968, 19; "Rep. Stokes Tells of 'New Battlefields,'" *Los Angeles Sentinel*, June 9, 1966, A1.

8. United Press International, "King Warns of Racial Violence in Cleveland"; United Press International, "Dr. King Says Police Invite Riots In Ohio"; United Press International, "Mayor Stokes Calls for War on Two Fronts"; "Rep. Stokes Tells of 'New Battlefields,'" *Los Angeles Sentinel*.

9. Carl B. Stokes, *Promises of Power: A Political Autobiography* (New York: Simon & Schuster, 1973), 96.

10. Ibid., 20–21.

11. Murray Schumach, "Martin Luther King Jr.: Leader of Millions in Nonviolent Drive for Racial Justice," *New York Times*, April 5, 1968, 25; James Reston, "Hate Cannot Be Burned Away," *Cleveland Plain Dealer*, April 7, 1968, 4A; Earl Caldwell, "Guard Called Out: Curfew Is Ordered in Memphis but Fires and Looting Erupt," *New York Times*, April 5, 1968, 1; "Negro Violence Hits US Cities in Wake of Dr. King Slaying," *Chicago Tribune*, April 5, 1968, 2; Thomas A. Johnson, "12 Are Arrested Here," *New York Times*, April 5, 1968, 1; Tom Wicker, "Thousands Leave Washington as Bands of Negroes Loot Stores," *New York Times*, April 6, 1968, 23.

12. United Press International, "Cleveland Mayor Takes to Streets: Stokes Praises His City for Avoiding Racial Disorder," *New York Times*, April 12, 1968, 20; James Yuenger, "LBJ Pleads for Racial Peace," *Chicago Tribune*, April 6, 1968, N2; Jesse W. Lewis Jr., "Baltimore Troubles Follow Washington Pattern," *Washington Post*, April 8, 1968, A2; Associated Press, "Group Bids Negro Athletes Help Calm Nation's cities," *New York Times*, April 9, 1968, 31; Associated Press, "Jim Brown's Group to Help in Riots," *Spokesman-Review*, April 9, 1968, 12; Associated Press, "Negro Professional Athletes Asked to Help Stem Tide of Racial Unrest," *Hartford Courant*, April 9, 1968, 24; United Press International, "Cleveland Mayor Takes to Streets: Stokes Praises

His City for Avoiding Racial Disorder," *New York Times*, April 12, 1968, 20; Associated Press, "Powell: 'Negroes' Face Extermination," *Cleveland Plain Dealer*, April 20, 1968, 15; "Brown's NIEU Praises MLK," *Los Angeles Sentinel*, April 11, 1968, B3; United Press International, "Don't Let Dr. King Die in Vain: Brown," *Chicago Daily Defender*, April 13, 1968, 3.

13. Associated Press, "Group Bids Negro Athletes Help Calm Nation's cities"; Associated Press, "Powell: 'Negroes' Face Extermination."

14. Owens, telephone interview, March 14, 2011.

15. Ibid.

16. Charles M. Roberts and Walter H. Pincus, "3 Slain in Chicago Many Fires Set," *Washington Post*, April 6, 1968, A1; Associated Press, "Baltimore, Pittsburgh Cool Again," *Cleveland Plain Dealer*, April 8, 1968, 1; "Violence Hits Nation's Major Cities," *Chicago Tribune*, April 6, 1968, N3; "55,000 Troops Employed to Put Down City Riots," *Cleveland Plain Dealer*, April 9, 1968, 4; Dave Brady, "Whitfield Shoots Holes in Big-Back Program," *Washington Post*, December 6, 1967, D1, D2; John B. Willmann, "It's Happening in Real Estate," *Washington Post*, September 28, 1968, D18; Dave Brady, "Whitfield Through as 1968 Redskin," *Washington Post*, November 23, 1968, E3; "Four Redskins Served in Area," *Washington Post*, April 18, 1968, C4; Owens, telephone interview, March 14, 2011; James Reston, "Hate Cannot Be Burned Away," *Cleveland Plain Dealer*, April 7, 1968, 4A. Whitfield and Owens were both drafted by the Dallas Cowboys in 1965 and traded the following year to the Washington Redskins.

17. Alton Hornsby Jr., "The Drum Major on the Mountaintop: A Tribute to Dr. Martin Luther King, Jr.," *Journal of Negro History* 62, no. 3 (July 1977): 213–16; Art Buchwald, "Bobby Tackles Redskin Problem," *Los Angeles Times*, November 14, 1963, C1; "Retarded Olympics Start Today," *Washington Post*, June 20, 1969, C3; Dave Brady, "Redskins' Mitchell Retires After 11 Years' NFL Play," *Washington Post*, September 9, 1969, D1; Claudia Levy, "'Black Union' Opens Here to Aid Businesses," *Washington Post*, November 19, 1968, C2; Alex Poinsett, "The Economics of Black Liberation," *Ebony*, August 1969, 152–53. According to Bobby Mitchell's daughter Traci, because her father was affiliated with the BEU from its inception, he believed he had the money to manage the difficulties and challenges he faced as the first black player for the Redskins. The two men had a relationship that lasted from 1962 to 1968 when Bobby Kennedy was assassinated. Theodore Robert Hagans Jr., the head of

the chamber of commerce for the District of Columbia; United States marshal Luke Moore; Simeon Booker, a journalist with *Washington Post*; and Bobby Mitchell, formerly of the Browns and then with the Redskins, also served on the board. Several city officials were also invested in the Washington office. Some notable figures were Mayor Walter E. Washington, Howard Samuels, the head of the SBA, and Reverend Walter E. Fauntroy, the vice chairman of the city council, were involved in the group's efforts. The Washington, DC, office was in the Anacostia area at 3230 Pennsylvania Avenue. Several professionals, volunteers, and members of the Washington Redskins staffed the chapter, accompanied by Arthur Mitchell.

18. Owens, telephone interview, March 3, 2011.

19. "BEU Sponsors Benefit for Scholarship Plan," *Cleveland Call and Post*, July 19, 1969, 10A; "Project JIM Expands," *Cleveland Call and Post*, June 14, 1969, 5C; "Cleveland: Now! 36 Programs Serve 35,000 Young Persons," *Cleveland Plain Dealer*, September 27, 1968, 14. Project JIM was given $9,600 by the Cleveland: NOW! money, which paid the salaries of twelve youth leaders who supervise youth in the program.

20. Van Deburg, *New Day in Babylon*, 117; Lawrence J. McAndrews, "The Politics of Principle: Richard Nixon and School Desegregation," *Journal of Negro History* 83, no. 3 (Summer 1998): 192; Hugh D. Graham, "Richard Nixon and Civil Rights: Explaining an Enigma," in "The Nixon Presidency," special issue, *Presidential Studies Quarterly* 26, no. 1 (Winter 1996): 95; Associated Press, "Nixon Chooses 2 Judges for the Courts of Appeals," *New York Times*, May 13, 1969, 2; Fred C. Allvine, "Black Business Development," *Journal of Marketing* 34, no. 2 (April 1970): 1–2.

21. Allen, *Black Awakening in Capitalist America*, 191–92.

22. Graham, "Richard Nixon and Civil Rights," 93–98; Ethel L. Payne, "Nixon Opens Minorities' Business Unit," *Chicago Daily Defender*, March 6, 1969, 1, 2.

23. Talmadge Anderson, "Black Economic Liberation under Capitalism," *Black Scholar* 2, no. 2, (October 1970): 13; "Black Capitalism Critics," *Sun Reporter*, January 17, 1970, 37; Robert E. Weems Jr. and Lewis A. Randolph, "The National Response to Richard M. Nixon's Black Capitalism Initiative: The Success of Domestic Détente," *Journal of Black Studies* 32, no. 1 (September 2001): 77; Dean Kotlowski, "Black Power-Nixon Style: The Nixon Administration and Minority Business Enterprise," *Business History Review* 72, no. 3 (Autumn 1998): 409–45.

24. Weems Jr. and Randolph, "The National Response to Richard M. Nixon's Black Capitalism Initiative"; Anderson, "Black Economic Liberation Under Capitalism."

25. Walter Rugaber, "Stans to Promote a Minority Business Enterprise: Commerce Chief to Set Up New Department to Direct Programs for the Poor," *New York Times*, March 6, 1969, 27; "Nixon Sets Up Agency to Help Blacks Own, Manage Businesses," *Jet*, March 20, 1969, 20–23; Graham, "Richard Nixon and Civil Rights," 95; Weems and Randolph, "National Response to Richard M. Nixon's Black Capitalism Initiative," 67; "Black Capitalism Critics," *Sun Reporter*, January 17, 1970, 37; Jan Nugent, "Unit Forms to Prod Black Capitalism," *Washington Post*, January 7, 1970, F7. Stans was named to his position on March 5, 1969.

26. "Business and Black Stagnation," *New Pittsburgh Courier*, November 23, 1974, A5; Brady Keys, telephone interview with the author, digital recording, September 29, 2011, Orlando, Florida, recording in possession of author; Associated Press, "Steelers Rout Cowboys, 37–7," *New York Times*, November 13, 1961, 45; United Press International, "Skoronski in Tough Spot, Replacing Packers' Ringo," *Washington Post*, July 21, 1964, B2; Eric B. Roberts, *From Football to Finance: The Story of Brady Keys, Jr.* (New York: Harcourt Brace Jovanovich, 1971), 2, 29–35; During the offseason, Keys worked with his real estate firm and as a personnel executive and employment interviewer with Douglas Aircraft. In 1966, he also read *The Franchise Boom* by Harry Kursh. This book helped him understand the possibilities of creating his own business. He believed that he had a recipe for fried chicken that people would love, and he decided to test his theory. Johnny Sample was also a financial contributor to the BEU.

27. Keys, telephone interview, September 29, 2011; Roberts, *From Football to Finance*, 42; "Rites Held in Los Angeles for 'Golden Bird' Founder Willie 'Bill' Stennis, 69," *Jet*, July 12, 1993, 51.

28. Robert Lipsyte, "Sports of the Times: All-Pro Chicken," *New York Times*, August 26, 1968, 50; Keys, telephone interview, September 29, 2011; "Brady Keys, Steelers Cornerback, 1961–67," *Pittsburgh Sports Daily Bulletin*, November 1, 2011; Associated Press, "Steeler Star: Keys Turns Chicken—Into Profits," *Washington Post*, August 20, 1967, C3; Robert Lipsyte, "Sports of the Times: All-Pro Chicken," *New York Times*, August 26, 1968, 50; "$2.2 Million Capital Set for All-Pro Chicken," *New Pittsburgh Courier*, May 30, 1970, 1, 4.

The All-Pro Chicken menu used football terminology for meals: first down, second down, third down, extra point, field goal, touchdown, and the Brady Keys all-pro special.

29. Keys, telephone interview, September 29, 2011.

30. Lipsyte, "Sports of the Times," 50.

31. Keys, telephone interview, September 29, 2011; "Brady Keys, Steelers Cornerback, 1961–67"; Roberts, *From Football to Finance*, 59–73.

32. Lipsyte, "Sports of the Times," 50.

33. Robert A. Wright, "Family Recipe Pays Off for a Negro Athlete," *New York Times*, June 7, 1969, 47; Philip H. Dougherty, "Advertising: Lots of Action on the Avenue," *New York Times*, June 20, 1969, 65; Roberts, *From Football to Finance*, 57–59; Allan Jaklich, "Chicken Outlets Pad Athletes' Roosts," *Chicago Tribune*, February 28, 1969, C10. He incorporated All-Pro Enterprises Inc. in 1968, which later served as the parent company of his Kentucky Fried Chicken and Burger King chains. He also owned a twin-engine Apache plane. Raymond League, the first Black account executive with J. Walter Thompson and executive of Zebra Associates, provided financing to Waldo Jeff for his All-Pro Chicken franchise in Bedford-Stuyvesant in New York.

34. "$2.2 Million Capital Set For All-Pro Chicken," *New Pittsburgh Courier*, May 30, 1970, 1, 4; Aaron Latham, "Black, White Firms Form Partnership," *Washington Post*, September 16, 1970, B1. Proceeds from the stock sales were used to build thirteen more restaurants.

35. John Wooten and Carole F. Hoover to Mayor Carl B. Stokes, Carl Stokes Papers, 1957–72, Container 29, Folder 519, April 20, 1970, Western Reserve Historical Society, Cleveland, Ohio. Jim Brown sent a letter to Stokes requesting a public endorsement of the Food First antipoverty effort. He believed the mayor's endorsement would "better enhance the cooperation of the Cleveland community" toward the program. The National Kickoff Dinner was held in Cleveland on June 14, 1970, at the Cleveland Sheraton Hotel. They invited Jesse Jackson and Coretta Scott King because both were "so articulate on the whole question of hunger in our nation." Stokes served as honorary chairman of the dinner. Senators George McGovern (Democrat from South Dakota), Jacob Javits (Republican from New York), and Walter Mondale (Democrat from Minnesota) were invited since these three men were part of the federal government's Committee on Hunger in the USA.

This provided a "tremendous boost financially and from a public relations standpoint."

36. Jim Brown to Mayor Carl B. Stokes, Carl Stokes Papers, 1957–72, Container 29, Folder 519, February 26 1970, Western Reserve Historical Society, Cleveland, Ohio; John Wooten to Mayor Carl B. Stokes, Carl Stokes Papers, 1957–72, Container 29, Folder 519, March 20 1970, Western Reserve Historical Society, Cleveland, Ohio, 2; John Wooten and Carole F. Hoover to Mayor Carl B. Stokes, Carl Stokes Papers, 1957–72, Container 29, Folder 519, April 20 1970, Western Reserve Historical Society, Cleveland, Ohio; Carole Hoover worked with the Cleveland branch of the union. An array of NFL players accompanied the BEU on this trip: James Shorter, Ray May, and Roy Jefferson of the Pittsburgh Steelers; Cid Edwards, Jamie Rivers, Lonnie Sanders, and Ernie McMillan of the St. Louis Cardinals; Erich Barnes, Leroy Kelly, and Sidney Williams of the Cleveland Browns; Jim Snowden and Brigman Owens of the Washington Redskins; Mike Taylor of the New Orleans Saints; and Irv Cross of the Philadelphia Eagles. Also accompanying the players were Maggie Hathaway, a longtime friend of Brown, social activist, and union contributor, and Ernest Thomas, a coordinator for the trip and community relations director of the BEU. The group gathered Wednesday morning at the Nite Nite Club, an establishment near the Lorraine Motel, to discuss the trip's logistics.

37. Charles Gillespie, "Jim Brown Comes to Mississippi," *The Nation*, September 21, 1970, 236–38.

38. Ibid.; J. Brown, telephone interview, February 25, 2011; Owens, telephone interview, March 14, 2011. The bus stopped at Rust College, where Arverne Moore, George Caldwell, and Henry Boyd, accompanied by other residents of the town, boarded with the group.

39. Gillespie, "Jim Brown Comes to Mississippi," 238; "Steeler Football Stars to Aid Miss. County," *Pittsburgh Courier*, February 21, 1970, 1, 8; Owens, telephone interview, March 14, 2011; Williams, telephone interview, March 29, 2011.

40. OJO, "Post Man," *Oakland Post*, March 5, 1970, 18; "Anacostia Picked for Project," *Washington Post*, March 31, 1970, C2; "Russell Coaches Again!," *Los Angeles Sentinel*, April 9, 1970, B2; "Mississippi-Glenville Link: 'Food First' Sunday Here to Be June 14," *Cleveland Plain Dealer*, May 11, 1970, 18A; "Food First Speaker Set," *Cleveland Plain Dealer*, May 17, 1970, 17A; "Soul

Golf: Charity Golf This Weekend at Skywest for Poverty," *Sun Reporter*, July 11, 1970, 35; Paul L. Montgomery, "Tennis Match Serves the Poor," *New York Times*, July 13, 1970, 33; "Two Champs," *New York Amsterdam News*, July 18, 1970, 34; "Happy Thanksgiving," *Los Angeles Sentinel*, November 26, 1970, B3; "BEU Food First a $12,885.25 Check," *Cleveland Call and Post*, November 28, 1970, 3A; J. Brown, telephone interview, February 25, 2011. When the Cleveland Browns visited the San Francisco 49ers during the 1970 season, a "Cleveland day" was created to raise money for Food First. The exact total of the American Freedom from Hunger Foundation Inc. check was $12,885.25.

41. "Black Economic Union Draws Support," *The Argus*, April 6, 1970, 10; "Jim Brown, Economic Union Cited in Congress," *Jet*, July 2, 1970, 4.

42. "Stokes Salutes Jim Brown in Congressional Record" *Jet*, July 9, 1970, 52.

43. BEU, Annual Report 1968, personal papers of Jim Brown. By 1969, the membership rate had changed to $2, $5, $25, $100, and $500 for a life membership.

44. Kaliss, *Beyond the Black Power Salute*, 22; Monica M. Dodge and Erika P. Pierson, "Activism Quiet on Mostly-White Campus," *Harvard Crimson*, May 23, 2011; Spencer Jourdain, telephone interview with the author, digital recording, April 13, 2011, Orlando, Florida, recording in possession of author. As a student at Harvard, Jourdain and his classmates did not see their presence there as part of a more significant movement or racial statement about America. As he recalled fifty years after graduating, "We were there to get an education and then to go out and be successful people in our chosen fields, not start a cohesive social movement." Because of the burgeoning civil rights movement, Jourdain remembers that the administration at Harvard made all necessary accommodations for Black students to ensure they were successful. This proactive response from the university was a strategy to limit unwanted protests or demonstrations about the school.

45. Monica M. Dodge and Erika P. Pierson, "Activism Quiet on Mostly-White Campus," *Harvard Crimson*, online edition, May 23, 2011; "Candidates for Queen," *Chicago Defender (National edition)*, October 18, 1952, 3; Jourdain, telephone interview, April 13, 2011; "Jim Brown's NIEU Opens in Harlem," *New York Amsterdam News*, July 22, 1967, 42; discussion with Spencer Jourdain, July 29, 2012. Jourdain had a history of family members committed

to the Black freedom struggle. His family oral history links an ancestor to abolitionists in the New England area and a male relative who fought with the Fifty-Fourth Regiment Massachusetts Volunteer Infantry. His grandfather, Edwin Bush Jourdain Sr., was a childhood friend of W. E. B. DuBois, as both grew up together in New Bedford, Massachusetts. Jourdain Sr. practiced law in the city where he joined DuBois to address White racial discrimination through a crusade called the Niagara Movement. Jourdain Sr. attended the conference, which led to the formation of the NAACP. Spencer Jourdain's father, Edwin Bush Jourdain Jr., was a race man who graduated from Harvard University in 1921. One of his earliest forms of activism came in the move to desegregate the dormitories at Harvard. Upon graduation, Jourdain Jr. moved to Evanston, Illinois, where he served as city alderman, becoming the first African American to serve as an elected official. Thus, for Spencer Jourdain, there was always a connection to engaging with the inequalities prevalent in African American communities. His family's history left a lasting impression on him about the role he was to play in US society.

46. Spencer Jourdain, telephone interview with the author, digital recording, June 22, 2012, Orlando, FL, recording in possession of author; Edward H. Jones, "A Status Report of the Equity Development Component of the Black Economic Union," September 25, 1970, Carl Stokes Papers, Manuscript Collection No. 4370. While Jourdain was an undergraduate at the Massachusetts institution, there was a rise in the number of international students, especially from Africa as many former African colonies became independent from 1955 to 1961. According to Jourdain, he and some of the African students "formed a vibrant social group" where they had "frequent discussions about the exciting potential of African economic development as newly independent nations and the potential role of America—and African Americans—to participate in helping create that exciting future." Ofia Nwali earned a PhD in economics from Harvard and helped develop joint ventures with emerging economic development activities in Africa, particularly to develop an East African housing venture. According to Spencer Jourdain, John Butler rendered an "early excellent analysis on behalf [of] a minority inventor trying to develop a 3D television."

47. Jourdain, telephone interview, June 22, 2012. Mitchell provided guidance and technical assistance to companies that came to the union for financial

help. While the BEU particularly helped businesses in the cities where it had offices, it also helped companies in the South. The BEU established relationships with such enterprises as the Cosby Wilson Corporation in Louisville, Kentucky; the Velberta's Wigs and Beauty Supplies in Dublin, Georgia; and Rural Mission Inc. on Johns Island in Charleston, South Carolina.

48. Peter Kihss, "$3.2-Million Is Granted by Ford to Help Antipoverty Programs," *New York Times*, March 8, 1968, 28; "Negro Industrial & Economic Union: Gets 4502,000 Ford Grant for Program Developments," *Cleveland Call and Post*, March 9, 1968, 1A, 2A; "$520,000 Grant Told for Industrial Union," *Los Angeles Sentinel*, March 21, 1968, A5; "Ford Foundation Grants $400,000," *New York Amsterdam News*, March 30, 1968, 31; "Playboy Gives NIEU $10,000," *Cleveland Call and Post*, May 18, 1968, 9A; "Jim Brown Opens Harlem Agency to Help Negro Businesses," *New York Times*, November 16, 1968, 29. Henry and Edsel Ford, the creators of the Ford Motor Company, initiated the Ford Foundation. There were White business owners who supported the union financially. *Playboy* founder Hugh Hefner made a $10,000 contribution to the union in May. At the time, he believed the objectives of the BEU were "worthy of support of all America."

49. "Premiere Benefit Helps NIEU Continue Loan Program," *Cleveland Call and Post*, October 12, 1968, 4A. Scholarships, or "educational loans," were given to students to help pay for their tuition, books, and school supplies. Recipients of the scholarship in 1968 were Charlotte Woods (Tennessee A&T University, now Tennessee State University), Deane Buchanan (Western Reserve University, now Case Western Reserve University), Margot Tillman (Cleveland State University), Dorothea Walker (Jane Addams Nursing School), and Phyliss Taylor (Ohio State University).

50. "Afro American Styles from New Breed," *Cleveland Call and Post*, May 18, 1968, 2B. New Breed group was greatly influenced by the philosophies of Marcus Garvey and Malcolm X. Outward expressions of this were seen in the red, black, and green flag attributed to the former and his self-improvement movement with the Universal Negro Improvement Association. A portrait of the latter was hung in the headquarters shops in Harlem. New Breed headquarters was located at 147th Street and St. Nicholas Avenue in Harlem, New York. For more on the "Black is Beautiful" movement, see Van Deburg's book *New Day in Babylon*.

51. Margaret Crimmins, "A 'New Breed' of Designers, Manufacturers," *Washington Post*, February 2, 1969, 113.

52. "Afro American Styles from New Breed," *Cleveland Call and Post*, May 18, 1968, 2B; Ann Geracimos, "About Dashikis and the New Breed Cat," *New Pittsburgh Courier*, May 17, 1969, 2; "Tomorrow's Designers Today!," *Chicago Daily Defender*, January 14, 1970, 21; Edward B. Fiske, "Finding Identity, Black Nuns Put Soul into Religious Life," *New York Times*, August 15, 1970, 22. Spencer Jourdain helped finance Maverick International, an "all-black couture house." For info on this business, see *Jet*, June 5, 1969, 63.

53. Crimmins, "'New Breed' of Designers, Manufacturers," 113.

54. Geracimos, "About Dashikis and the New Breed Cat," 28.

55. Crimmins, "'New Breed' of Designers, Manufacturers," 113; Stacy Kinlock Sewell, "The 'Not-Buying Power' of the Black Community: Urban Boycotts and Equal Employment Opportunity, 1960–64," *Journal of African American History* 89, no. 2 (Spring 2004): 138; The first line of the company catered solely to males. By the spring of 1969, they had expanded to female, baby, and unisex lines. As Geracimos mentions in her article, the definition of *dashiki* would not be found in *Webster's New World Dictionary* or at Brooks Brothers; the meaning of the word is "lost to history."

56. Geracimos, "About Dashikis and the New Breed Cat," 28; Spencer Jourdain, telephone interview with the author, digital recording, May 23, 2012, Orlando, Florida, recording in possession of author.

57. Geracimos, "About Dashikis and the New Breed Cat," 28; Crimmins, "'New Breed' of Designers, Manufacturers," 113. The company also sought to venture into other consumer goods, like food and furniture, but that aspect of the business did not develop. The BEU also helped several Black businesspeople get franchises with McDonald's.

58. Dave Brady, "Advocate of 'Scratch and Dig': Wooten on the Line On and Off Field," *Washington Post*, October 13, 1968, C4; "Display Ad 25," *Cleveland Call and Post*, August 24, 1968, 11B; "Atlanta Fans Rate No. 1," *Los Angeles Sentinel*, December 10, 1970, B3, B6; Gillespie, "Jim Brown Comes to Mississippi," 236; John Wooten to Ron Gault, February 6, 1970, Carl Stokes Papers, Manuscript Collection No. 4370. The company had offices in Cleveland at 10816 St. Clair and Watts, California, at 1314 East Forty-First Street. Dennis L. Taylor served as president of Magnificent. Wilbert Jackson,

his business partner, was the general manager. John Wooten served as sales director, while Jim Shorter, Sidney Williams, and Sumlor Harris managed sales and the promotion of products in different outlets.

59. Carl T. Rowan, Convocation Address, November 14, 1968, Colby College, Maine. The Better Homes for Cleveland Foundation was sponsored by the Catholic Diocese of Cleveland.

60. Ibid.; BEU, Annual Report 1968.

61. "Supreme Gifts with Dunbar Picture," *Cleveland Call and Post*, June 1, 1968, 7A; "Foreign Students Visit," *Cleveland Call and Post*, September 7, 1968, 5B; "Viewers Go on Tour of Black Businesses," *Cleveland Call and Post*, March 29, 1969, 7A; Ulf Goebel, "Black Community Leaders Deplore Hough Agency Series," *Cleveland Call and Post*, April 11, 1970, 1A. Namax Builders was located at 3970 East 177th Street. A young man who had been "fiddling around" in the tile business suddenly found himself a growing concern after receiving a $40,000 contract from Beavers.

62. Owens, telephone interview, March 14, 2011. Bobby Mitchell embraced the group's tenets, as seen in the formation of the Bobby Mitchell Insurance Agency at 3230 Pennsylvania Avenue, SE. The BEU received a $198,030 grant from the Department of Commerce on June 8, 1970, to assist its offices in DC, Kansas City, and Cleveland.

63. Owens, telephone interview, March 3, 2011; Owens, telephone interview, March 14, 2011; Joseph Whitaker, "BEU Plans Ad Clinic for Blacks," *Washington Post*, June 9 1970, A5; "Advertising Clinic," *Washington Post*, June 10, 1970, D11; "City and State: Md. Panel Will Probe Police 'Harassment,'" *Washington Post*, June 12, 1970, C6. Over two hundred proposals were sent to the office for help, but union board members deemed many of the applicants' ideas unworthy of financial support. Owens stated in an interview, "In the weekly clinics some of the focus was on [how] Black businessmen could improve how their dollars were spent. The bottom line of how important it was they could do things collaboratively and how effective it could be. It was the first of its kind in the country. It made national news."

64. Vernon C. Thompson, "Death of a Business: Rags-to-Riches Empire Succumbs to Over-Expansion," *Washington Post*, February 8, 1979, DC1; Owens, telephone interview, March 3, 2011; Owens, telephone interview, March 14, 2011.

65. Thompson, "Death of a Business."

66. Van Deburg, *New Day in Babylon*, 25.

5. Two Different Worlds: Kansas City and the BEU

1. "Super Bowl I Scoring Stats," January 15, 1967, Pro Football Hall of Fame; Vahe Gregorian, "The 1966 Chiefs," *Kansas City Star*, 10B; NFL Productions, *NFL America's Game.*

2. Gregorian, "The 1966 Chiefs."

3. Curtis McClinton Jr., telephone interview with the author, digital recording, June 15, 2010, Kansas City, Missouri, recording in possession of author; "Flash News in Brief: The Happiest News," *Baltimore Afro-American*, April 4, 1959, 1.

4. Gaylon White, "Curtis McClinton Looks Back," *Kansas City Town Squire*, November 1970, 79; Associated Press, "Missing Gridder Calls His Home," *Kansas City Star*, October 23, 1957, 13C; Curtis McClinton Jr., telephone interview with the author, digital recording, June 4, 2010, Kansas City, Missouri, recording in possession of author; McClinton, telephone interview, June 15, 2010; "Two Kansans Tell Secret AFL Draft," *Chicago Daily Tribune*, November 20, 1961, C1; Associated Press, "All-Star Football Selections," *New York Times*, November 23, 1960, 32; Associated Press, "24 Players Named to Western Eleven," *New York Times*, December 9, 1961, 31; "Four Negro Gridders Named All-Americans," *Cleveland Call and Post*, December 9, 1961, 4C.

5. Kent Pulliam, "McClinton's Strength Is Game of Life," *Kansas City Star*, February 26, 1995, C2; Donald M. Gamet, "Leader: Curtis McClinton," *Kansas Citian*, August 1970, 15.

6. McClinton, telephone interview, June 4, 2010, Kansas City, Missouri.

7. "Was Roommate of Junius Buchanan," *Philadelphia Tribune*, September 10, 1963, 12; Pulliam, "McClinton's Strength Is Game of Life," C2.

8. Pulliam, "McClintn's Strength Is Game of Life."

9. Vahe Gregorian, "The 1966 Chiefs," *Kansas City Star*, 10B; NFL Productions, *NFL America's Game.*

10. Greogrian, "The 1966 Chiefs"; United Press International, "Ex-Grambling Star Dies from Broken Neck," *Chicago Daily Defender*, September 10, 1963, 24; Randy Covitz, "Chiefs' Haynes Left Lasting Mark: Newest Member of Team's Hall of Fame Led Way for Black Player," *Kansas City Star*, February 24, 1991, 1.

11. Gregorian, "The 1966 Chiefs."

12. White, "Curtis McClinton Looks Back," 77–78; Ivan Carter and Blair Kerkhoff, "Athletes Who Succeeded On Field Had to Run through Obstacles Off It," *Kansas City Star*, February 23, 2003, C1, C17.

13. Mark Dent, "The Chiefs Proudly Broke Kansas City's Racial Barriers," *Kansas City Star*, 22A; Gerald Astor, "Kansas City's Mike Garrett: Big Little Chief," *Look*, November 14, 1967, 112–20; White, "Curtis McClinton Looks Back," 76, 79; Carter and Kerkhoff, "Athletes Who Succeeded On Field Had to Run through Obstacles Off It," C1, C17.

14. White, "Curtis McClinton Looks Back," 76, 79.

15. Astor, "Kansas City's Mike Garrett," 112–20; Mike Garrett, interview with the author, digital recording, July 14, 2023, KC, Missouri, recording in possession of author; Dent, "Chiefs Proudly Broke Kansas City's Racial Barriers," 22A.

16. Pulliam, "McClinton's Strength Is Game of Life," C2; Geri Gosa, "Goals for Blacks: Ex-Chief Still a Winner," *Kansas City Star*, August 3, 1972, 10.

17. Dent, "Chiefs Proudly Broke Kansas City's Racial Barriers," 22A.

18. Anderson, "America's Blackest Child."

19. "Jim Brown See Hard Choices for Nation," *Kansas City Call*, July 18, 1969, 1; Curtis McClinton Jr., telephone interview with the author, digital recording, October 5, 2010, KC, Missouri, recording in possession of author.

20. Gosa, "Goals for Blacks," 10.

21. Manning Marable, *How Capitalism Underdeveloped Black America: Problems in Race, Political Economy, and Society* (Chicago: Haymarket, 2015), 130; McClinton, telephone interview, June 4, 2010; White, "Curtis McClinton Looks Back," 78.

22. Dick Wade, "Negro Grid Stars Join in Fight on Poverty," *Kansas City Star*, June 2, 1968, S1.

23. "Pro Fullback McClinton Joins Bank Staff," *Jet*, February 25, 1965, 57; White, "Curtis McClinton Looks Back," 78, 79; Susannah Walker, "Black Dollar Power: Assessing African American Consumerism since 1945," in *African American Urban History since World War II*, ed. Kenneth L. Kusmer and Joe W. Trotter (Chicago: University of Chicago Press, 2019), 376–403; Pulliam, "McClinton's Strength Is Game of Life," C2. In February 1966, he received the charter to open his bank.

24. Walker, "Black Dollar Power."

25. Fred Fitzsimmons, "New Swope Parkway National Bank to Have New Building," *Kansas City Star*, September 17, 1967, 8F; "Swope Parkway Bank Invests in Bonds for State of Israel," *Kansas City Call*, November 8, 1968, 10; KU Athletics, "LaVannes Squires, KU's First African-American Men's Basketball Player, Passes Away at 90," *The Voice*, February 28, 2021. They were capitalized for $375,00, with a surplus of $225,000 and undivided profits of $150,000. Dr. Walter R. Peterson served as chair of the board. McClinton served as director and vice president. Kapable Inc. was the investment group with holdings over the land the bank was placed, and with the backing of a constituency of investors (e.g., the Lutheran Church provided $100,000). It was located at 4920 Swope Parkway in a 2,400-square-foot building, with off-street parking for thirty cars and two drive-through windows. The bank's size aimed to reflect its importance to the community.

26. Kaliss, *Beyond the Black Power Salute*, 21; Jackie Robinson and Alfred Duckett, *I Never Had It Made* (New York: HarperCollins, 1995), 183–84.

27. White, "Curtis McClinton Looks Back," 76, 79; Willie Lanier, telephone interview with the author, digital recording, July 27, 2023, Richmond, Virginia, recording in possession of author; "In the Field of Religion," *Kansas City Star*, October 5, 1968, 3.

28. White, "Curtis McClinton Looks Back," 78; Levin and Spellun, *Public and Private Support for the Development of Minority and Poverty Group-Owned Businesses*.

29. "Score a Choice on Bank Funds," *Kansas City Star*, March 2, 1969, 32A; Vernon E. Rice to Curtis McClinton, June 17, 1969.

30. "Presbyterians Ponder Supporting B.E.U. Goals," *Kansas City Star*, February 4, 1970; Bernard Hoffman to American Jewish Committee member, November 21, 1968; "B.E.U. Receives Federal Grant," *Kansas City Call*, March 7, 1969, 1; Some of the other companies were Shirley's Florist and Gift Shop at 3127 Swope Parkway, Lithon Color Press at 4344 Clary Boulevard, and International Fish Fry House at 3631 Prospect. Willie Mitchell, a member of the BEU and defensive back for the Chiefs, joined with McClinton to build a bridge with the KC chapter of the American Jewish Committee.

31. "Man Is Killed during Holdup," *Kansas City Times*, August 24, 1968, 3A.

32. "Making Good Start in Business," *Kansas City Call*, June 6, 1969, 2; "SBA Helps Three Local Men Start Auto Parts Businesses," *Kansas City Call*, June 6, 1969, 2; "Black Economic Union Moves to New Site," *Kansas City*

Call, June 13, 1969, 1; "Looking for More Black Chevrolet Dealers, Says G.M. Vice President," *Kansas City Call*, June 23, 1972, 5.

33. "The B.E.U.'s First Year," *Kansas City Call*, July 18, 1969, 10; "Jim Brown See Hard Choices for Nation," *Kansas City Call*, July 18, 1969, 1, 12.

34. John H. Wandless, *Minority Economic Development: Opportunities and Approaches* (Kansas City: Office of Economic Opportunity, 1969), 1–2, 24; Brian Burnes, "The Rev. John Wandless, Urban Ranger Corps founder, dead at 79," *Kansas City Star*, last modified December 28, 2015, https://www .kansascity.com/news/local/article51952920.html.

35. Wandless, *Minority Economic Development*, 1.

36. Ibid., 3, 24–26.

37. Jo McGuff, "Willie Lanier—A Man among Men," *Kansas City Star*, December 16, 1977, 25; Milton Gross, "Pro Football Goes Cloak & Dagger," *Boston Globe*, December 7, 1964, 31; Bill Nunn Jr., "Change of Pace," *Pittsburgh Courier*, February 6, 1965, 23; "Tough Chiefs 55 Per Cent Black: Set Record in Signing Non-Whites," *New Pittsburgh Courier*, November 1, 1969, 15; Paul Harasim, "Remembering Muhammad Ali, Boxing's Glory Days with George Foreman," *Las Vegas Review-Journal*, June 9, 2016; Vahe Gregorian, "Whether You Know His Name or Not, Lloyd Wells Belongs in the Chiefs' Hall of Fame," *Kansas City Star*, June 20, 2020; "Under the Banner," *Jacksonville Free Press*, March 23, 2023, 8.

38. Milton Gross, "Pro Football Goes Cloak & Dagger," *Boston Globe*, December 7, 1964, 31; Nunn, "Change of Pace," 23; "Tough Chiefs 55 Per Cent Black: Set Record in Signing Non-Whites," *New Pittsburgh Courier*, November 1, 1969, 15; Paul Harasim, "Remembering Muhammad Ali, Boxing's Glory Days with George Foreman," *Las Vegas Review-Journal*, June 9, 2016; Gregorian, "Whether You Know His Name or Not, Lloyd Wells Belongs in the Chiefs' Hall of Fame"; "Under the Banner," 8.

39. NFL Productions, *NFL America's Game*.

40. Richard Nixon to Curtis McClinton, January 22, 1970, LaBudde Special Collections and Archives, University of Missouri–Kansas City; "Praise from Nixon for B.E.U. Here," *Kansas City Star*, February 1, 1970.

41. White, "Curtis McClinton Looks Back," 79; Gosa, "Goals for Blacks," 10.

42. Dick Wade, "Negro Grid Stars Join in Fight on Poverty," *Kansas City Star*, June 2, 1968, S1; Joe McGuff, "Sporting Comment," *Kansas City Star*,

September 15, 1970, 13; Robert Moore, "McClinton Happy Off Field," *Kansas City Times*, August 7, 1971, 2D.

43. McGuff, "Sporting Comment"; Moore, "McClinton Happy Off Field."

44. McClinton, telephone interview, June 4, 2010.

45. Flournoy Coles Jr., "The Unique Problems of the Black Businessman," *Review of the Black Political Economy* 5, no. 1 (1974): 49; "N.I.E.U. Becomes the Black Economic Union," *Kansas City Call*, December 6, 1968, 2; "B.E.U. Launches Program to Create Black Unity," *Kansas City Call*, December 10, 1968, 3.

46. "Contract Let for St. Regis," *Kansas City Star*, December 30, 1969, 4.

47. "Operation Rehabilitation; Both Housing and Human," *Kansas City Call*, September 5, 1969, 5.

48. "Minority Housing Specialists on European Tour," *Kansas City Call*, March 13, 1970, 8.

49. US Census Bureau, "Consumer Income," Series P-60, No. 77, May 7, 1971, 1.

50. Arthur I. Blaustein and Geoffrey P. Faux, *Star Spangled Hustle* (Garden City, NY: Doubleday), 1972, 202–203; Mehrsa Baradaran, *The Color of Money: Black Banks and the Racial Wealth Gap* (Cambridge, MA: Belknap Press, 2017), 184.

51. "B.E.U. Plans Opening of New Center," *Kansas City Call*, October 9, 1970, 4; Campbell Gibson and Kay Jung, Historical Census Statistics on Population Totals by Race, 1790 to 1990, and by Hispanic Origin, 1970 to 1990, for Large Cities and Other Urban Places in the United States (Washington, DC: US Census Bureau, February 2005), 71; US Census Bureau, *1970 Census of Population* (Washington, DC: US Census Bureau, 1974), 3; "B.E.U. Seeks Business Applicants," *Kansas City Call*, January 2–8, 1970; "Business Class Completed by 18 At Black Union," *Kansas City Star*, January 17, 1970; Robert Moore, "McClinton Happy Off Field," *Kansas City Times*, August 7, 1971, 2D.

52. Moore, "McClinton Happy Off Field," 2D; "Black Attorneys and B.E.U. Solve Their Differences," *Kansas City Call*, November 26, 1971, 1.

53. McClinton, telephone interview, June 15, 2010; "37 African Nations Join in a Fair in Nairobi in Attempt to Build New Trade with One Another," *New York Times*, February 27, 1972, 13; Gosa, "Goals for Blacks," 10; Bill Pritchard, "B.E.U. Here Offers Assistance to Kenya in McClinton Visit," *Kansas City Call*, May 5, 1972, 18.

54. Pritchard, "B.E.U. Here Offers Assistance to Kenya in McClinton Visit."

55. Pritchard, "B.E.U. Here Offers Assistance to Kenya in McClinton Visit"; M. DeVonne French McClinton and Curtis McClinton Jr., telephone interview with the author, digital recording, July 23, 2023, Pentagon City, Virginia, recording in possession of author.

56. Louis Blue, "Swope Park Bank Insolvent; Still Operates Under F.D.I.C.," *Kansas City Call*, January 10, 1975, 1; "Swope Parkway Bank Building to Be Home of Health Center," *Kansas City Call*, May 14, 1976, 1; "Swope Parkway Bank Promotes 2 Employees," *Kansas City Call*, March 23, 1973, 3; "Milton Bledsoe Jr. Is Named Vice President of Ohio Bank," *Kansas City Call*, April 13, 1973, 4; "F.D.I.C. Saves the Day!," *Kansas City Call*, January 10, 1975, 12. This led the US comptroller of currency to close the bank, followed by the FDIC takeover. Willie Thomas was assigned as the liquidation officer to oversee this process. She was given a two-year window to achieve this task.

57. M. DeVonne French McClinton and Curtis McClinton Jr., telephone interview with the author, digital recording, July 23, 2023, Pentagon City, Virginia, recording in possession of author; "Swope Parkway Bank Building to Be Home of Health Center," *Kansas City Call*, May 14, 1976, 1; The Metropolitan Life Insurance Company sold the SPNB building to the city for $735,000. It was later remodeled and became the Model Cities Comprehensive Neighborhood Health Center.

58. McClinton, telephone interview, June 4, 2010; "B.E.U. Cites Accomplishments in Document Giving Its History," *Kansas City Call*, June 18, 1971, 17.

59. "New Pediatrician Joins Staff at Doctor's Clinic," *Kansas City Call*, January 20, 1978, 6; "Dr. M. DeVonne French to Staff of Doctor's Clinic," *Kansas City Call*, January 27, 1978, 6; "Anniversary Dinner: 'Economic Union Model for Blacks,'" *Kansas City Times*, November 18, 1978, 19B; "Dr. Anne Lamber Johnson to Introduce Dental Facilities in Open House Sunday," *Kansas City Call*, May 5, 1978, 7; Cynthia Newsome, "Kansas City Woman Is Trailblazer for African Americans in Dentistry," KSHB, February 15, 2021, https://www.kshb.com/news/black-history-month-2021/kansas-city-woman-is-trailblazer-for-african-americans-in-dentistry.

60. "Dr. Anne Lambert Johnson to Introduce Dental Facilities in Open House Sunday," 7; Newsome, "Kansas City Woman Is Trailblazer for African Americans in Dentistry."

61. "Private Sector Investors Awarded," *Washington Informer*, April 17, 1980, 16; "Black Business: A New Beginning?," *Black Enterprise*, January 1980, 21; "Curtis McClinton Honored," *The Skanner*, May 14, 1980, 19; "Receives Doctorate," *Jet*, July 17, 1980, 16; Eric Pianin and LaBarbara Bowman, "Curtis McClinton Jr. May Succeed Donaldson: Former Chiefs Star Expected to Take Deputy Mayor's Job," *Washington Post*, September 21, 1983, C1, C8; "Black Super Bowl History," *Miami Times*, January 24, 2007, 10D; McClinton, telephone interview, June 4, 2010. McClinton also received an honorary doctorate from Miles College in 1980.

62. Gosa, "Goals for Blacks," 10.

63. Ibid.

64. Ball, *Myth and Propaganda of Black Buying Power*, 93.

Epilogue

1. "Black Builders Contending for More of the Construction Pie," *Pittsburgh Courier*, December 1, 1973, 28; Claudia Levy, "Units Funded By OMBE Back Agency," *Washington Post*, May 31, 1975, D7; "BEU Grant," *Cleveland Call and Post*, March 8, 1984, 15A; Judge A. Deane Buchanan, in-person interview with the author, digital recording, September 24, 2010, Cleveland Heights, Ohio, recording in possession of author; "Two Rehabilitated Buildings Bring New Life to University Circle Area," *Cleveland Call and Post*, November 8, 1980, 9B; Williams, telephone interview, March 29, 2011.

2. "John Wooten Directs NFL Player Programs," *Pittsburgh Courier*, September 7, 1991, 6; Gerald Eskenazi, "Sale of Cowboys Expected Today, and Landry Might Be Out," *New York Times*, February 25, 1989, 49; Associated Press, "Cowboys' Buyer Hires a New Coach," *New York Times*, February 26, 1989, S5; "Cowboys Name Wooten Director of Pro Personnel," *Los Angeles Sentinel*, August 24, 1989, B4; "Charlie Cherokee Says," *Chicago Daily Defender*, April 3, 1971, 5; "BEU Moves Main Office," *Los Angeles Sentinel*, April 15, 1971, B6; "BEU Moves National to L.A.," *New York Amsterdam News*, August 14, 1971, A12; "John Wooten Directs NFL Player Programs," *Pittsburgh Courier*, September 7, 1991, 6; "Wooten Named Eagles V.P.," *Pittsburgh Courier*, April 9, 1994, 7; "Ex-Football Pros Seek Hire Ground in NFL," *Afro-American Red Star*, March 22, 2003, A1; Daniel Gray, "NFL's First Black Head Coach Inducted into Football Hall of Fame," *Tennessee Tribune*, August 11, 2005, B1. In this position as director of NFL player programs, Wooten reported to the

NFL executive vice president of labor relations Harold Henderson. Wooten represented "outstanding players," such as Otis Armstrong (drafted by the Denver Broncos in 1973, first round, ninth overall), Charley Taylor (NFL Hall of Fame, class of 1984), Darryl Stingley (drafted by the New England Patriots in 1973, first round, nineteenth overall), and Buddy Bell (Cleveland Indians, MLB).

3. "Wilkinson Released in Salary Cap Saga," *New York Times*, July 30, 2003, D7; Christine Brennan and Neil H. Greenberger, "Williams Released in Redskins' Youth Movement," *Washington Post*, March 31, 1990, G1; David Aldridge, "Redskins' Monk Gets Browns' Attention," *Washington Post*, February 26, 1994, G1, G3; Leonard Shapiro, "Monk Aims for Record Grab Today," *Washington Post*, December 10, 1994, C7; Display Ad 22, "How Do You Convince Kids in DC They Can Actually Go Further in the Seat on the Right?," *Washington Post*, December 16, 1994, A23; Clifton Brown, "Smith and Knicks: Bad Blood Still Flows," *New York Times*, December 28, 1996, 37.

4. Danyella Davis, "Indiana Black Expo Reaches 40-Year Milestone," *The Recorder*, July 9, 2010, 3; Ron Wynn, "NFL Legend Passes," *Tennessee Tribune*, July 14, 2011, 5B; Ken Denlinger, "Outcasts No More, Mackey, Davis Enter Hall Today," *Washington Post*, August 1, 1992, D2; Jack Chevalier, "Football Hall of Fame to Honor Former Inductees," *Philadelphia Tribune*, July 28, 2000, 2C; "Hall of Famer Mackey Dies at 69," *La Prensa*, July 10, 2011, 3B.

5. Sam Doku, "Bobby Mitchell Honored for 44 Years of Diligence to the Redskins," *Washington Informer*, March 26, 2003, 25; Marvin Wamble, "NFL's Bobby Mitchell Honored with FPA's Younger Award," *Michigan Chronicle*, April 9, 2003, C1; Dave Brady, "Redskins' Mitchell Retires after 11 Years NFL Play," *Washington Post*, September 9, 1969, D1; Sam Doku, "As Doku Sees It: Bobby Mitchell and the Fight to Retire His Number," *Washington Informer*, March 26, 2003, 24. A sports field in the Congress Heights neighborhood of Washington, DC, was named in honor of Mitchell in 2000.

6. Walter Beach III, "Stop Preening," *New York Times*, December 21, 2003, SP9; Amy Waldman, "Bias Case Gains against the City: US Agency Finds Evidence of Parks Dept. Discrimination," *New York Times*, February 5, 2001. In 1986, Walter Beach was inducted into the Central Michigan University Hall of Fame.

7. Associated Press, "Pro Football Hall of Fame Inducts 7 Saturday," *Washington Post*, July 25, 1971, C7; "Jim Brown Enters Hall of Fame," *Sacramento*

Observer, February 11, 1971, B11; Jodie Valade, "Finding Holes: Jim Brown Had a Way of Making Something Out of Nothing. These Days, He's Trying to Do the Same Thing Off the Field," *Cleveland Plain Dealer*, September 5, 2004, C1; A. S. "Doc" Young, "Jim Brown: Part I," *Los Angeles Sentinel*, August 4, 1977, A7.

8. Valade, "Finding Holes: Jim Brown Had a Way of Making Something Out of Nothing," C1.

9. Tony Grossi, "Cleveland's 'Goal' Model," *Cleveland Plain Dealer*, October 15, 2006, C8.

10. Pat McManamon, "Jim Brown on Colin Kaepernick: 'I Am with Him 100 Percent,'" ESPN, August 30, 2016; "Jim Brown on Colin Kaepernick's Anthem Protest: 'I Would Not Challenge Our Flag,'" *Sports Illustrated*, September 22, 2016, https://www.si.com/nfl/2016/09/22/jim-brown-colin-kaepernick-protest-national-anthem.

11. Sean Wagner-McGough, "Jim Brown: Colin Kaepernick Has to Decide If He's an Activist or a Football Player," CBS Sports, August 25, 2017, https://www.cbssports.com/nfl/news/jim-brown-colin-kaepernick-has-to-decide-if-hes-an-activist-or-a-football-player/; Jenna West, "Jim Brown: 'I Don't Think That We Should Take Knees in Protest,'" *Sports Illustrated*, October 11, 2018, https://www.si.com/nfl/2018/10/11/jim-brown-protests-kneeling-national-anthem.

12. West, "Jim Brown."

13. Sopan Deb, "N.B.A. Blames Economy for Hiring Freeze and Budget Cuts," *New York Times*, April 11, 2023, https://www.nytimes.com/2023/04/11/sports/basketball/nba-budget-cuts.html; Mike Ozanian, "NFL National Revenue Was Almost $12 Billion In 2022," *Forbes*, July 11, 2023, https://www.forbes.com/sites/mikeozanian/2023/07/11/nfl-national-revenue-was-almost-12-billion-in-2022/?sh=510c1d542d74; The Nielsen Company, *Amplifying Black Voices in Media: Creating Informed, Thoughtful, and Authentic Experiences* (New York: Nielsen, 2022), 3.

14. Louis Moore, *We Will Win the Day: The Civil Rights Movement, the Black Athlete, and the Quest for Equality* (Lexington: University Press of Kentucky, 2021), xxiii.

Bibliography

Government Documents

Federal Bureau of Investigation Surveillance Files, FBI Files on Black Extremist Organizations, Part I: COINTELPRO Files on Black Hate Groups and Investigation of the Deacons for Defense and Justice.

US Census Bureau. *Sixteenth Census of the United States: 1940—Population*, vol. 1, Number of Inhabitants. Washington, DC: US Census Bureau, 1942.

Special Collections

Black Archives of Mid-America. Kansas City, Missouri.

Curtis McClinton Jr. Papers, Kenneth Spencer Research Library. University of Kansas.

Joseph Vaudrey Baker papers, 1935–1974. Manuscript, Archives, and Rare Book Library, Emory University.

LaBudde Special Collections & Archives, University of Missouri–Kansas City.

Mayoral Manuscript Collections: Carl B. Stokes, Western Reserve Historical Society.

Oakland History Collection, Oakland History Room. Oakland Public Library.

Schomburg Center for Research in Black Culture, Harlem, New York.

Special Collections, Michael Schwartz Library. Cleveland State University.

Walter Cooper Papers, Rush Rhees Library, Rare Books & Special Collections. University of Rochester Libraries.

Unpublished Documents

Wooten, John. "History of Negro Industrial and Economic Union." Appendix 2, 2. The Western Reserve Historical Society, Carl B. Stokes Papers, Manuscript Collect No. 4370.

Video Recordings

Berman, Brigitte. *Hugh Hefner: Playboy, Activist, and Rebel.* Produced by Brigitte Berman. 124 min. Metaphor Films, 2009. Digital videodisc.

Lee, Spike. *Jim Brown: All American.* Produced and directed by Spike Lee. 140 min. 40 Acres & A Mule Filmworks/HBO Sports, 2002. Digital video disc.

Moore, Theresa. *Third and Long: The History of African-Americans in Pro Football 1946–1989.* Produced and directed by Theresa Moore. 180 min. T-Time Productions, 2011. Documentary.

NFL Productions *NFL America's Game The Super Bowl Champions: 1969 Kansas Chiefs Super Bowl IV.* Produced by NFL Films. 60 min. NFL Network, 2012. Documentary.

Audio Recordings

Brown, Jim, and Jeff Baxter. *Jim Brown Tells It Like Is.* Cleveland, OH: Main Line, 1968.

Books

Abdul-Jabbar, Kareem, with Peter Knobler. *Giant Steps.* Toronto: Bantam, 1983.

Abdul-Rauf, Mahmoud. *In the Blink of an Eye.* New York: Kaepernick, 2022.

Adelman, Melvin. *A Sporting Time: New York City and the Rise of Modern Athletics, 1820–70.* Urbana: University of Illinois Press, 1986.

Alexander, Rae Pace, ed. *Young and Black in America.* New York: Random House, 1970.

Ali, Muhammad, with Richard Durham. *The Greatest: My Own Story.* New York: Random House, 1975.

Allen, Frederick L. *Only Yesterday: An Informal History of the 1920s.* New York: John Wiley & Sons, 1931.

Allen, Robert L. *Black Awakening in Capitalist America: An Analytic History.* Garden City, NY: Doubleday, 1969.

Anderson, Sheldon. *The Politics and Culture of Modern Sports*. Lanham, MD: Lexington Books, 2015.

Andrews, David L., ed. *Michael Jordan Inc.: Corporate Sport, Media Culture and Late Modern America*. Albany: State University of New York Press, 2001.

Austin, Curtis. *Up Against the Wall: Violence in the Making and Unmaking of the Black Panther Party*. Fayetteville: University of Arkansas Press, 2008.

Baker, Aaron, and Todd Boyd. *Out of Bounds: Sports, the Media, and the Politics of Identity*. Bloomington: Indiana University Press, 1997.

Ball, Jared A. *The Myth and Propaganda of Black Buying Power*. Cham: Palgrave Macmillan, 2020.

Baradaran, Mehrsa. *The Color of Money: Black Banks and the Racial Wealth Gap*. Cambridge, MA: Belknap Press, 2017.

Bass, Amy. *Not the Triumph but the Struggle: The 1968 Olympics and the Making of the Black Athlete*. Minneapolis: University of Minnesota Press, 2002.

Batchelor, Denzil. *Jack Johnson and His Times*. London: Phoenix Sports, 1956.

Bell, William K. *Fifteen Million Negroes and Fifteen Billion Dollars*. New York: William K. Bell, 1956.

Biondi, Martha. *To Stand and Fight: The Struggle for Civil Rights in Postwar New York City*. Cambridge, MA: Harvard University Press, 2003.

Blaustein, Arthur I., and Geoffrey P. Faux. *Star Spangled Hustle*. Garden City, NY: Doubleday, 1972.

Bontemps, Arna. *Famous Negro Athletes*. New York: Dodd, Mead, 1964.

Branch, Taylor. *At Canaan's Edge: America in the King Years 1965–68*. New York: Simon & Schuster, 2006.

Branch, Taylor. *Parting the Waters: America in the King Years 1954–63*. New York: Simon & Schuster, 1988.

Branch, Taylor. *Pillar of Fire: America in the King Years 1963–65*. New York: Simon & Schuster, 1998.

Brown, Jim, with Myron Cope. *Off My Chest*. Garden City, NY: Doubleday, 1964.

Brown, Jim, with Steve Delsohn. *Out of Bounds*. New York: Kensington Publishing, 1989.

Brown, Paul, with Jack Clary. *PB: The Paul Brown Story*. New York: Atheneum, 1979.

Burns, Stewart. *To the Mountaintop: Martin Luther King Jr.'s Sacred Mission to Save America 1955–1968*. New York: HarperCollins, 2004.

Burgos, Adrian, Jr. *Cuban Star: How One Negro-League Owner Changed the Face of Baseball*. New York: Hill and Wang, 2011.

Capparell, Stephanie. *The Real Pepsi Challenge: The Inspirational Story of Breaking the Color Barrier in American Business*. New York: Wall Street Journal Books, 2007.

Carlos, John, with Dave Zirin. *The John Carlos Story*. Chicago: Haymarket, 2011.

Carmichael, Stokely, with Michael Thelwell. *Ready for Revolution: The Life and Struggles of Stokely Carmichael (Kwame Ture)*. New York: Scribner, 2003.

Carrington, Ben. *Race, Sport and Politics: The Sporting Black Diaspora*. Los Angeles: Sage, 2010.

Carson, Clayborne, ed. *The Autobiography of Martin Luther King, Jr.* New York: Warner, 1998.

Carson, Clayborne. *In Struggle: SNCC and the Black Awakening of the 1960s*. Cambridge, MA: Harvard University Press, 1981.

Cashin, Sheryll. *The Failures of Integration: How Race and Class Are Undermining the American Dream*. New York: Public Affairs, 2004.

Chafe, William. *The Unfinished Journey: America since World War II*. 5th ed. New York: Oxford University Press, 2003.

Chatelain, Marcia. *Franchise: The Golden Arches in Black America*. New York: Liveright, 2020.

Clegg, Claude Andrew. *An Original Man: The Life and Times of Elijah Muhammad*. New York: St. Martin's Griffin, 1998.

Coakley, Jay. *Sports in Society: Issues & Controversies*. Boston: McGraw Hill, 2007.

Collier-Thomas, Bettye, and V. P. Franklin. *Sisters in the Struggle: African American Women in the Civil Rights–Black Power Movement*. New York: NYU Press, 2001.

Conyers, James L., Jr., ed. *Race in American Sports: Essays*. Jefferson, MO: McFarland, 2014.

Cooky, Cheryl, and Michael A. Messner. *No Slam Dunk: Gender, Sport, and the Unevenness of Social Change*. New Brunswick, NJ: Rutgers University Press, 2018.

Countryman, Matthew J. *Up South: Civil Rights and Black Power in Philadelphia*. Philadelphia: University of Pennsylvania Press, 2006.

Demas, Lane. *Integrating the Gridiron: Black Civil Rights and American College Football*. New Brunswick, NJ: Rutgers University Press, 2010.

Denlinger, Ken, and Paul Attner. *Redskin Country: From Baugh to the Super Bowl*. New York: Leisure Press, 1983.

Dionisopoulos, P. A. *Rebellion, Racism, and Representation: The Adam Clayton Powell Case and Its Antecedents*. DeKalb: Northern Illinois University Press, 1970.

Dittmer, John. *Local People: The Struggle for Civil Rights in Mississippi*. Urbana: University of Illinois Press, 1995.

Dudziak, Mary L. *Cold War Civil Rights: Race and the Image of American Democracy*. Princeton, NJ: Princeton University Press, 2000.

Duru, N. Jeremi. *Advancing the Ball: Race, Reformation, and the Quest for Equal Coaching Opportunity in the NFL*. New York: Oxford University Press, 2011.

Edwards, Harry. *The Revolt of the Black Athlete*. New York: Free Press, 1969.

Eig, Jonathan. *Ali: A Life*. Boston: Houghton Mifflin Harcourt, 2017.

Eisen, George, and David K. Wiggins, eds. *Ethnicity and Sport in North American History and Culture*. Westport, CT: Greenwood, 1994.

Ezra, Michael, ed. *The Economic Civil Rights Movement: African Americans and the Struggle for Economic Power*. New York: Routledge, 2013.

Ezra, Michael. "Main Bout, Inc., Black Economic Power, and Professional Boxing: The Cancelled Muhammad Ali/Ernie Terrell Fight." *Journal of Sport History* 29, no. 3 (2002): 413–37.

Ezra, Michael. *Muhammad Ali: The Making of an Icon*. Philadelphia: Temple University Press, 2009.

Fairclough, Adam. *To Redeem the Soul of America: The Southern Christian Leadership Conference and Martin Luther King, Jr.* Athens: University of Georgia Press, 1987.

Farmer, James. *Lay Bare the Heart: An Autobiography of the Civil Rights Movement*. Fort Worth: Texas Christian University Press, 1998.

Feinstein, John. *Raise a Fist, Take a Knee: Race and the Illusion of Progress in Modern Sports*. New York: Little, Brown, 2021.

Freeman, Mike. *Football's Fearless Activists: How Colin Kaepernick, Eric Reid, Kenny Stills, and Fellow Athletes Stood Up to the NFL and President Trump*. New York: Sports Publishing, 2020.

Freeman, Mike. *Jim Brown: The Fierce Life of an American Hero*. New York: HarperCollins, 2006.

Garrow, David J. *Bearing the Cross: Martin Luther King, Jr., and the Southern Christian Leadership Conference.* New York: Perennial Classics, 1999.

Garvey, Marcus, and Robert Blaisdell. *Selected Writings and Speeches of Marcus Garvey.* Mineola, NY: Dover, 2004.

Gems, Gerald R. *Before Jackie Robinson: The Transcendent Role of Black Sporting Pioneers.* Lincoln: University of Nebraska Press, 2017.

Gems, Gerald R. *Viet Nam Vignettes: Tales of the Magnificent Bastards.* Haworth: St. Johann, 2005.

Gibson, D. Parke. *The $30 Billion Negro.* London: Macmillan, 1969.

Glick, Brian. *The War at Home: Covert Action against U.S. Activists and What We Can Do about It.* Boston: South End Press, 1989.

Gorn, Elliot J., ed. *Muhammad Ali: The People's Champ.* Urbana: University of Illinois Press, 1995.

Goudsouzian, Aram. *King of the Court: Bill Russell and the Basketball Revolution.* Berkeley: University of California Press, 2010.

Gregory, James N. *The Southern Diaspora: How the Great Migration of Black and White Southerners Transformed America.* Chapel Hill: University of North Carolina Press, 2007.

Grossman, James. *Land of Hope: Chicago, Black Southerners, and the Great Migration.* Chicago: University of Chicago Press, 1989.

Grundy, Pamela. *Learning to Win: Sports, Education, and Social Change in Twentieth-Century North Carolina.* Chapel Hill: University of North Carolina Press, 2001.

Hahn, Steven. *A Nation Under Our Feet: Black Political Struggles in the Rural South from Slavery to the Great Migration.* Cambridge, MA: Harvard University Press, 2003.

Hamilton, Charles V. *Adam Clayton Powell, Jr.: The Political Biography of an American Dilemma.* New York Atheneum, 1991.

Harlan, Louis R. *Booker T. Washington; the Making of a Black Leader, 1856–1901.* New York: Oxford University Press, 1972.

Harlan, Louis R. *Booker T. Washington: The Wizard of Tuskegee, 1901–1915.* New York: Oxford University Press, 1983.

Harris, David. *The League: The Rise and Decline of the NFL.* New York: Bantam, 1986.

Hartmann, Douglas. *Race, Culture, and the Revolt of the Black Athlete: The 1968 Olympic Protests and Their Aftermath*. Chicago: University of Chicago Press, 2003.

Hauser, Thomas. *Muhammad Ali: His Life and Times*. New York: Simon & Schuster, 1991.

Haygood, Wil. *King of the Cats: The Life and Times of Adam Clayton Powell, Jr.* Boston: Houghton Mifflin, 1993.

Haygood, Wil. *Sweet Thunder: The Life and Times of Sugar Ray Robinson*. Chicago: Lawrence Hill, 2011.

Henderson, Edwin B., ed. *The Negro in Sports*. Washington, DC: Associated Publishers, 1939.

Henderson, Simon. *Sidelined: How American Sports Challenged the Black Freedom Struggle*. Lexington: University Press of Kentucky, 2013.

Henderson, William L., and Larry C. Ledebur. *Economic Disparity: Problems and Strategies for Black America*. New York: Free Press, 1970.

Hill, Lance. *The Deacons for Defense: Armed Resistance and the Civil Rights Movement*. Chapel Hill: University of North Carolina Press, 2004.

Hill, Laura W., and Julia Rabig, eds. *The Business of Black Power: Community Development, Capitalism, and Corporate Responsibility in Postwar America*. Rochester, NY: University of Rochester Press, 2012.

Hodges, Craig, with Rory Fanning. *Long Shot: The Triumphs and Struggles of an NBA Freedom Fighter*. Chicago: Haymarket, 2017.

House-Soremekun, Bessie. *Confront the Odds: African American Entrepreneurship in Cleveland, Ohio*. 2nd ed. Kent, OH: Kent State University Press, 2009.

Isaacs, Stan. *Jim Brown: The Golden Year 1964*. Englewood Cliffs, NJ: Prentice Hall, 1970.

Jackson, Thomas F. *From Civil Rights to Human Rights: Martin Luther King, Jr., and the Struggle for Economic Justice*. Philadelphia: University of Pennsylvania Press, 2007.

Jeffries, Hasan K. *Bloody Lowndes: Civil Rights and Black Power in Alabama's Black Belt*. New York: NYU Press, 2010.

Jones, Charles E., ed. *The Black Panther Party [Reconsidered]*. Baltimore: Black Classic, 1998.

Jones, Edward H. *Blacks in Business*. New York: Grosset & Dunlap, 1971.

Joseph, Peniel E. *Waiting 'Til the Midnight Hour: A Narrative History of Black Power in America*. New York: Henry Holt, 2006.

Kaliss, Gregory J. *Beyond the Black Power Salute: Athlete Activism in an Era of Change*. Urbana: University of Illinois Press, 2023.

Katz, Milton S. *Breaking Through: John B. McLendon, Basketball Legend and Civil Rights Pioneer*. Fayetteville: University of Arkansas Press, 2007.

Kusmer, Kenneth L. *A Ghetto Takes Shape: Black Cleveland, 1870–1930*. Urbana: University of Illinois Press, 1976.

Lackritz, Marc E. *The Hough Riots of 1966*. Cleveland: Regional Church Planning Office, 1968.

LaFeber, Walter. *Michael Jordan and the New Global Capitalism*. New York: W. W. Norton, 1999.

Lapchick, Richard. *Broken Promises: Racism in American Sports*. New York: St. Martin's/Marek, 1984.

Lapchick, Richard E., ed. *Fractured Focus: Sport as a Reflection of Society*. Lexington, KY: Lexington Books, 1986.

Lawson, Steven F. *Running for Freedom: Civil Rights and Black Politics in America*. New York: McGraw Hill, 1997.

Lazerow, Jama, and Yohuru Williams, eds. *In Search of the Black Panther Party: New Perspectives on a Revolutionary Movement*. Durham, NC: Duke University Press, 2006.

Litwack, Leon. *Trouble in Mind: Black Southerners in the Age of Jim Crow*. New York: Knopf, 1998.

Lomax, Michael E., ed. *Sports and the Racial Divide: African American and Latino Experience in an Era of Change*. Jackson: University Press of Mississippi, 2008.

Long, Michael G., ed. *First Class Citizenship: The Civil Rights Letters of Jackie Robinson*. New York: Times Books, 2007.

Lynd, Alice. *We Won't Go: Personal Accounts of War Objectors*. Boston: Beacon, 1968.

Maltz, Maxwell. *Psycho-Cybernetics: A New Way to Get More Living Out of Life*. Englewood Cliffs, NJ: Prentice Hall, 1960.

Marable, Manning. *Black Liberation in Conservative America*. Boston: South End Press, 1997.

Marable, Manning. *How Capitalism Underdeveloped Black America: Problems in Race, Political Economy, and Society.* Chicago: Haymarket, 2015.

Marable, Manning. *Malcolm X: A Life of Reinvention.* New York: Viking, 2011.

Marable, Manning. *Race, Reform and Rebellion: The Second Reconstruction in Black America, 1945–1990.* Jackson: University Press of Mississippi, 1991.

Maraniss, David. *Clemente: The Passion and Grace of Baseball's Last Hero.* New York: Simon & Schuster, 2006.

Marc, David. *Leveling the Playing Field: The Story of the Syracuse 8.* Syracuse, NY: Syracuse University Press, 2015.

Marqusee, Mike. *Redemption Song: Muhammad Ali and the Spirit of the Sixties.* 2nd ed. London: Verso, 2005.

Martin, Charles H. *Benching Jim Crow: The Rise and Fall of the Color Line in Southern College Sports, 1890–1980.* Urbana: University of Illinois Press, 2010.

Martin, Waldo, Jr. *Brown v. Board of Education: A Brief History with Documents.* Boston: Bedford/St. Martin's, 1998.

Matlin, Daniel. "'Lift Up Yr Self!' Reinterpreting Amiri Baraka (LeRoi Jones), Black Power, and the Uplift Tradition." *Journal of American History* 93, no. 1 (June 2006): 91–116.

McCullough, Bob. *My Greatest Day in Football: The Legends of Football Recount Their Greatest Moments.* New York: Thomas Dunes, 2001.

Melanson, Philip H. *The Murkin Conspiracy: An Investigation into the Assassination of Dr. Martin Luther King, Jr.* New York: Praeger, 1989.

Miller, Patrick B., and David K. Wiggins, eds. *Sport and the Color Line: Black Athletes and Race Relations in Twentieth-Century America.* New York: Routledge, 2004.

Moore, Leonard N. *Carl B. Stokes and the Rise of Black Political Power.* Urbana: University of Illinois Press, 2002.

Moore, Leonard N. *The Defeat of Black Power: Civil Rights and the National Black Political Convention of 1972.* Baton Rouge: Louisiana State University Press, 2018.

Moore, Louis. *We Will Win the Day: The Civil Rights Movement, the Black Athlete, and the Quest for Equality.* Lexington: University Press of Kentucky, 2021.

Morris, Aldon D. *The Origins of the Civil Rights Movement: Black Communities Organizing for Change.* New York: Free Press, 1984.

Murphy, Frank. *The Last Protest: Lee Evans in Mexico City.* Kansas City, MO: Windsprint, 2006.

Ofari, Earl. *The Myth of Black Capitalism.* New York: Monthly Review Press, 1970.

Ogbar, Jeffrey O. G. *Black Power: Radical Politics and African American Identity.* Baltimore: Johns Hopkins University Press, 2005.

Olsen, Jack. *The Black Athlete, A Shameful Story: The Myth of Integration in American Sport.* New York: Time-Life, 1968.

Oriard, Michael. *Bowled Over: Big-Time College Football from the Sixties to the BCS Era.* Chapel Hill: University of North Carolina Press, 2009.

Oriard, Michael. *Reading Football: How the Popular Press Created an American Spectacle.* Chapel Hill: University of North Carolina Press, 1993.

Orr, Jack. *The Black Athlete: His Story in American History.* New York: Lion Press, 1969.

O'Toole, Andrew. *Fight For Old DC: George Preston Marshal, the Integration of the Washington Redskins, and the Rise of a New NFL.* Lincoln: University of Nebraska Press, 2016.

Owens, Jesse, with Paul G. Neimark. *Blackthink: My Life as a Black Man and White Man.* New York: William Morrow, 1970.

Owens, Jesse, with Paul G. Neimark. *I Have Changed.* New York: William Morrow, 1972.

Parrish, Bernie. *They Call It a Game.* New York: Dial Press, 1971.

Payne, Charles. *I've Got the Light of Freedom: The Organizing Tradition and the Mississippi Freedom Struggle.* Berkeley: University of California Press, 1995.

Payne, Charles, and Adam Green. *Time Longer Than Rope: A Century of African American Activism, 1850–1950.* New York: NYU Press, 2003.

Pluto, Terry. *When All the World Was Browns Town: Cleveland's Browns and the Championship Season of '64.* New York: Simon & Schuster, 1997.

Polite, Fritz G., and Billy Hawkins. *Sport, Race, Activism and Social Change: The Impact of Dr. Harry Edwards' Scholarship and Service.* San Diego, CA: Cognella, 2012.

Quirk, James, and Rodney D. Fort. *Pay Dirt: The Business of Professional Team Sports.* Princeton, NJ: Princeton University Press, 1992.

Ransby, Barbara. *Ella Baker & the Black Freedom Movement: A Radical Democratic Vision*. Chapel Hill: University of North Carolina Press, 2003.

Reichley, A. James. *Conservatives in an Age of Change: The Nixon and Ford Administrations*. Washington, DC: Brookings Institution, 1981.

Remnick, David. *King of the World: Muhammad Ali and the Rise of an American Hero*. New York: Random House, 1998.

Rhoden, William. *Forty Million Dollar Slaves: The Rise, Fall, and Redemption of the Black Athlete*. New York: Broadway, 2007.

Roberts, Eric B. *Football to Finance: The Story of Jr.* New York: Harcourt Brace Jovanovich, 1971.

Roberts, Randy, and Johnny Smith. *Blood Brothers: The Fatal Friendship between Muhammad Ali and Malcolm X*. New York: Basic Books, 2016.

Robinson, Jackie, and Alfred Duckett, *I Never Had It Made*. New York: HarperCollins, 1995.

Ross, Charles K. *Mavericks, Money, and Men: The AFL, Black Players, and the Evolution of Modern Football*. Philadelphia: Temple University Press, 2016.

Ross, Charles K. *Outside the Lines: African Americans and the Integration of the National Football League*. New York: NYU Press, 1999.

Ross, Charles K. *Race and Sport: The Struggle for Equality On and Off the Field*. Jackson: University Press of Mississippi, 2004.

Runstedtler, Theresa. *Jack Johnson, Rebel Sojourner: Boxing in the Shadow of the Global Color Line*. Berkeley: University of California Press, 2012.

Rushin, Steve. *The Caddie Was a Reindeer and Other Tales of Extreme Recreation*. New York: Atlantic Monthly Press, 2004.

Russell, Bill, and Taylor Branch. *Second Wind: The Memoirs of an Opinionated Man*. New York: Random House, 1979.

Russell, Bill, and William McSweeny. *Go Up for Glory*. New York: Coward-McCann, 1966.

Sample, Johnny, with Fred J. Hamilton and Sonny Schwartz. *Confessions of a Dirty Ballplayer*. New York: Dial Press, 1970.

Schulman, Bruce. *The Seventies: The Great Shift in American Culture, Society, and Politics*. Cambridge, MA: Da Capo Press, 2001.

Sellers, Cleveland, with Robert Terrell. *The River of No Return: The Autobiography of a Black Militant and the Life and Death of SNCC*. Jackson: University Press of Mississippi, 1990.

Sheppard, Harold L., ed. *Poverty and Wealth in America*. Chicago: Quadrangle Books, 1970.

Shropshire, Kenneth L. *In Black and White: Race and Sports in America*. New York: NYU Press, 1996.

Smith, Thomas G. *Showdown: JFK and the Integration of the Washington Redskins*. Boston: Beacon, 2011.

Smith, Tommie, with David Steele. *Silent Gesture: The Autobiography of Tommie Smith*. Philadelphia: Temple University Press, 2007.

Snyder, Brad. *A Well-Paid Slave: Curt Flood's Fight for Free Agency in Professional Sports*. New York: Penguin Group, 2006.

Staudohar, Paul D., and James A Mangan, ed. *The Business of Professional Sports*. Urbana: University of Illinois Press, 1991.

Stokes, Carl B. *Promises of Power: A Political Autobiography*. New York: Simon & Schuster, 1973.

Sullivan, Patricia. *Days of Hope: Race and Democracy in the New Deal Era*. Chapel Hill: University of North Carolina Press, 1996.

Taylor, Otis, with Mark Stallard. *Otis Taylor: The Need to Win*. New York: Sports Publishing, 2003.

Taylor, Ula Y. *The Veiled Garvey: The Life & Times of Amy Jacques Garvey*. Chapel Hill: University of North Carolina Press, 2002.

Thomas, Damion L. *Globetrotting: African American Athletes and Cold War Politics*. Urbana: University of Illinois Press, 2012.

Thomas, Evan. *The Man to See: Edward Bennett Williams Ultimate Insider; Legendary Trial Lawyer*. New York: Simon & Schuster, 1991.

Ture, Kwame, and Charles V. Hamilton. *Black Power: The Politics of Liberation*. New York: Vintage, 1992.

Tyson, Timothy. *Radio Free Dixie: Robert F. Williams & the Roots of Black Power*. Chapel Hill: University of North Carolina Press, 1999.

Van Deburg, William. L. *Black Camelot: African-American Culture Heroes in Their Times, 1960–1980*. Chicago: University of Chicago Press, 1997.

Van Deburg, William L. *New Day in Babylon: The Black Power Movement and American Culture, 1965–1975*. Chicago: University of Chicago Press, 1992.

Washington, Booker T. *Up from Slavery: An Autobiography*. New York: Doubleday, Page, 1901.

Washington, James M., ed. *A Testament of Hope: The Essential Writings and Speeches of Martin Luther King, Jr.* New York: HarperSanFrancisco, 1991.

Watterson, John S. *The Games Presidents Play: Sports and the Presidency.* Baltimore: Johns Hopkins University Press, 2006.

Weems, Robert E., Jr. *Desegregating the Dollar: African American Consumerism in the Twentieth Century.* New York: NYU Press, 1998.

Weinberg, Kenneth G. *Black Victory: Carl Stokes and the Winning of Cleveland.* Chicago: Quadrangle Books, 1968.

Westheider, James. *The African American Experience in Vietnam.* Lanham, MD: Rowman & Littlefield, 2008.

Whitaker, Matthew C. ed. *African American Icons of Sport: Triumph, Courage, and Excellence.* Westport, CT: Greenwood, 2008.

White, Derrick E. *Blood, Sweat, & Tears: Jake Gaither, Florida A&M, and the History of Black College Football.* Chapel Hill: University of North Carolina Press, 2019.

Wiggins, David K. *Glory Bound: Black Athletes in White America.* Syracuse: Syracuse University Press, 1997.

Wiggins, David K. *More Than a Game: A History of the African American Experience in Sport.* Lanham, MD: Rowman & Littlefield, 2018.

Wiggins, David K. *Out of the Shadows: A Biographical History of African American Atheltes.* Fayetteville: University of Arkansas Press, 2006.

Wiggins, David K., and Patrick B. Miller, *The Unlevel Playing Field: A Documentary History of the African American Experience in Sport.* Urbana: University of Illinois Press, 2003.

Williams, Robert F. *Negroes with Guns.* Detroit: Wayne State University Press, 1998.

Winford, Brandon K. *John Hervey Wheeler, Black Banking, and the Economic Struggle for Civil Rights.* Lexington: University Press of Kentucky, 2020.

Witherspoon, Kevin B. *Before the Eyes of the World: Mexico and the 1968 Olympic Games.* DeKalb: Northern Illinois University Press, 2008.

Woodward, Komozi. *A Nation within a Nation: Amiri Baraka (LeRoi Jones) and Black Power Politics.* Chapel Hill: University of North Carolina Press, 1999.

Zinn, Howard. *A People's History of the United States.* New York: Harper, 2005.

Zirin, Dave. *A People's History of Sports in the United States: 250 Years of Politics, Protest, People, and Play.* New York: New Press, 2008.

Zirin, Dave. *What's My Name, Fool? Sports and Resistance in the United States.* Chicago: Haymarket, 2005.

Articles

Allvine, Fred C. "Black Business Development." *Journal of Marketing* 34, no. 2 (April 1970): 1–7.

Anderson, Talmadge. "Black Economic Liberation under Capitalism." *Black Scholar* 2, no. 2 (October 1970): 11–14.

Bartok, Richard E. "NFL Free Agency Restrictions under Antitrust Attack." *Duke Law Journal* 1991, no. 2 (April 1991): 503–59.

Blackman, Dexter. "African Americans, Pan-Africanism, and the Anti-Apartheid Campaign to Expel South Africa from the 1968 Olympics." *Journal of Pan African Studies* 5, no. 3 (2012): 1–25.

Bond, Julian, Eugene Walton, Anita Cornwell, Conrad Kent Rivers, Sterling Stuckey, Brooks Johnson, Francis Ward, Nathan Hare, Eloise Greenfield, Ronald Fair, Dudley Randall, and John Killens. "A Symposium: Black Power—It's Meaning and Measure." *Negro Digest* (November 1966): 20–37, 81–96.

Coles, Flournoy, Jr. "The Unique Problems of the Black Businessman." *Review of the Black Political Economy* 5, no. 1 (1974): 45–55.

Covan, Michael. "The Emergence of the Black Athlete in America." *Black Scholar* 3, no. 3 (November 1971): 16–28.

Creedon, Pam. "The Super Bowl and War: Change in the Theatre for the Masculine Myth." *Football Studies* 7, no. 1/2 (2004): 108–21.

Daniel, Pete. "African American Farmers and Civil Rights." *Journal of Southern History* 73, no. 1 (February 2007): 3–38.

Dorinson, Joseph. "Black Heroes in Sport: From Jack Johnson to Muhammad Ali." *Journal of Popular Culture* 31, no. 3 (Winter 1997): 115–35.

Dyerson, Mark. "The Emergence of Consumer Culture and the Transformation of Physical Culture: American Sport in the 1920s." *Journal of Sport History* 16, no. 3 (Winter 1989): 261–81.

Evans, Arthur S., Jr. "Blacks as Key Functionaries: A Study of Racial Stratification in Professional Sport." *Journal of Black Studies* 28, no. 1 (September 1997): 43–59.

Garvey, Edward R. "From Chattel to Employee: The Athlete's Quest for Freedom and Dignity." *Annals of the American Academy of Political and Social Science* 445 (September 1979): 91–101.

Graham, Hugh D. "Richard Nixon and Civil Rights: Explaining an Enigma," in "The Nixon Presidency," special issue, *Presidential Studies Quarterly* 26, no. 1 (Winter 1996): 93–106.

Hall, Jacquelyn Dowd. "The Long Civil Rights Movement and the Political Use of the Past." *Journal of American History* 91, no. 4 (March 2005): 1233–63.

Harpalani, Vinay. "The Athletic Dominance of African Americans—Is There Genetic Basis?" *Journal of African American Men* 2, nos. 2–3 (Fall 1996–Winter 1997): 39–56.

Heard, George Alexander. "St. Simons Island during the War between the States." *Georgia Historical Quarterly* 22, no. 3 (1938): 249–72.

Hornsby, Alton, Jr. "The Drum Major on the Mountaintop: A Tribute to Dr. Martin Luther King, Jr." *Journal of Negro History* 62, no. 3 (July 1977): 213–16.

Hunter, David W. "Race and Athletic Performance: A Physiological Review." *Journal of African American Men* 2, nos. 2–3 (Fall 1996–Winter 1997): 23–38.

Kahn, Lawrence M. "The Effects of Race on Professional Football Player's Compensation." *Industrial and Labor Relations Review* 45, no. 2 (1992): 295–310.

Kahn, Lawrence M. "Discrimination in Professional Sports: A Survey of the Literature." *Industrial and Labor Relations Review* 44, no. 3 (April 1991): 395–418.

Kotlowski, Dean. "Black Power-Nixon Style: The Nixon Administration and Minority Business Enterprise." *Business History Review* 72, no. 3 (Autumn 1998): 409–45.

Lewis, Richard, Jr. "Racial Position Segregation: A Case Study of Southwest Conference Football, 1978 and 1989." *Journal of Black Studies* 25, no. 4 (March 1995): 431–46.

Lomax, Michael E. "The African American Experience in Professional Football." *Journal of Social History* 33, no. 1 (Autumn 1999): 163–78.

Lomax, Michael E. "Revisiting the Revolt of the Black Athlete: Harry Edwards and the Making of the New African-American Sports Studies." *Journal of Sport History* 29, no. 3 (2002): 469–79.

McAndrews, Lawrence J. "The Politics of Principle: Richard Nixon and School Desegregation." *Journal of Negro History* 83, no. 3 (Summer 1998): 187–200.

Miller, Patrick. "The Anatomy of Scientific Racism: Racialist Responses to Black Athletic Achievement." *Journal of Sport History* 25, no. 1 (Spring 1998): 119–51.

Mogull, Robert G. "Football Salaries and Race: Some Empirical Evidence." *Industrial Relations* 12, no. 1 (1973): 109–12.

"Releasing Superstars from Peonage: Union Consent and the Nonstatutory Labor Exemption." *Harvard Law Review* 104, no. 4 (1991): 874–95.

Sailes, Gary A. "Betting against the Odds: An Overview of Black Sports Participation." *Journal of African American Men* 2, nos. 2–3 (Fall 1996–Winter 1997): 11–22.

Sewell, Stacy Kinlock. "The 'Not-Buying Power' of the Black Community: Urban Boycotts and Equal Employment Opportunity, 1960–64." *Journal of African American History* 89, no. 2 (Spring 2004): 138.

Smith, Thomas G. "Civil Rights on the Gridiron: The Kennedy Administration and the Desegregation of the Washington Redskins." *Journal of Sport History* 14, no. 2 (1987): 189–208.

Smith, Thomas G. "Outside the Pale: The Exclusion of Blacks from the National Football League, 1934–1946." *Journal of Sport History* 15, no. 3 (1988): 255–81.

Vertinsky, Patricia, and Gwendolyn Captain. "More Myth Than History: American Culture and Representations of the Black Female's Athletic Ability." *Journal of Sport History* 25, no. 3 (Fall 1998): 532–61.

Walker, Susannah. "Black Dollar Power: Assessing African American Consumerism since 1945." In *African American Urban History since World War II*, edited by Kenneth L. Kusmer and Joe W. Trotter, 376–403. Chicago: University of Chicago Press, 2019.

Weems, Robert E., Jr., and Lewis A. Randolph. "The National Response to Richard M. Nixon's Black Capitalism Initiative: The Success of Domestic Détente." *Journal of Black Studies* 32, no. 1 (September 2001): 66–83.

Weistart, John C. "League Control of Market Opportunities: A Perspective on Competition and Cooperation in the Sports Industry." *Duke Law Journal* 1984, no. 6 (December 1984): 1013–70.

Weistart, John C. "Judicial Review of Labor Agreements: Lessons from the Sports Industry." *Law and Contemporary Problems* 44, no. 4 (Autumn 1981): 109–46.

Wiggins, David K. "'Great Speed but Little Stamina': The Historical Debate over Black Athletic Superiority." *Journal of Sport History* 16, no. 2 (Summer 1989): 158–85.

Wiggins, David K. "Vince Matthews, Wayne Collett, and the Forgotten Disruption in Munich." *Journal of African American History* 106, no. 2 (2021): 278–303.

Wooten, John. "The Human Environment: Poverty." *Nation's Business* 56 (June 1968): 60–61.

Dissertations

Corson, Keith. "Trying to Get Over: African American Directors after Blaxploitation, 1977–1986." PhD diss., New York University, 2012.

Suchma, Philip C. "From the Best of Time to the Worst of Times: Professional Sport and Urban Decline in a Tale of Two Clevelands, 1945–1978." PhD diss., Ohio State University, 2005.

Wright, Leah Michele. "The Loneliness of the Black Conservative: Black Republicans and the Grand Old Party, 1964–1980." PhD diss., Princeton University, 2009.

Reports

Gibson, Campbell, and Kay Jung. *Historical Census Statistics on Population Totals by Race, 1790 to 1990, and by Hispanic Origin, 1970 to 1990, for Large Cities and Other Urban Places in the United States*. Washington, DC: US Census Bureau, 2005.

Lapchick, Richard, with Philip Costa, Tamara Sherrod, and Rahman Anjorin. *The 2012 Racial and Gender Report Card: National Football League*. Orlando: Institute for Diversity and Ethics in Sport, 2012.

Lapchick, Richard, with Antoinette Lecky and Aaron Trigg. *The 2012 Racial and Gender Report Card: National Basketball Association*. Institute for Diversity and Ethics in Sport, 2012.

Levin, Felice, and Arnold Spellun. *Public and Private Support for the Development of Minority and Poverty Group-Owned Businesses: A Study with Special Emphasis on the Role of Foundations*. Project Evaluation (A-73). Sleepy Hollow, NY: Division of National Affairs, Ford Foundation Archives, 1975.

National Football League. "Super Bowl I Scoring Stats." Canton, OH: Pro Football Hall of Fame, 1967.

The Nielsen Company. *Amplifying Black Voices in Media: Creating Informed, Thoughtful and Authentic Experiences.* New York: Nielsen, 2022.

US Census Bureau. *1970 Census of Population.* Washington, DC: US Census Bureau, 1974.

Wandless, John H. *Minority Economic Development: Opportunities and Approaches.* Kansas City: Office of Economic Opportunity, 1969.

Newspapers

The Argus
Atlanta Daily World
Baltimore Afro-American
Boston Globe
Chicago Daily Defender
Chicago Daily Tribune
Chicago Defender
Chicago Tribune
Cleveland Call and Post
Cleveland Plain Dealer
Cleveland Press
Courier Journal
Detroit Free Press
Edwardsville Intelligencer
Final Call
Hartford Courant
Harvard Crimson
Jacksonville Free Press
Kansas City Call
Kansas City Star
Kansas City Times
Kansas City Town Squire
Kingsport New
Las Vegas Daily Optic
Las Vegas Review-Journal

Look
Los Angeles Sentinel
Los Angeles Times
Miami Times
Michigan Chronicle
The Nation
New Jersey Afro-American
New Pittsburgh Courier
New York Amsterdam News
New York Times
Oakland Post
Oakland Tribune
Philadelphia Tribune
Pittsburgh Courier
Pittsburgh Sports Daily Bulletin
Portland Skanner
La Prensa
The Recorder
The Skanner
Spokesman Review
St. Petersburg Independent
Sun Reporter
Tennessee Tribune
The Voice
Wall Street Journal
Washington Afro American
Washington Informer
Washington Post, Times Herald

Periodicals

Black Enterprise
Ebony
ESPN
Forbes
Jet

Playboy
Saturday Evening Post
Society Magazine
Sports Illustrated
Time

Podcasts

Anderson, Joel. "America's Blackest Child." *Slow Burn*, podcast audio, June 7, 2003. https://slate.com/podcasts/slow-burn/s8/becoming-justice-thomas/e1/clarence-thomas-journey-from-rural-georgia-to-the-supreme-court.

Index

Race and Sports

Series editors: Gerald L. Smith and Derrick E. White

This series publishes works that expand the boundaries of sports history. By exploring the intersections of sports and racial and ethnic histories through the racial dynamics of gender, culture, masculinity, sexuality, and power as represented in biography, community, film, literature, and oral history, the series opens a new analysis of American sport and culture.